T0164662

Pop's Story

Paul O. Peterson

Order this book online at www.trafford.com
or email orders@trafford.com

Most Trafford titles are also available at major online book retailers.

Printed in the United States of America.

ISBN: 978-1-4269-6611-8 (sc)
ISBN: 978-1-4269-6612-5 (hc)
ISBN: 978-1-4269-6610-1 (e)

Library of Congree Control Number: 2011906197

Trafford rev. 05/18/2011

www.trafford.com

North America & international
toll-free: 1 888 232 4444 (USA & Canada)
phone: 250 383 6864 • fax: 812 355 4082

Acknowledgements

To Diane Cooke, who encouraged me and helped me get started writing my memoirs.

To the members of the Memoirs writing class at Shell Point Retirement Community, who gave me constructive criticism and council concerning my life story.

To my sister-in-law Nellie Barr, son Glenn, Linda Vander Jagt, and Judy Munson who spent many hours editing and correcting my drafts.

To my son Craig who put together the Family's ancestry chart and provided information on A.F. Andersons early years in Chicago.

Without your help and encouragement my life story would not have been written.

Thank you all!

Thanks

Caroline Anderson "Mussie:" My grandmother who showed only unconditional love and never said a bad word about anyone.

Father Oscar: Dad taught me the joy of hard work and dedication to do my best in whatever I did.

Mother Alice: Her hours of prayer for me are eternally emblazoned in my memory. She passed her love of great music on to me, and that has given me great joys of my life. Her skill in cooking and baking Swedish breads and cookies were matched only by my wife, Carolyn. I regret that she never saw my sons grow up, and they never got to know her.

Wife Lee: My soul mate for over fifteen years, an introvert like me, a partner in our love of music, mother of my three wonderful sons. We were one in temperament and in our love for God and all that's beautiful. We were one flesh. What a beautiful lady she was with her face framed in a broad brimmed hat and white gloves. Much of her cooking skills were past to her by my mother, who loved her like a daughter.

Wife Carolyn: The wife God gave me, who brought me out of my grief and shell. She has the greatest gift of hospitality I have ever observed. If I hadn't married her I'd have nowhere near the number of friends I have today. She helped to get me involved in projects that gave me a chance to use my gifts, and this has given me great joy and fulfillment. She became my wife when my sons were 9, 10 and 14. Within a year of our marriage they stopped addressing her as Carolyn and called her Mother or Mom. She'd earned that right! An invitation for dinner at our home or gifts of baked goods is cherished by our friends.

I'm so thankful for my three sons who have given me pride and joy in the way they have lived their lives. They and their wives have given me seven beautiful grandchildren whom I love and pray for every day.

I'm thankful for the many friends who helped shape my life. I'm thankful for the college that helped me learn and gave me the desire to grow in knowledge and wisdom. What joy music has brought me! I'm glad for the opportunities that I've had to sing in many church choirs and choral groups.

What a privilege has been mine to be a citizen of the greatest country on earth, the United States of America. In all my travels I've never found a country that compares to it.

I thank God who has been with me since I was in my mother's womb. He brought me through the loss of my precious wife Lee and led me to Carolyn. After my sudden early retirement He guided my life into great avenues of service.

Table of Contents

Preface

The following is the story of my life. I write with the purpose of informing my children and grandchildren of what happened in my life and what was important to me, and in the hope that it will help them understand what I valued and what joy I had in living my life.

To begin it is necessary to give a short history of my roots. I began gathering data on my ancestors in the 1960s' Most of the early information came from my mother and father and Aunt Elvira. From my father I got a few pictures and some verbal history with very little documentation. Some of this information, especially on grandfather Peterson was inaccurate. On my mother's side I got much more data. The addendum contains much of this material.

In 1977 I got in touch with a researcher that worked in the genealogical records department of the Church of Jesus Christ of Latter-day Saints (Mormons). They believe that I Corinthians 15:29 (baptism of the dead) allows them to help achieve salvation for those already dead through the baptism of someone living in the name of the dead person. Because of this belief, the gathering of information regarding genealogy becomes very important. So it is the member's desire to aid as many of their forebears as possible to enter into the glory of the hereafter with them. In Sweden the Mormons have had permission to microfilm public records all the way back to 1590.

They gave me documentation on the Anderson branch of the family back to the 1830's

With that information I contacted the Svenska Emigration institutet in Vaxjo, Sweden to find the dates of their emigration. In the 1980's I went to the National Archives in Washington and found by going through passenger ship lists, the date of their embarkation, and the vessel they came on. While there I also got 1880 and 1900 census records of Chicago. In them I found data on where they lived, and information on each family member on both the Anderson and Peterson side.

In February 1978 I sought additional information on my grandfather Peterson who I had been told came from the same area as my grandmother, Trolle-Lungby. No trace of him was found. There things stood until 2006 when working with the genealogy librarians at Shell Point I was encouraged to contact the people in Vaxjo to do a broader search of Sweden. I went back with two other bits of data that I had recalled my father relating: That his father was a twin and that his father's father had been in the army. Bingo!!! This was the key to finding him. My grandfather Anderson was born in Habo, on the SW side of Lake Vattern. My grandfather Peterson was born in Rok, slightly inland from the same lake; on the NE side. This information was received in March of 2007. This ended my 28 year search for my ancestral roots.

Going back to the 1700's all my ancestors were common people; farmers, laborers, maids, soldiers. On the Anderson side, both of my grandparents were converted to "Baptistic Christianity" before they left Sweden. On the Peterson side I have no evidence that this was the case.

Chapter 1

I Am Born

To paraphrase one of my favorite authors, Charles Dickens, 1929: it was the best of times, A time of peace; the stock market reached a record high in the last week of October: Herbert Hoover was sworn in as the 31st President of the US. Martin Luther King Jr., Andre Previn, Beverly Sills, Audrey Hepburn, Jackie Kennedy Onasis, Bob Newhart, Anne Frank, Arnold Palmer, Dick Clark, William Safire, and Grace Kelly were born. It was also the worst of times: In my birth city, Chicago, Al Capone's henchmen gunned down seven members of a rival gang on February 14th, known as the St. Valentine's Day Massacre. The Communists and members of the new Nazi party clashed amid gun fire on the streets of Berlin, and the U.S. Stock Market crashed on October 24th. In other news, the first Nudist organization in the U.S., the American League for Physical Culture, was founded in N.Y.C. In July, transcontinental air service began with scheduled flights between New York and Los Angeles. A $350 ticket would get you there in 48 hours.

For my father, the World Series that fall between his beloved Cubs and Connie Mack's A's was a major blow. The series stood at 2-1 in favor of the A's. In game four, after seven-and one half innings, the Cubs were cruising with an 8-0 lead. One out, two lost balls in the sun, and 13 batters later, the Cubs found themselves trailing

10-8. The A's had an improbable victory. Instead of a tied series they had a 3-1 lead. The Cubbies never recovered and lost the series 4-1.

Technological advances took place: Richard Byrd made the first flight over the South Pole, The Graf Zeppelin flew around the earth, penicillin was discovered by Alexander Fleming, and construction was started on the Empire State Building. In the arts, the first Academy Awards were held, and Mary Pickford, "America's Sweetheart," was voted best actress. The all- time, most popular Swing Era song was composed, "Stardust." The average annual income rose to $2,062, the average new car cost $450, a new house $7,246, a gallon of gas 12 cents, a quart of milk 14.5 cents and the average life expectancy had risen to 54.1 years. The cost to send a letter was two cents.

On the 16th of December it started snowing in Chicago, and by the 20th, 15 inches had fallen, the 6th heaviest snowstorm in Chicago's history. On the evening of the 19th my Dad took my Mother to the Lying- In Hospital as she had gone into labor. After 20 hours and 20 minutes I was born at 9 pm, weighing 7lbs, 13ozs, and was 19 and a half inches long with long blonde hair. My parents named me Paul Oscar Peterson, giving me the initials POP which I've lived with all my life. Because of this, I've titled my autobiography "POP's Story."

The LYING- IN HOSPITAL was the "Ritz" of Maternity Hospitals in Chicago. Mothers stayed a minimum of 10 days after delivery. My Mother and I were there 12 days. The doctor who delivered me was named Hagens. He charged $159, and the hospital bill was $75!

My mother was 31 and my father 47 when I was born. They brought me home to their apartment at 7140 Peoria on Chicago's south side. When I was two we moved to 8234 Champlain Ave, further south and east. The house was on a 30'x 120' lot, built of brick with a full attic and basement. It had six rooms; a living room, dining room, kitchen, two bedrooms and a den that we used as an all purpose room, where we listened to the radio. The length of the house was 66 feet and the width 26 feet, giving us a floor area of about 1'600 sq.ft. There was one bathroom for us to share. It had a tub but no shower. Generally each house on our street abutted the house next to it, with an alley between every other house. Our neighbor on the south, the DeMuyts, shared an alleyway that led to our small back yard and garage. Stairs at the back of the house led up to an enclosed porch that measured about 8x12 ft.; one walked through it to get to the back door. About ten feet in back of the house there was a garage that fronted on a concrete driveway that serviced houses on the west side of Champlain and the east side of St. Lawrence. I and my family lived in that house for 19 years.

My brother Willard was born on September 11th 1932. I was three years old when we began sharing a 9'X 12'room and a double bed and closet. We each had our own dresser and night stand. We slept in the same bed until I went off to college in 1948. Even then we shared the bed when we were home. It seems sort of weird now that we did this. Today most children in our country have their own room or at least their own bed. Amazingly, we both turned out quite normal. This is not to say that we did not have battles over space, but I don't recall that any blood was spilled over it.

My mother recorded many milestones about my first years in a book entitled: "Our Baby's First Seven Years". She noted that I started making imitative noises at eight months, like Dada, and began speaking words at18 months and saying sentences I'd memorized at two, like "Humpty Dumpty sat on the wall", "Mary, Mary quite contrary," and the table blessing we used for years, "Be present at this table Lord, be here and every where adored. These blessings take and grant that we may feast in Paradise with thee. Amen. One of my first questions was, "When was God made?" At two years nine months, I was three feet tall and weighed 28 lbs.

Every Sunday we'd get into our green Hupmobile coupe and drive five miles to the Swedish Baptist Church of Engelwood. This church had been founded by a group of Swedish Baptist emigrants, that included my maternal grandparents, who came in the 1890's. The church service was conducted in Swedish, but for the children's sake the Sunday school was in English. I learned songs such as: "Jesus loves the little children, all the children of the world; red and yellow, black and white, they are precious in His sight. Jesus loves the little children of the world." I'd look out the window of our kitchen at an Oak tree and sing: "I shall not be, I shall not be moved. Just like the tree planted by the water. I shall not be moved." Then I'd add "Just like Demuyt's tree."

My favorite toys were: a Teddy bear, a toy tractor trailer truck, an automobile, an ABC book and a sled (It was not named "ROSEBUD"). I made my first public speech at the 1932 Christmas program: "I like to go to Sunday school, I'm always there you know, unless I happen to be sick and then I cannot go." Edith Malcolm was the head of the beginners' department. She will get a big reward in heaven for all the lives she touched with her love and teaching. Some of her teachings have come back to me when I needed them. She corrected me one time when she heard me pray: "and deliver us from eagles instead of evil."

The first playmates I had were Nancy Vagness, who was a classmate of mine through all 8 grades of Arthur Dixon Grammar School, and Bruce Bing, who lived five houses north of us.

I have two sharp memories of my pre-school years. Nancy lived across the street from us and her house had a sloping driveway down to the street. One day she sat in her wagon and coasted into the street. A car coming down the street hit the wagon throwing her into the street where she lay motionless. I ran into our house screaming that a car had killed Nancy. My Mother and I ran out to the street along with other neighbors just in time to see her revive.

She suffered only a few scrapes and bruises. That was a great lesson to me regarding the danger of playing in the street.

The scariest memory of my early childhood occurred at the Chicago Worlds Fair in 1933. One of the spectacular attractions of the fair was the Sky Ride. It had a cable car that went back and forth between two steel towers 90 feet off the ground. My folks and Uncle Dave and Aunt Alta went up the elevator to the platform where we waited to get on the cable car. My Uncle Dave decided to give me a thrill by holding me out over the railing of the tower. I screamed in terror and he brought me back to the platform. Many times over the next few years, I relived that experience in my dreams and woke up thrashing and crying. I never saw my Dad so angry with his brother, who did such a foolhardy thing to his nephew. It took me several years before I was able to get over my fear of him.

At the height of the depression, ragged, suffering men came to our back door and begged for food. Each day when Mom made my Dads' lunch, she made several more sandwiches that she would give to these poor men when they knocked on our door. She also told them that God loved them, and she would pray for them to find work.

On my fifth birthday I was 3' 8" tall and weighed 38 pounds. I got a very important gift on that day, a red "Streak O Lite" steel coaster wagon. It was to serve me when I got into my first business in 1942, hauling newspapers and magazines to our garage. It was later used by my sons in the 60s at Bass Lake for their recreation. They don't make them like that anymore.

In February 1935 I entered the Arthur Dixon grammar school, which was about a block from our home. I searched the internet to find out who Arthur Dixon was and what fame he had achieved in order to get a school named for him. I got three listings: A famed British Mathematician, who died in 1955, a famous art auctioneer in London, and an Irish emigrant who was a Chicago Alderman in the late 1800s. (I'll bet that the last one is the correct one, because he was a Democrat.) I was in a class of 25 with Mrs. Wilkes as my teacher. She was the major reason that I liked going to school.

A dark day came when some of my schoolmates discovered that my initials were PP. My reaction to those who taunted me was to cross them off my friend list, to strike out at them or run away. I learned quickly that I was a better runner than fighter. Later in my life, when my children were born that was good reason not to have a junior or to give them first names starting with P.

There were no bullies in my class, but an older boy down the street, Buddy Wethered, was a big one. I did everything possible to avoid him. One day he and his buddy caught me and tied me to a big iron gate. After they teased me for a while they left and after a few minutes I freed myself. I never reported this to my parents or the school, but fortunately they left me alone after that. I noticed that a few of the smaller boys in the school were bullied almost every day. One was Harold McQuinny, He carried a leather briefcase with a handle on it. In my mind, I remember seeing him spinning around with his briefcase at arm's length fending off several bullies. I've often wondered how much this affected him in his adult life. That's sad!

In my grammar school years few days were missed because of sickness. I had the flu a couple of times, chicken pox and measles but nothing serious. Having Uncle Dave around was beneficial to the family as he was a sales rep of Upjohn, a major drug company. He had a well- stocked basement with medicine and vitamins. We'd visit him when our stocks ran low on cod liver oil, which mother made us take every day, and Miladol and Chericol cough syrup to medicate us when we were sick. If we had a head or chest cold a routine was followed every night: a wet hot towel was applied to our chest to open our pores, then mentholated "Vicks Salve" was rubbed on, then flannel cloths put on and pinned to our P.J's. That and lots of sleep helped us get well. No doctor visits or antibiotics were needed.

Uncle Dave never said that we seemed to visit only when we needed medicine. Huh!

Most birthdays and holidays were celebrated at our house with Aunt Elvira and Mussie or at their place. At those times I received many of my favorite toys. They were: wooden alphabet blocks, plain 4x6 plywood boards; and my all- time favorite, an American Flier freight train with enough tracks plus an X crossing to make an 8- shaped layout. Every birthday or Christmas brought more cars, tracks, switches, crossing gates, stations, etc. With the blocks and boards I'd build tunnels and viaducts. A couple of years later I was given an Erector Set that made it possible to make additional structures.

I started to enjoy reading books: *Black Beauty, Robinson Crusoe, Tom Sawyer, The Sugar Creek Gang* series, which taught Christian morals, and my favorite bed time story book, *A Hive of Busy Bees.* These stories emphasized the importance of being kind, helpful, honest, helpful, perseverant and grateful. Will and I were allowed to listen to one hour of radio serials each Monday thru Friday, including "Jack Armstrong, the All-American Boy," "The Lone Ranger", "Tom Mix," and on the weekend, "The Shadow" and "The Green Hornet." We'd go into the family room, light a candle, turn on the radio at 4:55 to let it warm up, turn out the light, pull the shades if necessary and get ready to fantasize through the voices and sound effects of the heroes and villains. They were very effective in helping us paint a picture of how justice and virtue triumphed over the bad guys. It beat TV all to pieces. Our minds conjured up images that went beyond any visual picture. To stretch our minds we also read the square Big Little Books, and comic books which we also exchanged with friends. Even with all these activities I enjoyed playing by myself most of the time rather than with friends.

In the fall of 1939, I made the most important decision of my life when I decided to personally accept Jesus Christ's atoning sacrifice for me on Calvary's cross.

The year 1940, was a watershed year for our family. We bought a new maroon Dodge car and took our first trip to foreign territory, Wisconsin. On the way to the Dells, on separate signs along the road, we read poetry: "He lit a match — to check the tank — that's why they call him — Skinless Frank — Burma–Shave". Or, "She kissed the hairbrush — by mistake — she thought it was — her husbands face — Burma-Shave". We saw Starved Rock, Lover's Leap, spectacular red rock formations and were spectators at Indian Dances. Then we headed east through the city of Green Bay, the home of the hated "Packers" who had Cecil Isbell and Don Hudson as "Bear" killers. We headed north to Door County. There we stayed for a week at the Little Sister Resort. We played with other boys and girls, swam, and did some boating. The most important thing we did on that trip was to buy a collie-sheltie puppy that my mother named "Sharp". That was the name of one of Queen Elizabeth's dogs she said, and that was that.

Then another major event occurred: Dad took me to my first ball game at Wrigley Field to see the team he and I loved, THE CUBS. As we reached the top of the ramp, suddenly the field opened up like heaven before me with the gigantic centerfield scoreboard looming over it. The only pictures I'd seen of it were in black and white. Now I saw the lush, green ivied walls, smoothly raked brown infield and the perfect white striped foul lines and batter's box. On the field were my heroes: "Smiling" Stan Hack, Phil Cavaretta, "Gabby" Hartnett, (who had hit the home run in the last of the ninth two years before to win the pennant). In the outfield were Andy Pafko (The Kid from Boyceville), Augie Galan and Bill (Swish) Nicholson. In the bullpen warming up was their best pitcher, Claude Passau. My Dad bought me a scorecard so that when Pat Piper said, "Get your pencils and score-card ready for the lineup for today's ball game," I correctly wrote in every name. (My teachers in school would have been amazed to see me more attentive than they'd ever seen me in class. I could be a top student when properly motivated.) The Cubs won, of course, and I was hooked for life.

The newspapers during the season would print individual pictures of each Cub player and most of the opposing team members also. I'd cut out these pictures and paper- clip each team together. I kept all these pictures in a tin cracker box. There were eight teams in the National League: The Boston Braves, Brooklyn Dodgers, N.Y.Giants, Cincinnati Reds, Philadelphia Phillies, Pittsburgh Pirates, Chicago Cubs and the St. Louis Cardinals (who had the best looking uniforms and a guy named Stan Musial). In the summer I'd get the box out and place the pictures of the players at their position and fantasize a ballgame, which the Cubs always won. When Hal Totten or Ronald Reagan broadcast the "ticker tape" games, I'd have each player's picture before me as they would come to bat. The announcers would fantasize and create each pitch, as the tape would only read: Hack 2-1 singles to rf, Herman 0-2 pops to ss, Pafko 3-1 triples to right, Hack scores. The great announcers of the game Jack Brickhouse, Mel Allen, Russ Hodges and Red Barber, used recorded crowd cheers that really made the game come alive.

Most all of our summers were spent at Bass Lake, Indiana. On highway 30 we'd get more poetry. "A man, a miss— a car, a curve.— he kissed the miss— and missed the curve.— Burma Shave". A few miles later, "Hardly a fool— is still alive— who passes on a hill— at 65— Burma Shave". On the last straight section of the road there were a couple of hills we'd all strain to get our first sighting of the lake. Bass Lake is the third largest lake in Indiana, ten miles around. It is shallow except for a 35- foot deep channel that was dredged in the early 1900's to allow a shallow draft steamer to go the length of the lake. There was a little town at the north end of the lake called Winona. In that town was a Bar and Grill, a bowling alley, Rupstorff's General Store, (which had a great soda fountain), a gas station, and a riding stable. There was also a fish hatchery in back of the town.

As you headed south up a slight hill, you came to "Swede's town", made up mostly of my maternal uncles, aunts and cousins. In order were the cottages of the Sundbergs, Larsons, Christensens,

Mortensons, AF Andersons, Roy Andersons, Charles Andersons and Bernard Andersons. When school let out in Chicago, the families that owned these cottages would go to the lake. The wives and children of most families would stay there until Labor Day. This included my nine cousins and the two children of the Mortenson's who were considered part of our "bunch." Our family stayed at my grandmother Mussies's cottage. Up to 1940, when the older cousins began working or went into the service we played, swam and hung out as a group. We played all the ball games kids play plus croquet, badminton, horse shoes and the chase and tag games. The driving trip from Chicago took about three hours until Hwy 30, the Lincoln Hwy, was improved to be a divided double lane road. This improvement took an hour off the trip.

Even when we were on vacation our parents insisted that we go to Sunday school at a Pilgrim Holiness Church which was two miles east of the lake. Sometimes, before going to Sunday school we'd drop in at Uncle Bunny's for his Swedish Pancakes A few years ago I got his recipe from my cousin Carol and many of our friends have been treated to "Uncle Bunny's Pancakes". The church was Pentecostal. When the Pastor or other leaders would pray they would start slowly and softly; as they continued the speed increased as well as the volume. By the time they said "Amen" the windows were rattling. If the prayer well- reflected the congregation's spirit, many in the congregation shouted "Hallelujahs" and "Praise the Lord." Most of those who prayed made God a two-syllable word, God-ah. The farmer who taught us kids was really good at making the Old Testament stories live, and referred several times in the course of the summer to his damn tractor, car or truck. This was sure a lot different than our Baptist Sunday School teachers in Chicago. We never told our parents about his swearing, as his teaching held our attention. The farmer was a God fearing man, as were all the congregation. It was good for us to see how others worshipped and depended on God. For five years they had a fund raiser going, collecting a mile of pennies, which amounted to $850, to repair the roof. God was good to them.

Our next door neighbors, the Mortenson's were Swedish Covenant folks. They had two children, Elmer Jr. whom we called Mort, and a girl, Lois who was a year younger than me. Elmer Sr. called his son Junior, even when Mort was an adult. I never heard his father refer to him as Elmer or Mort. Strange!! Lois was a pretty girl who had a cyst on her lung. The cyst had to be drained periodically through a hole in her back. This hole was just below her shoulder blade and was covered by a 4 inch square cloth bandage. When we went swimming she could not go out deeper than her waist and could not swim. She never complained about her condition and I admired her for that. When she was 15 she had surgery that removed part of her lung and the cyst, and the hole was closed.

The Mortenson's neighbors were the Christensen's. The man who lived there was a Danish Naturist. Our parents knew he liked to swim in the nude and worship the sun in the same way. We would alert all the cousins when he was about to go swimming. This was done by word of mouth as none of our cottages had telephones. He'd come out of his boat- house wearing a black wool bathing suit with only one strap over his shoulder, cave man style. He'd go to his row boat, sit astraddle the prow, and paddle with an oar out to deeper water. He would then drop the anchor and slip into the water. In a minute the black suit would be thrown into the boat and he'd swim for a while. At the end of the swim he'd reach into the boat, get the suit and usually not pull it above his waist. When he got to shore and walked to the boat house all we cousins would swim or crawl to the embankment and get a spot where we could lay and get a sight line to the open door. Soon he would walk out naked and hang the suit on a tree branch. Sometimes, if the sun was high, he'd grab a towel and lay on the grass for awhile. But most of the time his favorite way to dry was to face the western afternoon sun and stand in the doorway with one extended arm to the top door frame. It was quite a show, and we quietly laughed ourselves sick. Once my cousin Rod laughed so hard he did get physically sick. One day when he was laying on his towel, our dog wandered over to him, sniffed him, and licked his face. He really got upset about that and shooed him away.

Most of us got this free show at least once a week. His wife did not share his enthusiasm for naturism. I don't ever remember seeing her in a bathing suit.

On many evenings we would get together and tell ghost stories. My brother Will was the youngest of the cousins and was most affected by these tales. One night cousin Larry said that he had seen a ghost come out of Swanstrom's well just after sunset the previous night. After much bantering and statements of disbelief, we decided as a group to go over and investigate. About ten of us went over and stood warily, a safe distance away and watched for a few minutes. After some time, big cousin Larry took Will by the hand to the well and boosted him up so he could look down into it. When Larry turned on a flashlight, the ghost, his buddy Ralph Swanstrom wearing a sheet let out a banshee scream and leapt out of the well. Poor Will, the smallest of us, was left in the dust as we ran home. I don't know if he ever forgave us for leaving him alone to be caught by the ghost.

It's tough being the youngest cousin. When we older cousins went places where we didn't want him with us, my parents would say, "Paul, he's only two years younger than you. Conversely, when I'd put him down for not being able to do what we older cousins could do, they would say "Well Paul, you have to remember he's three years younger than you." Actually he's 2years nine months younger than me.

Another summer ended and we got into car for the trip back to Chicago. "Her Chariot raced — at ninety per — they hauled away — what had Ben Hur — Burma Shave" and a few miles later. "The hero was strong — and she was willin — She felt his face — and married the Villain — Burma Shave" It was beautiful to come home to our Elm-tree lined street and show off our new dog, Sharp, but I knew the fun was over and that tomorrow I'd be starting grade 5B.

In September, my favorite Aunt, Elvira, married a man she had met in our church Albin Person. He had emigrated from Sweden in the early 30s. He was a carpenter/contractor. When I first met him I had a hard time believing he was Swedish as he had a dark complexion, was bald and resembled Mussolini. I liked him but was hurt when Aunt Elvira told me that Will was going to be ring bearer for their wedding because he was closer in age to Cousin Adele, who was to be the flower girl. Aunt Elvira and Uncle Albin were married in the Windemere East Hotel as my Mother and Dad had been in 1927.

That winter nearly every boy in the class badgered his parents to get them Hi-Tops. These laced up boots resembled Army boots: they came up high on the calf At about mid- calf was a beautiful snapped pocket that held a three-inch pocket knife. My parents were very kind and bought a pair for me. (I told my grandsons about this last summer, they could not believe we were allowed to take a knife into school. Once again I was reminded that America was a better land in the 30s and 40s than it is today.)

It was decided that we should attend the Wednesday prayer meeting at our church as a family. After singing a couple songs and hearing scripture read, prayer requests were given by several. The Pastor then asked those who were physically able to kneel at our chairs and pray. Unless you had white hair it behooved you to get on your knees, unless you wanted to be judged to be less spiritual. The floor was wooden, and my knees were bony. Do you think less of me when I say that, after ten minutes of this, my upper torso and elbows were used to relieve my pained knees? At nearly every prayer meeting one of the regular "prayer warriors" would pray, "God wipe the cob webs of sin from our minds." One night another saint who had heard this often prayed loudly, "God kill the spider." That ended the prayers on cob webs.

On Christmas of 1940 I got a stamp book and a lot of cancelled stamps to put into it. Dad also gave me a lot of stamps on paper to soak off and add to my collection, starting me on my long enjoyed hobby of philately. Every few weeks I'd take a handful of the stamps on paper into the bath tub, as I'd bathe and play, I'd put the soaked off stamps on the tiled walls to dry. This did not please my mother as there would be a mark where each stamp had been. Stamps taught me a lot of geography and history. Learning was fun and easy that way rather than from a dull book or lesson in school. I got a wonderful new toy as a result of my parents buying a new refrigerator, a big cardboard box. I took it to a corner of the basement and it became my sanctum sanctorum for several years. I used a serrated steak knife to cut a door and window that flapped up. Unless you were invited in, it was a place for me, Sharp, my books and treasures. No brother or parents allowed!!

My sixth grade school year was not auspicious. During a snowball fight at recess I threw at an opponent, who ducked, and the snowball hit a little girl in the face. She reported me to her teacher. The teacher went to the principal and in short order I was summoned to the principal's office. His name was Otto Shank, a tall, bald German. (By the end of the year we referred to him as the Nazi.) He grabbed me by the chin and pulled me to a chair where he gave me a severe rebuke, and said I'd be suspended if I were caught throwing snowballs again. I told the girl I was sorry for what I'd done and asked her forgiveness. The rest of the day I prayed that Otto would not call my folks about the incident. He did, and that night my father administered his razor strap to my bare bottom. My report card for that semester was the worst I ever received. My teacher, Ms. Petersen, wrote on the card that she gave me low grades because she knew I could do much better. She said I was a good, smart boy, but I spent too much time dreaming and detached from the subject being taught. As I look back on those years, she was correct in that criticism.

That year we got a new Pastor, Carl Olson. He persuaded the Church to change from Swedish to English in all the worship services and all Sunday school classes except for the old ladies class that my grandmother taught in Swedish. He also persuaded the church to allow all children sixth grade and over to attend the morning worship service. This did not bring the improvement the Pastor expected. Our church had a wooden floor that slanted to the front and rows of wooden seats that were supported by cast iron frames. We boys who sat in the back row learned quickly that if we dropped a marble on the floor it would roll down to the front and pin ball off the iron frames. Marbles fell out of our pockets, by accident, more often than one would expect.

The first Sunday of each month was Communion Sunday. The Elders of the Church would pass a loaf of bread wrapped in a linen cloth to each row. The communicant would break off a piece and pass the loaf on until all were served. Each person would then eat the bread. The grape juice was then passed in a golden cup with a napkin. Each person would sip from the cup, wipe the lip of the cup and pass it on to the person next to them. A good number of younger families thought this practice should be changed. Several of the older men had big mustaches which went into the cup when they drank. Also, some older members did not wash very often.

A church business meeting was called to discuss this matter. It was proposed that we serve cubed pieces of bread on a tray, and that trays containing small individual glasses of juice be used in place of the common cup. Several mothers spoke about their concerns for good hygiene and pleaded that we make this change. A bony, "old country" Swede rose to his feet and in a trembling voice read 1 Cor.11:23-25: "*The Lord Jesus the same night in which he was betrayed took break and when he had given thanks, he brake it and said, take eat: this is my body, which is broken for you: this do in remembrance of me After the same manner also he took the cup, when he had supped saying, this cup, NOT CUPS, is the new testament in my blood: this do ye, as often as ye drink it, in remembrance of me*" He said if we adopted the proposed way, we would deny the infallibility of God's Word and he would no longer participate in the communion service. In spite of his passionate plea the church voted to make the change. I was glad that fire did not fall from heaven on us when we took communion the next month.

That spring my cousin Rod got a full size, two-wheel bike and gave me his smaller one, which I enjoyed riding to school, stores and friend's homes. We took it with us when we again drove to Bass Lake for the summer. We read more great Burma-Shave poetry. Within this vale — of toil and sin — your head grows bald — but not your chin; and Dinah doesn't — treat him right — but if he'd shave — Dinah mite! The Baseball Season of 41 may have been the greatest ever. I spent a lot of time listening to games and reading of DiMaggio's 56- game hitting streak, Williams' batting average of .406, and tremendous pennant races. Times were changing for us cousins. Burt, Ralph and Larry were either working or going into the service. Mort, Wiggs, Rod and I spent a lot of time making model airplanes out of Balsa wood, glue, and tissue paper. We went without a shirt for most of the summer and got terrific tans. (I'm paying for that now. I've had a couple dozen skin cancers taken off me over the past ten years.) We heard Reveille and Taps from a boys camp, Camp Gridley, each day, and saw them parade or row to Winona every Saturday evening. War was going on in Europe and China and threatening the U.S. We had some great "Rubber Gun" fights and "Fish" marble games. Many contests ended in soda fights with either Pepsi, Coke or R.C. the ammunition. That's when I developed a preference for the 12oz Pepsi over the 6 oz Coke. It was a no-brainer. I got twice as much ammunition with Pepsi, than I did with Coke. The Jingle went: "Pepsi Cola hits the spot; 12 full ounces that's a lot; Twice as much for a nickel too; Pepsi Cola is the drink for you. Nickel, nickel, nickel, trickle, trickle, trickle"

One day my dad took us on a trek to pick wild blueberries. After walking a couple of hundred feet we came to a barbed wire fence. My dad stepped on the bottom strand and pulled up on the top one between two wooden fence posts and directed us to pass through the opening. As I was about to do so, one of the posts broke and a swarm of Yellow Jackets streamed out and attacked us. We ran as fast as we could back to our cottage, flaying our arms at the bees as we entered the house. As you might expect a few of them got into the house on our clothes. Mother seeing this chased us out of the house. We ran to the lake and jumped in to escape them, keeping only our face above water. After about ten minutes they left, and we went back to the house to treat our bites with a wet bicarbonate poultice.

One Sunday we had only one car to take eight of us to Sunday school so Mort and I got a chance to ride on the running board while holding on to the window frame. That was my fun ride for the summer. It sure beat any carnival ride I'd ever taken. Another great summer was over with Labor Day, back to the big city and more great poetry: The wolf is shaved — so neat and trim, Red Riding hood — is chasing him — and:" If you drive — while your drunk. — carry a coffin — in your trunk — Burma Shave".

The Baseball "Fall Classic" started the first week in October, with games played in the afternoon, as God meant them to be. School boys could get sick or ditch school. Older boys, their dads could, for a variety of reasons, leave work early to get to a radio and enjoy the game The series matched the Yankees and the Dodgers. Most fans cheered for the underdog Dodgers. Alas, like the Cubs in 29, The Dodgers though down 2 games to 1 were ahead 4-3 with two outs and nobody on for the Yanks in the ninth inning. Tommy Henrich swung at strike 3, but Catcher Mickey Owens missed catching the ball and Henrich ran to first base and made it safely. Four batters later, the Yankees were ahead and won 7-4. The Yankees won the next day and won the series 4-1. That was ironic in the year of '41.

In September I started getting an allowance of a quarter a week. In return it was expected, that I would scrub the kitchen and den floor each Saturday and do outside jobs when requested like cutting grass, raking leaves and shoveling snow.

On the first Sunday of December, Mussie, Aunt Elvira and Uncle Albin came over for dinner after church and spent much of the afternoon visiting. I was in our bedroom when I heard a Paper boy calling, "Extra, Extra." I went to the den and announced that something important must have happened and we should turn on the radio. We heard of the attack on Pearl Harbor, which brought tremendous changes to all our lives in the next four years.

Christmas at "A. F.'s" with Lutfisk, Peppakakor & Santa

My maternal grandfather A. F. Anderson emigrated from Sweden to America in 1887. He settled in Chicago and soon had saved enough money to pay for his fiancee's fare to come over. During the next 14 years he founded an Iron Works, married, had five children and became fairly wealthy. In his spare time with his brother and other friends they founded the Chicago City Bank and Trust Co. He ran for state senator in Illinois on the Republican ticket in 1914. When I came along in 1929 his five children had presented him with eight grandchildren. Each Christmas was celebrated in his enormous three story brick home in the Hyde Park section at 6841 Bennett Ave. You entered the house via a large green marbled vestibule. The living room was paneled with stained glass and mahogany and the ceiling had beams of mahogany. For the Christmas Eve dinner the table was set for upwards of twenty.

When the dinner was ready my grandmother, "Mussie" would bid us to come to the table. A.F. would tell us where each family would sit. We would stand by our chairs while he seated Mussie, then he would go to the other end of the table and sit down. Then we could sit. Woe be to any of us grandkids who sat down before he did. When all were seated, he would say grace and then the food would be brought in and served. By Swedish tradition we always had potato sausage, (a veal and pork concoction which was stuffed into hog intestines and boiled.) I liked the sausage as it was well seasoned with pepper. I loved the Swedish meatballs, and still do. That was not the case with the other dish, Lutfisk, a boiled cod. This dish my cousins and I hated but were forced to eat, because if we didn't eat it, Santa Claus would not come with our presents.

Let me tell you about Lutfisk: One purchased it at the local Scandinavian delicatessen, a large side of a cod, up to a yard long, which had been dried outdoors until it was as stiff as a board, smelling like a dead fish should. Now I'll give you the instructions from a Swedish cook book on the preparation of Lutfisk:

Soaking of Lutfisk

To every two pounds of dried fish have a half lb. of soda, a half lb. of slaked lime and water. To get the fish ready for Christmas eve, begin December ninth. Divide the fish in two or three pieces and put in a tub. Add cold water to cover and place in a cool place, change the water every day for four days. Then scrub the fish on both sides and remove. Empty tub. Cover the bottom with lime; arrange a layer of fish skin down on lime. Cover with lime, add another layer of fish, skin side up, and cover with lime. Dissolve soda in a little warm water; add cold water. Pour slowly over fish until very well covered. Solution should always cover all of fish. Last of all put light press on fish (board with a stone on top)

Soak fish 5-7 days or until soft enough to let fingers penetrate thickest part easily. Remove. Rinse tub, return fish and cover with fresh cold water. Change water every day first five days, later twice every week. Fish is ready to cook after 4-5 days in fresh water. Cook small piece first to test. Fish may be kept in water a long time but becomes hard if kept too long. Now the fish is ready to prepare for dinner.

Recipe for: Boiled Lutfisk

3 lbs soaked Lutfisk. Skin and cut up fish. Place pieces close together in cheese cloth and sprinkle with salt. Place on fish rack. Cover fish with water, bring water slowly to boiling point and simmer 10 to 15 minutes. When ready, drain and remove from cheese cloth

to hot platter. Always serve with salt, black and white pepper, boiled potatoes, melted butter and white sauce.

When this was brought to the table it looked and smelled like a fish jelly with bone holding it together. All the adults' oo'd and ah'd, hoping their enthusiasm would cause their children to take a large helping. It never happened, but we eventually with the help of the cream sauce and potatoes got enough down to make sure Santa would come in the next couple of hours. (It boggles my mind to think of the thousands of grandchildren of emigrant Swedes that went thru this rite of passage every Christmas. Maybe the Lutfisk cartel paid our grandparents off.) Our meal ended with our payoff of several Pepperkakor cookies (a ginger cookie).

After dinner conversation continued around the table for some time before one of us children had the courage to ask our parents to ask A.F. if we could be excused from the table. The world would have ended if we'd had the temerity to address him directly with this request. Finally he would consent to us grandchildren being excused and we'd go off to play hide and seek in the upper rooms of the house.

While the dishes were being washed by the aunts the men retired to the living room. Many times they fell asleep as they digested the conglomeration of lutfisk, potato sausage, herring, etc. that was now churning in their stomach. I don't know of any of my cousins who inflicted Lutfisk on their children, once they left the nest.

I must say in its defense, I never heard of anyone dying from eating it.

Shortly after the ladies were done in the kitchen, they and we cousins joined our uncles and AF in the living room to await Santa's arrival. After a seemingly endless time of waiting, the back doorbell rang and Santa was ushered in with his bag of gifts.

We cousins had an age range of 14 years. Some of the older ones smirked as we younger ones were in awe of Santa's appearing and the timeliness of his arrival. Sooner or later the right of passage occurred for us as we noticed that Uncle Lawrence was missing from the circle, and Santa was wearing brown shoes like he wore. These magical Christmas gatherings ended for several reasons; the death of AF, marriages of some of the older cousins, and the coming of WW II. Five of my cousins went into the service, four returned, Ralph missing an arm; and his brother Burt, the oldest, best and brightest, never came back. On April 11, 1944, on a bombing run over Halberstadt, Germany, the B-24 that he piloted was blown out of the sky, only two of the crew of ten were able to bale out and survive. When the news of that tragedy came to our family, something died in all of us.

Chapter 2

The War Years

On Monday the eighth of December, all the children in our school gathered in the school auditorium to hear President Roosevelt's address to the Congress and the nation. I can hear it now. "Yesterday, December seventh 1941 — A date that will live in infamy — The United States was suddenly and deliberately attacked by naval and air forces of the Empire of Japan. — I ask that the Congress declare that since the unprovoked and dastardly attack by Japan on Sunday, December seventh 1941, a state of war has existed between the United States and the Japanese Empire." The following day the U.S. also declared war against Germany and Italy. Those three countries were referred to as the Axis nations. America was at war. Until that war ended with the defeat of the Axis in 1945 America, was united as it had never been before and there was great pride in being an American. In millions of windows white flags with blue borders appeared. A blue star on the white field represented someone from that home who was serving in the armed forces. If a silver star or a gold star appeared on the flag that meant that a family member was missing in action or had given their life for their country.

Early in 1942 there was only bad news from the battlefields. The Philippines, an American possession, was quickly overrun by the Japanese. On the Bataan peninsula many Americans were killed or captured. Our Russian allies armies were pushed back to Moscow and Leningrad. In North Africa the Germans, led by their brilliant General Rommel were sweeping our British allies back to Egypt.

On April 18th came the thrilling news that a squadron of 18 B-25s, commanded by Col. Jimmy Doolittle, had taken off from the aircraft carrier Hornet and dropped their bombs on Tokyo, to the complete surprise of the enemy. This did not amount to much militarily, but it was a wonderful morale builder for America.

On the home front all Americans were affected by rationing of such things as meat, coffee, sugar, gasoline and tires. No new cars were manufactured from 1942 thru 1945.

Unless you had to use the car to run a business, you were only allowed to purchase four gallons of gas a week. Each family was allowed to buy five pounds of sugar every three months. Red tokens were used to buy meat and butter. Only essential use of the automobile was encouraged. A national speed limit of 35 mph was set. Everyone was asked to turn in scrap metal and old tires, and you had to go through all kinds of paper work to get new tires. We were asked to save newspaper and cardboard and sell it to scrap dealers. Housewives were asked to save fat from frying meat and were paid four cents a pound for the fat they turned in to the butcher shop. Signs appeared on the windows of the markets," Ladies turn in your fat cans here." Comedians like Bob Hope had a great time making jokes about those signs.

Used newspaper, magazines and cardboard were sold to junk dealers at forty to fifty cents a hundred weight. That fact started me on my first business. I went to the back doors of all the three-story apartment buildings on Langley and Eberhart, between 82nd and 83rd and left notices that I would pick up all their newspaper and magazines on the back porch and haul them away on a scheduled day of the week. My Dad and I modified my Streak-O-Lite wagon with three-foot high wooden sides. Dad also gave me an old bathroom scale and twine so I could bundle the papers in 50- pound units. When I had a few tons in the garage we'd call scrap dealers and make our deal with the highest bidder. From 1942 to 1946 I made several hundred dollars from this business and bought War Bonds.

In the spring and summer we played softball in the alley, street, or school playground. For most of you, a softball is12 inches in circumference is fast pitched and fielders use gloves. The softball used in Chicago was 16 inches round and was slow pitched. One of the best players in our neighborhood was Beatie Bowman who lived across the alley from us. She was cute tomboy and as good an athlete as any of the boys. She was generally one of the first ones chosen in our pick up games. Most of us boys also noticed that she was well put together. I should also mention that she was a good piano player. In the next couple years I asked her to go out on a date, but she turned me down. This was my first disappointment in the romance area.

Many times on cold afternoons, I'd come home and walk into a warm kitchen permeated with the smell of goodies baking. Our dog, Sharp, would be lying under the high- legged stove basking in the warmth from the oven. I'd take off my coat and get under the stove and cuddle up to her warm, soft-furred body. When mother would announce that a treat and a glass of milk were on the table, Sharp and I'd get up and go to the table. I'd enjoy a chocolate chip cookie, Swedish coffee bread or, best of all, her great Limpa rye bread. Sometimes I'd give a crust to Sharp. My memories of those times are especially precious to me.

When school was out we felt it was essential for us to drive to Bass Lake so off we went. Again we enjoyed the Burma Shave signs: "If hugging on highways — is your sport — trade in your car — for a Davenport." — Burma Shave." And later, "Grandpa's beard — was stiff and coarse — and that's what caused — his fifth divorce — Burma Shave."

Boys started collecting war gum cards instead of baseball cards. There were five cards to a pack with a stick of pink bubble gum. Such heroes as MacArthur and Colin Kelly, who as a Navy Dive Bomb pilot dropped a bomb down the stack of a Japanese battleship, thus sinking it, Audie Murphy, the most medaled G I of WWII, Patton. and Eisenhower were the most sought after cards to be traded. We also in a game of skill, lagged cards to see who could get closest to the third line ahead on the sidewalk, the closest card to the line took all the cards. We did the same with pennies.

Summer was not all fun and games. Many of the farmers' sons had gone off to war so there was a labor shortage. (In the Forties twenty per cent of the U.S. population were farmers.) At the country church we went to one of the farm boys, Eldon asked Will and I if we'd like to earn some money working on his father's farm. Our job would be to hoe and weed crops and slop the hogs for 25 cents an hour. We accepted the offer. We usually worked there a couple of days a week. After working all day, Eldon, Will and I would ride our bikes home to our cottage and swim and play together.

One day we had to catch all the male pigs and pen them in. The vet was coming to neuter them. They set up a V shaped trough and slanted it at about 30 degrees. We'd catch the pigs and drag them by their hind legs to the trough, where we'd place them on their backs. As we held them as still as we could the vet cut off their male equipment. It was quite a circus with the pigs kicking and squealing and the vet hollering at us to hold them still. The Palmers' dogs also knew what was going on and scrapped and barked, vying to get the morsels the vet removed. Sometimes it took two of us to hold the bigger pigs, one on each leg. A lot of blood and sweat was involved in that task. When we went home that summer I had a lot more muscle on me.

Palmers grew 25 to 30 acres of peppermint in a mucky soil. The entire crop was contracted to Wrigley's for their gum flavors. A week before it was cut, their inspectors came to make sure that the field was weed free. They did not want weed flavors to contaminate the mint oil. In the days before the inspectors came we crawled through the itchy, mucky soil and pulled out every thing growing that was not peppermint. The following week the mint was cut and the hay rake put it in rows. After a day of sun drying, the hay wagon came and we pitch forked it onto the wagon. We sat on the mint and the tractor pulled it to the mint cooker plant 10 miles away. There the oil was pressure cooked out of it. The pressure cooker was 12-15 feet in diameter and 12 feet deep. We loaded the cut mint into the vessel, and they had us walk on it to pack it down. Then more could be put into the vat as steam was let into the bottom. As the hot vapors came up to us it made our eyes tear up. Finally the plant manager would judge that we had as much as we could get into the vat. The lid was closed and clamped down. The cooker took out the mint oil and water, which drained into drums. The mint oil separated from the water and was decanted off. The mint oil was the most important cash generator for the Palmers' farm.

When Will and I came home from that job we smelled so strongly of mint that Mom made us undress on the porch. We'd put on our bathing suits, take a bar of Fels Naptha soap and go down to the lake to try to get rid of the over powering odor that was on our bodies. The harvesting of the mint crop usually took several days.

Palmers also had 10 to 12 Guernsey cows for milk and about 100 hens. Twice a year, usually, we'd buy six dozen eggs from them. They would send them to us in egg crates by mail. Amazingly, only rarely was an egg broken in the shipment. I looked forward to these shipments, because for postage they used high denomination stamps which I'd add to my collection. Mr. Palmer was also a bee keeper and sold a lot of honey at his roadside stand.

When working at the farm, we'd go to the barnyard at lunch time to wash up in the cattle watering tank. After lunch we'd goof off sometimes and have cow pie fights. You tried to make sure when you picked one up that it had baked in the sun long enough to be hard, or else you'd get a mess on your hand. It was great fun. Then we'd wash up again, and go back to hoeing corn, picking vegetables or slopping the hogs.

In 1943, one of my biggest thrills was catching a 25- inch Walleyed Pike, but I was also disappointed, when no one had film in their camera to take a picture of it on my stringer. Film was almost impossible to get during the war years.

During those summers I read a number of baseball biographies plus: *TWO YEARS BEFORE THE MAST, THE BOUNTY TRILOGY, THE SPY, THE LAST OF THE MOHECANS, OLIVER TWIST, DAVID COPPERFIELD* and my favorite, *GREAT EXPECTATIONS* Dickens became my favorite author.

On one Fourth of July my older cousin, Rod, bought some M-80's and Cherry Bombs. We had a lot of fun watching him blow tin cans into the air and destroy milk cartons. He made a big mistake when he put one in a Wren house of Mussie's. The Cherry Bomb blew out the sides and bottom of the house. Feathers and straw along with the floor of the house were all on the ground. The roof was left hanging on a cherry tree branch. Mussie took a broom stick to Rod for that and Uncle Lawrence administered further punishment to his son that evening.

On every Friday evening we'd go to the town of Knox to pick up my dad arriving from Chicago. It was good to see the steam powered Nickel Plate RR train pull into the station. After picking him up, we'd drive back to the lake and stop at Roepstorff's for hot fudge sundaes topped with whipped cream and a cherry.

One summer day I got the worst whipping of my life. After a swim, Will and I were playing Croquet. As brothers are sometimes wont to do in these games, I noticed my brother nudging his ball with his foot in order to get a better line up for the next wicket. I called him on it. Things escalated to the point that he hit me on the shin with his mallet. I fell down screaming and writhing in pain. Mother came to the door just in time to see me pick up a ball and throw it at him as he was running away. It hit him in the kidney area and he fell screaming in pain. As Mother came down the hill she went to a maple tree, ripped off a branch and stripped the leaves as she advanced toward me. I quickly tried to explain why I had thrown the ball at him. All my protestations did no good as she got to me and applied the Maple switch to my bare legs 6 to 8 times. The welts that switch raised were visible the rest of the summer. As I lay there crying and writhing in pain I spied Will peeking around the corner of the boat house laughing at my suffering. That event did not engender brotherly love.

During the war years my Uncle Lawrence would get 16mm sound "March of Time" movies from the library and invite the relatives over to see the newsreels, mostly of the war, in his basement movie room. My Aunt Judy would provide our supper prior to the movie. I still picture Uncle Lawrence prior to the supper, sitting in front of his green eyed Philco. In the winter months he wore an olive colored wool knit cap on his bald head and over his cap he wore ear phones. Every few minutes he'd announce loudly to all that he was listening to Hong Kong or Calcutta etc. on the shortwave radio. After dinner he'd set up his flood lights and Speed Graphic to take family pictures. Everybody hated these sessions except him. His four children especially never wanted their picture taken. I don't think any of my Larson cousins owned a camera until well after they'd flown the nest.

My mother continued to play the Northwestern 400 hour on the radio and I started my record collection with 78 rpm recordings of: *MARCH SLAV,*, *The1812 OVERTURE* and other Wagner and Von Suppe' overtures. I got a portable record player for my birthday and the *TSCHAIKOVSKY'S PIANO CONCERTO #1* on four records. Each side of a record had a maximum of 5 minutes of music. It was my favorite piece of music; Rubenstein was the pianist. I also got a few of Rossini's overtures, *La GAZZA LADRA* and *WILLIAM TELL.*

The war news turned generally for the better in mid 1942, as US Navy Carriers found the Japanese fleet of Carriers off Midway Island and sank all but one of them. That was the beginning of the end for Japanese expansion in the Pacific area. From then on they were on the defensive as the US Marines attacked the Japanese held islands and won them from them. The Russians turned the tide of battle against the Germans at Stalingrad in the winter of 1941-42, inflicting heavy casualties on them, and by the end of 44 had pushed them back to Germany. At El Alamein in Egypt the British won a big battle, and by 1943 had pushed the Germans out of Africa.

My Uncle Bernard's family received very bad news, my cousin, Ralph's lower arm had been blown off by a faulty hand grenade. Even worse news came that son Burt's B24 (Liberator) bomber had gone down over Germany, and only three of the ten aboard had been able to parachute out and the ten were now listed as missing in action.

In the sixth grade we had Mrs. Agnes Olney as our home room teacher. Her teaching assignment was to educate us on the facts of US History starting with Columbus's discovery of the continent, up through Colonial times, and the calling of the first Continental Congress in 1774. She spent so much time talking about the colonies and their troubles that someone dubbed the lady, "Agony Olney the Hag of the colony." Isn't it sad that that's what I remember most about her?

When we got to sixth grade field trips were made to the Field Museum, The Museum of Science and Industry, and The Brookfield Zoo. In the next school year we toured the Union Stock Yards where we were all shocked by what we saw. The pigs had one of their back legs shackled to a chain, and were then upended and conveyed while squealing down a cable to the butchering floor. There men with bloodied knives slit their throats. The blood gushed out and splattered their knee high rubber boots. As the pigs moved down the line they were put in boiling water and the hair was removed. They were then cleaved down the middle and their guts spilled out on the floor. We then went to where the cattle were killed and butchered. The cattle were herded into a wedge shaped corral that eventually became a single file chute. At the end of the chute a man astride the chute hit them on the top of the head with a sledge hammer. The unconscious animal then slid out of the chute, was shackled on both legs, and upended on a conveyor line. There they were stabbed in the heart and gutted like the pigs.

It was impressive to see iron ore turn into ingots and finally into bars or rolls of steel. We also saw hot, dirtied, sweating men working at very dangerous jobs. After the tours of the Stock Yards and the Steel plant our teachers pointed out we'd better study or we might end up butchering hogs or pouring red hot steel the rest of our life. I did a lot better in school in the 7 and 8th grades; Mrs Cohn and Mrs Harris were my teachers and they knew how to make learning exciting. I got top grades in history and general science.

In October of 1944, I and most of my Sunday school buddies got to our rebellious stage. We went against our church and parent's teaching that movies were sinful. One Sunday afternoon, when our parents thought we had gone to a young peoples meeting at church, we went to a double feature at the Southtown Theatre. We saw "Hail the Conquering Hero" and "Tall in the Saddle" featuring actors John Wayne, Gabby Hayes and a stunning tall brunette "cowgirl," Ella Raines. I remember praying while sitting in the darkness that my folks would not find out where I was and that Jesus would not come and find me in a MOTION PICTURE show. To my knowledge my folks did not find out, but Jesus knew and that left me with a guilty conscience.

That fall most of our teenage Sunday school class gave their testimonies of faith to the Deacons and were baptized into the church. Our middle-aged Pastor Olson had enlisted in the Navy, and we were left with Pastor Dr. Hagstrom, who was well into his 70's. One of our class members, Frank Kumlander, was a 200-pound football lineman. When Dr. Hagstrom lowered him into the waters of baptism, he could not lift him out of the water and he lost his grip on him. The word passed back through our line of baptismal candidates, "Hagstom lost Frank." Fortunately, Frank did pull himself up to newness of life.

During Halloween week our Sunday school teacher invited us to his house for a party. His son was in our class. Their house was on Claremont Ave a half block from Western Ave., a major street in Chicago, with streetcars running on it. At some point in the evening it was suggested we go out for a walk. We crossed vacant lots. Many local people had "Victory Gardens" on these lots. Frost had killed the tomato plants but there were many tomatoes, red and green laying on the ground. Most of us athletes decided it would be fun to throw the tomatoes at passing streetcars and cars. When one car was hit, the driver pulled over and ran toward us. We ran back toward our teacher's house. Poor Frank tripped over one of the low fences people had around their gardens and fell face down, knocking the wind out of him. Fortunately, the person chasing us gave up the chase and we escaped. We learned that night that it was dangerous to do that kind of mischief, as we might have been attacked by the people we were throwing at or reported to the police and arrested. In the next few years I never threw anything other than snowballs at cars. I can't say that was a good thing to do either.

I graduated from Dixon school in February 1944, and the next week started my high School studies at Hirsch. Mother insisted I take Latin as she explained it was the mother of all languages. All I remember from that course is hic, haec, hoc and amo, amas, amat. Half the time the teacher gave us the thrill of conjugating verbs. I'm sure you are not surprised when I report that I ended up that course with a grade of D.I also took Algebra, taught by one of the worst teachers I ever had. That, combined with my poor study habits resulted in a C-.

We church buddies had an embarrassing winter night when we told our parents we were going bowling and instead went to another picture show at the Southtown theatre. When we came out, Paul Brown's car wouldn't start. Our teacher at church was his father.

Paul called him to come to jump start the car. For this our Paul got grounded for a couple of weeks, and the entire class got another lesson on the commandment regarding bearing false witness. We young Baptist boys also smoked cigarettes when we went out in order to emulate John Wayne, GI's and other movie tough guys. Fortunately, when we got out of high school only one or two of us had acquired a nicotine addiction, and we gave up something that could have eventually killed us.

Most of my friends at church went against the teaching of our church and parents on social issues. I'm glad to say, however, that we never drank alcoholic beverages, and we didn't know anything about drugs. The worst thing we did was to lie to our parents when we went out as to where we were going and what we were doing. I believe they knew what we were doing, but that only encouraged them to pray all the more. When my brother found out I was going to movies, he told me I was going to hell.

In all those teen years I was in leadership of our young peoples group at the church. I had head knowledge of the faith. I talked the talk on Sunday but did not walk the walk the rest of the week. I was a hypocrite.

A major crisis arose for me in March of '44. On the way home from Hirsch, while walking down the alley with a couple of buddies, I had smoked a cigarette. I entered the house through the kitchen door. In the middle of the room Mother was ironing, and I had to squeeze by her. She smelled the smoke odor on my clothes. There was no way to hide my guilt. When she asked if I'd been smoking, I confessed. She started crying and sent me to my room to await my Father. When he came home he asked me to give him my Cigarettes. We went down to the furnace and threw them into the fire. Then he led me upstairs and gave me the last and hardest whipping I ever received from him. After baring my backside he laid into me with his razor strop. In a conference a few days later my parents informed me that they were going to enroll me in Chicago Christian High

School in the fall. The ironic thing about that was the school was run by the Dutch Reformed Church, and a greater percentage of the boys at that school smoked than did at Hirsch.

It took me only 15 minutes to walk to Hirsch. To get to CCHS it was a half mile walk to the 79th streetcar line and three and a half mile ride on the streetcar. The student fare on the street car was four cents, and it took about 45 minutes door to door. There were no school buses to any of the city schools. Several good things happened because of the move to Chicago Christian. I got teachers who taught their subjects well. I took courses in Old and New Testament and my knowledge and understanding increased. I got good grades in zoology and physics and at least average grades in Geometry. I went out for the basketball team in the fall but did not make the cut.

Also that fall, mom decided that since we had a grand piano, Will and I should learn to play it. It was one of the few mistakes she made in our rearing. Esther Nelson was our teacher. She was not successful in inspiring us to become pianists. She tried to challenge us by telling us how well the Brunzell boys, Ed and Wayne, were doing. Sylvia their mother was a good friend of mom's, and was always bragging about how well her sons were doing on the piano. Before I'd practice each afternoon mom set up the alarm clock that went off after a half hour of bungled scales and pieces. I never saw clock hands move so slowly. All of Miss Nelson's students had to participate in the spring recital, where the poor parents had to sit through an hour of memorized, butchered pieces in order to hear the Brunzell boys dazzle them with their artistry. We endured this for a couple of years. Thankfully, at our second recital, Will bailed us out. He had a simplified version of the first movement of the Grieg Piano Concerto to perform. It opens with seven descending chords. He did them beautifully and then went blank. Ester had him start three more times but it did not work. He got up from the piano bench and returned to his seat next to our family. He got the biggest ovation that evening from the adults who were glad he'd shortened the program. That ended our drive to be child protégés on the piano.

During June of 1944, before my transfer to CCHS, the war news improved. US and British forces landed on Normandy's Beaches in France, and the Italians surrendered as US forces invaded Italy. Now the Germans had to fight the Allies on three fronts. By the end of '44, the Russians had pushed the Germans out of Russia and were only a few hundred miles from the German border on the east. The US and British forces were on the German border on the west, and Allied forces were almost to the Italian Alps on the South. The Japanese were being defeated in the Philippines, and US B29s were daily bombing the Japanese homeland. My cousin Larry Larson was a Bombardier on one of those B29s.

In November, dad helped me to build a rectangular shack under the back porch that was MINE. Dad bought the plywood and siding and in return I offered to bank the coal furnace at night, take out the clinkers in the morning, and refuel with coal. The shack was built on a concrete slab that was under the porch. The ceiling was the porch floor. Later I found a junked carpet runner that I cut to fit the area, which was about four by eight feet. I put a latch lock on the door and no one was allowed in but our dog. I had a four-inch high box to sit on. In there I read my comic books and other books, looked at and updated my collection of clippings of baseball players and beautiful women such as Rita Hayworth and Betty Grable. I also fantasized on my Cubs being the World Series Champs. It also helped me become more of an introvert.

1945 was a pivotal year in history. In April President Roosevelt died of a stroke, and Harry Truman became president. On May eighth Germany surrendered, and the fighting in Europe ended. On August 8th the first atomic bomb was dropped on Hiroshima, Japan, and as a result Japan surrendered on August 14th. It is estimated that 45 to 50 million people were killed as a result of WWII. My Uncle

Bernard's family received confirmation that cousin Burt was killed when the plane he piloted was shot down over Germany. What a terrible price that family paid because of the war. Burt's brother Ralph had lost an arm to a grenade and his brother, "Wiggs", had been on a ship that was attacked by Japanese suicide bombers.

When the war ended I was sad that I had not had the thrill of fighting in it. However, as I heard my cousins and others tell their stories about the war, and learned more by study, I became thankful that I had not been born a few years earlier, or I might have experienced the horrors of war as they had.

Come September my prayers were answered. The Cubs were in the World Series. They owed a special debt of gratitude to the Reds who lost 21 of 22 games to the Cubs. They were National League champs and their opponents from the American league were the Detroit Tigers. Both teams had lost most of their best players to the armed forces. At the end of six games they were tied 3 games to 3. The series went to the final game at Wrigley Field. Hal Newhowser the top lefty in the American League was to be opposed by Hank Borowy of the Cubs. Bleacher seats were available for the game and went on sale at ten am. Will and I and a couple of friends convinced our parents to let us take the El at three am so we could get in line for tickets. We got there at four am and stood in line for six hours. We were about three quarters of a block away when the box office opened. We moved up as the tickets were sold and there were ten ahead of us when the last ticket was sold. We went home sad. Later in the day we were sadder yet as we listened to the game. The Tigers scored five runs in the top of the first and the game ended 9-3. The Tigers were World Champions.

I have in my memorabilia two, cheepo Woolworth scrapbooks with the box scores of every Cubs game in the 1945 season and every article in the sport section about the World Series. Unfortunately, the acid in the scrapbook paper continues to embrittle the paper and more and more of it is crumbling away. It's been 66 years since the

Cubs were in the World Series and over100 years since they won it. If they don't win it before I shuffle off this mortal coil, maybe I should have the scrapbook's ashes buried with my remains.

Alleys, Garbage Cans, & Fires *

The first twenty years of my life our family lived in a bungalow on the far southeast side of Chicago. We were halfway between the stockyards to the northwest and the steel mills of South Chicago and Gary, Indiana. When the wind blew from the northwest we got the stench of rotting offal from the Union Stock Yards, and when the wind came from the southeast we got the sulfurous smoke of the blast furnaces. To compensate for this the city fathers gave us smooth concrete alleys off our back yards. This made a wondrous rink to play roller skate hockey. We made pucks by sawing off discs from four inch asbestos pipe insulation tubes. When the pucks abraded down too much we just sawed off another one. OSHA didn't stop us once. Telephone poles had cut off bushel baskets nailed to them ten feet off the ground for our basketball games, the pole also served as "home" for, hide and seek, chase one chase all, and free the bunch games.

Baseball was a challenge as you could only hit to centerfield. Neighbor's yards, some of which had ferocious barking dogs, were "out," and the one who hit it there had to fetch it. This also tried the patience of neighbors when we flipped over their fence to retrieve a ball in their flower beds. A number of balls were lost when they went through garage windows. Naturally, with our father's assistance, we replaced the windows thus learning how to do that job correctly.

There were spirited games of kick the can. I remember one game when we used a near empty paint can and set it on fire to get an added bang out of the game. (Oil based paints wet and dry, burn wondrously and smoky.) The can when kicked caused the burning paint to be sprayed around increasing our delight. One of my friends still has a scar on his leg where he was branded by a red hot can.

In the thirties, the depression, it was common to have beggars come to the door asking for work or a sandwich. My mother made a couple extra sandwiches each day when she made my dad's lunch and would give them to the men with a Christian tract when they asked for help. Rag, newspaper and scrap metal dealers, along with Milkmen and Icemen, came down the alley in their horse- drawn wagons. These horses many times left fertilizer for my father's roses and dahlias.

Garbage cans were put just inside the back fence and were public property for young boys looking for hidden treasure. I once found an old "22" rifle and used it when we played cops and robbers or cowboys and Indians. That treasure was taken from me when a squad car came down the alley and two of Chicago's finest asked me to surrender my weapon. It did no good for me to tell them I had no bullets and to point out that the firing pin was missing from the gun. They disposed of my weapon by putting it between two bricks and running over it a couple of times. It's fortunate that that incident didn't make me a cop hater and lead me into a life of crime. We had a lot of police protection in our ward; Al Capone lived a half mile west of us.

Garbage containers were either square concrete receptacles with a steel top lid, or 30 to 40 gallon drums. Containers sometimes got full before collection time, so some neighbors set their trash on fire in order to make more room. This smoke added to the ambience of the neighborhood.

A good garbage can was hard to come by. The recently introduced galvanized 30 gallon cans were no match for Chicago's sanitation engineers, who would empty them by banging them down on the back lip of the truck. A year of this abuse turned them into 20 gallon containers looking like they were designed by Dali. The best garbage cans were used 40 gallon oil or grease drums that you could get from your local gas station.

Just before the Pearl Harbor attack, the bottom of our garbage can rusted out. I asked the local Sinclair station owner to let me have a waste drum that was quite a mess. He let me take it when I told him I wanted to clean it up so it could be used as a garbage can. My plan was to give it to my parents as a Christmas present. He was nice enough to give me a top that clamped on to it. So, how was I to get it cleaned up? I couldn't use my mother's rags. They were too valuable. The best answer was to burn up the oil and grease. I rolled the drum down the alley until it was about ten feet from the back of our garage, then tipped it up and set it on fire. I soon found out how much smoke and fire this would cause.

Kids from blocks away came to find the source of the pillar of smoke. Soon there was quite a crowd seeing my fire works. I'm still amazed that no one called the fire department, which would have probably dashed my dream of giving this present to my folks.

After about a half hour I heard my mother calling me to supper. I knew I couldn't leave the fire burning unattended. I had to put it out. How do you put out a fire? You pour water on it. I tried the hose but it was all frozen up so I got the biggest bucket of water I could carry, lifted it to the top of the almost red hot drum and dumped it in. BABOOM!! A column of burning oil and steam whooshed past my face all the way up to the telephone wires. For that I achieved instant fame with my friends. I also got a singed wool cap and eyebrows. The explosion blew out the fire and the oil and grease from the drum. When I came into the house I had to explain my red face, singed cap and eyebrows. My parents went out and saw their new garbage can. They also said they were glad that I hadn't scarred my face for life.

That can lasted ten years. We left it when we moved to a new home in Beverly Hills, on the southwest side of Chicago. The burned spot and oil stain was still on the alley as a reminder of my escapade.

* Or: How Children had fun before TV, Nintendo, X Box and Cell Phones.

Chapter 3

Some Ups and Mostly Downs

I had high hopes of making the team in basketball and even greater hopes to make the baseball team at Chicago Christian, but neither dream was realized. As a junior in 1947, our school had the best pitcher in the state, George Zoetterman. He pitched two no- hitters that year, and in three games had over 20 strikeouts. He made the front page of the sports section of the Chicago Tribune on several occasions. The last time he was pictured was when he signed with the White Sox for the highest bid that had ever been offered a Chicago prep star. With all the fame he got for his 90 + MPH fast ball it never went to his head and he was the most popular guy in our class. I would love to have played on that team but that did not happen. In his second year in the minors George got a sore arm that ended his baseball career. Fortunately, George had saved most of his bonus money and used it to start a private scavenger business in Chicago's southeast suburbs. He became one of the most successful of the graduation class in February 1948.

The assistant basketball coach, who was also, the track coach, asked me to try out for the track team and I made it as a middle distance runner. I was the number two or three runner on the mile relay team and the number one half- miler. My best time for the half mile was run in a three team race which I won with a time of 2:08. My most important race was for the parochial high schools' city championship which was held at Stagg Field on the U.

of Chicago campus. In that race I ran a time of 2:11 and finished third. That season I won all but three of my races. (Stagg Field received immortality when it was revealed that in 1942, under the stands of that field, the first sustained nuclear reaction had taken place. Enrico Fermi and his fellow scientists had brought to birth the Atomic age a few feet from where I had run.)

When the worst war in history ended in 1945, the whole world breathed a sigh of relief, but it wasn't long before our former allies, communist Russia, took over other countries such as Poland, Hungary, and Austria. The Chinese Communists defeated the nationalist government and also fomented revolution in other countries in Asia. For a few years the US and its democratic allies held the edge because they had the atomic bomb, but by 1950, the Communist countries also had this terrible weapon. As a result the whole world now lived under the fear of nuclear destruction. That terrible sword still hangs over the world and wars and rumors of war still go on to trouble our lives and bring death to many.

In 1946, I had my first toothache in a lower right molar. Our family dentist, Dr. Runyon, found it was so decayed that he had to pull it. After that he gave my teeth a further exam. When he was done he asked me how old I was. I answered 16. He factiously congratulated me for having a cavity for every birthday. In order to help my folks out, he offered me a job working in his office in order to pay off my up coming bills. At that time there wasn't any fluorinated water or toothpastes, which greatly reduced tooth decay; plus most families could not afford regular six month check ups to detect dental problems early. Most of the calcium I was taking into my body was going to the bone division. It didn't help either that there were days when I forgot to brush my teeth to get rid of food and candy particles, chewed Bazooka bubble gum and drank a lot of acidic, sweet Pepsi. I accepted his offer and for about two years worked four to six hours a week as his lab technician. I helped him make amalgam fillings, impressions of upper and lower jaws for full and partial dental plates and crowns. I also cleaned and waxed floors once a week.

On my sixteenth birthday I received a top of the line Gilbert Chemistry set. Dad gave me about five feet of his work bench to do the experiments their book suggested. At the same time I found I was enjoying doing the lab work for Dr. Runyon. I soon decided that I wanted to go to college to major in Chemistry and to spend my life discovering new products that would, as the DuPont slogan said: "Make better things for living through Chemistry."

Another of my friends, Ken Bell, also had an interest in chemistry, but he had expanded from the listed experiments. He got a good recipe for gun powder, went to a laboratory supply store and bought the ingredients. (I hope no one can do that today. It had the make-up of the bomb that was used in Oklahoma City a few years ago) He mixed the chemicals together in his basement and encapsulated them in various sized capsules which he then taped. He gave me some of them to have fun with, throwing them against walls, etc. A bomb the size of a standard vitamin capsule was equivalent to a "Cherry Bomb." When we'd walk down the alley and throw them against a wall or drop them on pavement from 20 to 30 feet above, they'd give an impressive bang.

One afternoon a few of us buddies were in his basement as he was filling capsules. The powder stuck in the funnel neck and he shook it to loosen it up. The funnel end hit a solid surface and it exploded. None of us bystanders were hurt except that some of us had our ears ringing for a couple of days. Luckily for him, only the neck of the funnel had blown off, the main force of the explosion had gone out the wide part of the funnel. He had a severe cut and a powder burn on his hand but did not suffer loss of any fingers or use of his hand. That ended our fooling around with explosives. Thank God that He gave us a lesson before we did more serious damage to ourselves and others, or got in trouble with the police.

On Sunday afternoon the teens met for what was hoped would engender spiritual growth and good Christian fellowship. I imagine that I did get some good teaching, but the only positive lesson I remember is the one about filling the Mason jar. The teacher first poured as many golf balls into the jar as he could and asked us if the jar was full. We said, yes. Then he poured marbles into the same jar while shaking it. Quite a few marbles filled the voids between the golf balls, and he asked again if the jar was full; most again said yes. Then he put in a couple handfuls of dried peas were poured in the jar. Again the question; not many said yes this time as we got the point. He said the majority were right that time as he then poured in sand. Again the question came, this time most again said yes. He then poured a full glass of water into the jar before it overflowed. His lesson was that we may feel we have enough of God in us and not realize that if we want more of Him, He is ready to give us above and beyond what we can ask or imagine. That is very true. I just wish I could remember more of what he taught us, but I don't remember the good episodes as well as I do the bad. For example: Oscar Ostling was a deacon in the church, and a gentleman's gentleman. It fell to him to give us a temperance lesson. He set two glasses on the table. One contained water, and the other Ethyl alcohol. He then took two big earth worms and put them in the glass of water. They wiggled around for a couple minutes. Then he fished them out and put them in the alcohol. Within a few seconds, they lay dead on the bottom of the glass. When he asked us if we got the point, one of my buddies answered," If you drink alcohol, you won't have worms." Poor Mr. Ostling, rest his soul. I'm sure he knew we got the point, but what we all remembered was the wise guy's reply.

Paul, one of my friends had a model A Ford with a rumble seat; unless it was raining or below freezing we all vied to ride in the rumble seat. We'd drive around looking for girls, and in order to look macho, we'd smoke. One night we were pulled over by a policeman. When he started lecturing us on our behavior, one of our group had the gall to speak up. "Sir, we're a Sunday School class." Our friend never lived that down.

One Sunday afternoon at church, Ken Bell used gas filled balloons to illustrate a lesson. When the meeting was over we had about an hour to kill, so we played with the balloons. We went up to the sanctuary to goof off and accidentally two of them settled at the apex of the ceiling about 40 feet up and directly over the pulpit. Word spread to the young people about this. Consequently, when the service began the front of the church was filled with young people who were looking up at the balloons. This was observed by the adults as they sat down. When Pastor, Dr. Olson came in, he was probably the only person in the sanctuary who was unaware of the balloons. You guessed it! In the middle of his sermon one of the balloons slowly descended and Ken's sisters rushed forward to catch it. Pastor Olson, filled with righteous anger, departed from his sermon and gave those responsible a stern lecture on the sanctity of God's house. God was surely offended by this action and those responsible for it needed to fall on their faces before Him and beg for forgiveness. He did not ask those who had done this to step forward, and I think that was wise. It had been a joint effort and we had all been rightly chastised. It was a long and quiet ride home with my mom and dad that night.

The summer of 1947, I spent a lot of the weekdays scraping and painting the wood on our house and garage. On the weekends, dad and I would take the train and spend Saturday and Sunday at Bass Lake. I spent most of August at the lake. Those weeks were to be eventful to say the least.

My grandmother's cottage sat on a slight bluff that arose about 100 feet from the lake. Within fifty feet of the cottage were two enormous oak trees. The circumference of each tree was 12 to 13 feet. One Sunday afternoon a thunderstorm hit us that out-did all we'd ever seen; boats, canoes, and lawn furniture were blown across the yard. The cottage did not have a cellar so we just had to sit in the living room and observe the storm's fury. My grandmother sat in her rocking chair with her eyes closed. I'm sure she was asking God to protect us. Suddenly, there was a loud crack as the oak nearest us split. One half went toward the other oak and knocked it over. When the trees hit, the ground shook and we felt the force. If either of those trees had come down on our cottage it would have reduced it to splinters and we might have been killed. Grandmother's fervent prayers may have saved us that afternoon. The only damage to the neighbor's cottage were, some shingles blown off, a gutter torn away, and a few holes in the screens of the porch. A large maple tree next to our garage was also toppled over. The roots of the tree lifted the concrete slab, so the garage was three feet off the ground on the south end. The weather experts later said that our area had experienced several "tree-top tornados." It took a couple of weeks, using the largest chain saws to cut up the three trees.

One of the cottages close to us was occupied by the Larson family. My cousins, Larry, Debbie and Rod came out on the weekends, but my youngest cousin Adele, was there most of the summer with her girlfriend, Joan Dilly. Joan was the cheer leader captain of Hirsch High School. Think of the most enticing teenage girl you ever saw and square it and you'll approximate Joan. She was mouth- gapingly seductive and had most all the boys at Hirsch dangling on her leash. She dated only a few of the football heroes. She lived to drive boys with hopping hormones to distraction. I was one of them!

At the lake I was privileged several times to apply our favorite tan lotion, which was Johnson's Baby Oil with a few cc's of Iodine in it, to her skin. She reciprocated that favor to me several times. At those times I was transported to heights of fantasy and joy. I never asked her for a date as I knew I would be turned down and that would have destroyed my dream. For years I had romantic dreams about us together, but if I couldn't fulfill that dream I was willing to be her baby oil slave. Mother warned me to stay away from girls like her, and I know she would have been on her knees all night praying if I'd ever dated Joan. On many nights Adele, Joan, and I would walk downtown to the bowling alley where the teenagers hung out. Many nights Joan would go off with the hood of the group, a dark Greek kid named Carly Newey. How could she choose him when I was available? At that time I would describe myself as a skinny Ron Howard. Adele told me that Betty Conners thought that I was a wow and would like me to take her on a hay ride that Adele and Joan were also going on. I asked Adele to set it up. I'd meet Betty at the stable at 8 on Saturday night. The following chapter is an account of that first date. Another summer ended at Bass Lake. As we drove home we smiled when reading: "The chick he wed—let out a whoop—felt his chin—and flew the coop—Burma Shave.

When we came home on that Labor Day weekend we found that our home had been burglarized. The thieves had entered by breaking a back window of our den. The police said that the robbery had been very professional. It made us sick to see that in the bedrooms they had dumped every dresser drawer on the beds. They had pawed through all our possessions. They even scooped out Noxema and Vaseline to see if jewels had been hidden in the creams. To get that off their hands they wiped them on the drapes. When mother saw that she cried. What they took they put into pillow cases that were missing from my folks bed. They didn't get much of value, but they messed up our home so badly that it took us a couple of weeks to put it back together. We felt violated and afraid that it could happen again.

My First Date, Kiss, Etc

I was fixed up to go on my first date by my cousin Adele with a girl named Betty Conners. Betty lived in back of the "Conners Garage and General Store", about a mile south of us on Bass Lake. The Conners garage could be described as a run down type" 7-11". Betty and her mother ran the store and Hank, her father, and her grandfather, Harv, ran the garage. Hank was the best handyman or mechanic on our end of the lake. He also was the garbage collector who came every Tuesday to pick up our trash. His father Harv worked in the garage and manned the gas pump. The gas pump was an old type that had a glass tank on top of the pump. Harv would pump the number of gallons you wanted into the glass tank and then empty it into the auto's tank; you could see what you were getting. Harv was also known as the town drunk. Every Saturday night about 6 o'clock he'd walk by on his way to Jaxx's bar and restaurant in Winona, He'd stagger home between 10 and midnight, talking or arguing with himself. One night my cousin Rod and I stumbled over him as he lay on the shoulder of the road.

Betty told my cousin Adele that she'd like to go on a hay ride with me that Adele and Joan were planning. Betty thought that I was a "wow". It was set up that I would meet her at the stable and be her date for the night. After the ride, she would go to the bar and get a ride home with her dad. When I spied her at the stable, she could well have been a stand in for Daisy Mae of Li'l Abner. She had short blonde hair, and was wearing a red kerchief around her neck, a peasant blouse and very short, cut- off blue jeans. She was quite a package.

When everyone was there, the wagon driver took our two dollars and set the rules for behavior: No drinking or smoking and no throwing of hay would be allowed. Our behavior was to be proper, and if a couple got too passionate he'd have the boy come to the front of the wagon and sit beside him for the rest of the ride. He said we would have a rest stop in about an hour, and at that place we could get a drink of water or buy a soda. There were about 10 to 12 couples that got on the wagon.

Betty and I got on the wagon about half way back on the far side. There was one pleasant surprise, the hay was about a foot deep so it was comfortable. The only other hay ride I'd been on was with our church youth group, there was only a couple of inches of hay on the wagon, and that was quickly disposed of by a few idiots who got into a hay throwing fight, or thought it was great fun to stick a hand full of it down one's back. By the end of the ride no hay was left on the wagon and many had itching eyes and backs from the scratchy hay; some fun!

We layed on the hay and looked up at the stars for a while, but then she rolled toward me and pulled some hay up to cover us. What a surprise I got when she rolled on top of me and kissed me. I kissed back and the next thing I knew she was pushing her tongue through my closed lips. Shock, pleasure, guilt, and hopping hormones in my engine room were exploding all at once. I as a young boy I had debated at length with my Baptist buddies about how many dates you should have with a girl before you kissed her goodnight. (Our general consensus was three.) After a couple more of these kisses she took my hands and put them on places they had never been before, and said; "I want to go all the way." I said I was afraid the driver would see that and I'd have to go up front, so we'd better not do it. I'd passed a defining moment in my life, but I gave her the wrong reason. I should have said, "I believe it's a sin to do that, but I didn't. So I passed that defining moment with a D minus.

Betty was cool to me for the rest of the hay ride, and when I walked her back to the tavern where her father waited I didn't even try to give her a peck on the cheek. I never dated Betty again. She told Adele that I was a goody-goody boy. Well, I wasn't that good, but God saved me from doing something that night that could have changed the entire course of my life for the worst.

I've thought about that experience many times in my life. Why was I able to stop going further with Betty? My cousin Adele and Joan Dilly were on that wagon and I didn't want to be embarrassed in front of them. The thing that scares me is what we might have done if we'd been alone, and what might have resulted if we'd had sex. I've known enough people who for a few minutes of pleasure messed up the rest of their lives in doing something they knew was wrong. The book of Proverbs says: "Train up a child in the way he should go, and when he is old he will not depart from it." Our Church, Sunday school and especially my parents, taught me the Ten Commandments, the Sermon on the Mount, the Epistles of Paul, especially those to the Romans and Corinthians, I knew the Old Testament accounts of Joseph and Potiphar's wife, and David and Bathsheba. All this was in my mind as I was being tempted. I had goals in life that I wanted to achieve: a college education leading to a degree in chemistry. That dream might have ended if I'd become a father at 18. Last but not least, I had great pride and love for my family and their reputation, and I did not want to do anything that would bring sorrow and shame to them.

Now, as I near the end of my life what disappoints me is the fact that in the early years of my life I was not a good witness for Jesus Christ. The Question haunts me, what happened to Betty, where is she now?

Chapter 4

Tragedy and Triumph

During the summer of '47 at Bass Lake my mother taught me to drive and in June of '48 I got my driver's license. It was not until August, when they traded in their Dodge for a sky blue '48 Chrysler, that I was allowed to drive with them as passengers in the car.

I applied to Wheaton College for entrance in the fall of 1948. At that time there was no such thing as SAT, and the sole criterion Wheaton had to judge me on were my grades. Wheaton responded that my grades were not good enough to prove I could do college level work and urged me to go to another college to prove I could do better. If my grades improved, they would consider my entrance for the fall of '49. I had saved $900 toward my college education, but I knew that was only enough for one year. I'd have to work as much as possible to get myself through. Others suggested that I go to Illinois Institute of Technology and take their aptitude test. They would give me guidance on what my major could be. Many, including my parents, advised me to apply to Bethel College for admission. They accepted me for the Spring quarter of 1948.The IIT Test showed I had aptitude in music, chemistry and other sciences, and I scored high in history and geography. The devastating news was that I was poor in math, which I needed to take to get a degree in chemistry. My dad suggested I take the Civil Service exam so that if all else failed I could get a government job. This turned out to be a great suggestion. In my last semester at CCHS, I made pretty good grades.

I celebrated my 18th birthday on December 20th. I was a quarter- inch short of six feet tall and weighed 130 pounds.

Our class of 45 students graduated in February. My folks presented me with my first wrist watch, a Lord Elgin engraved suitably for the occasion. I was ready to go to college. In the fall my best friend in the class, Bruce Brown, a "brain," would go to Wheaton, where we both had planned to major in chemistry. Dr. Runyon for whom I had worked gave me $50 to help send me off to college in style.

My father and I took a great train, the Vista Domed Burlington Zephyr, up to St. Paul. On the trip he told me that mom and he had saved four thousand dollars for my college education. They believed that would cover my room, board and tuition. I would have to work to pay for books and incidentals. I was in shock that they had been able to save this much on his meager government pay. He also said they had set aside the same amount for brother, Will. He advised me to study hard so that I could prove to Wheaton College that I could get good grades and be accepted by them the following year. They had confidence that I could be a good student. Their generosity was a great motivator for me to do my best.

At college I finally learned to study and got good to excellent grades in that first spring quarter. That first quarter my only extra-curricular activity was track, and I ran the half mile. I declared my major as chemistry and took a rigid course schedule which included remedial English (You who are reading this treatise may wonder if I passed that course.) The only subject I struggled with was college algebra. I had to be tutored in basic algebra as I had barely passed that in high school. On Saturday mornings I took a course at the U of Minnesota on WWII history in Europe. The course was taught by a former lieutenant in the German army who fought most of the war on the Russian front. He made that history so exciting for me that I have been a reader of WWII and Civil War history all my life. At Bethel I also took music appreciation and sang in a church choir. That got me started in singing in many choirs for most of my life. From 1949 to 1972, every Christmas, with various choirs, I sang Handel's Messiah. I was taught Old Testament by Dr. Sam Schultz. Fifty three years later he was one of the first people I met when we moved to Shell Point Village.

When I got home from Bethel I registered for the army draft and after my physical was classified 1A, which meant that unless I continued in college the army would be my next occupation. This gave me an additional reason to study hard.

In July of 1948, our family took our second vacation trip. We went to the east coast stopping first at Niagara Falls, and then on to NYC. We went up the coast through Connecticut and stopped for a few days in Rhode Island. We had been invited to stay with a former sailor, Len Stuns. He had taught radar at the U. of Chicago during the war, and attended our church on Sundays. My folks invited him home for many Sunday dinners. He reciprocated their kindnesses by being our guide to Boston, Cape Cod, Lexington, and the rocky coast of Maine to Bar Harbor. At that point we headed west and spent two days in Montreal. It was the first time I had ever heard French spoken. We returned by way of Cooperstown and the Baseball Hall of Fame, and then took Hwys.5 and 20 across New York and Ohio. There were no Super Highways at that time. (They were built in the mid-fifties) We went through countless cities and hundreds of traffic lights before we reached Bass Lake and relaxed for a few days. I went home with Dad and finished my job of painting the house.

I came back to the lake for a couple of weeks before heading back to Bethel for the 48-49 school year. While there I had one of the most undesirable experiences of my life. Several cabins north of us, lived my Aunt Edna and Uncle Roy. They owned the 20 ft. sailboat that I sailed a few times each summer. They were the parents of Shirley, who was the glamour girl of all my cousins. She was on her third engagement at 21. Aunt Edna was at the cottage with Shirley and Frank, her fiancé who was in his late 20's. My aunt Edna had to go home to Chicago to have her hair done. She asked my mother if I would chaperone them the night she would be in Chicago. My wonderful, intelligent mother agreed that I would do this!!

As night fell I went over to their cottage to take on this weighty responsibility. I found them dressed in their pajamas sitting on the swing that was to be my bed for the night. I was introduced to Frank, a medical student. We played a game of Rook and then I went into the living room and read while they "Bill and Cooed" for a hour or so, then they went to their separate bed rooms. I went out to the porch and laid down to sleep. I didn't sleep very well that night: several times I heard the floor creaking, but I'm sure you'll understand that I did not turn on my flashlight or get up and investigate. When I went back to our cottage in the morning, mother asked me how things had gone. I told her, please, never ask me to do that again. That was the most unkind, unthinking thing my Mother ever did to me. I don't understand to this day why she couldn't see how impossible it was for me to do that task.

Shirley and Frank were married the next year. The marriage lasted three months when it was discovered that he had another wife and two children living on the far north side of Chicago. The marriage was annulled but by that time Shirley was pregnant. She moved to Texas, had a baby girl, and started life again.

I went back to Bethel and took general chemistry, physics, New Testament, and freshman composition. I tried out for baseball and made the team. I was not a starter but played in games at second and third base and got several hits, one being a triple that won a game. I earned my red "B" and wore it proudly. That spring at least one-third of our games were snowed out. If you go to college and want to play baseball don't go to a school in any state north of Chicago!

As I now had completed three quarters of college studies, with good grades, I applied to Wheaton College to be accepted as a sophomore beginning with the fall '49 semester. To my great joy I was accepted.

That summer Dad was able, because I had taken the Civil Service exam, to get me a job with the Department of Commerce. I spent most of the summer running a Mimeograph machine that printed out government needed equipment and requested bids on their requirements. On the week- ends I took the train to Bass Lake. Usually on those weekends I had a date with Lois Mortenson to see a play at the Maxinkuckee Playhouse, a Summer Stock group of actors put on plays such as, *Brigadoon, Dial M for Murder* and *The Mousetrap.*

I had pre-registered to take qualitative analysis, German, calculus, philosophical apologetics and Victorian-era literature that first semester so I got a head start by reading *War and Peace* and *Crime and Punishment* during the summer months. To this day the latter is my favorite novel, ever.

My first day at Wheaton was very traumatic, Bill, my roommate who I'd just met that evening, vomited on the floor of our room. I went to the R.A.; he called the nurse and doctor to come as we cleaned up the floor. They took him to the infirmary and later that night to the hospital. The next day they told me he had been diagnosed with Polio and would not be coming back to school.

For you who lived through those years before Drs. Salk and Sabin came up with the vaccines to stop that dreaded disease you probably all had family or friends that were struck by it. It seemed to be contracted mostly in the summer months by young people. Parents had us all take precautions so that we would not be paralyzed or killed by it. Bill had permanent disablement on the left side of his body. For the next few months every time I got a headache or upset stomach I feared I might be coming down with polio. This was not a good way to start my sophomore year. I soon got a new roommate, Bob Morrison, who was a physics major transferring from Shippensburg College in Pennsylvania. He was taller than I and almost as skinny. We got along real well. He was a whiz at math and we were both in the same calculus class. He tried to help me through the class but it was no use: he got an A and I flunked a course for the first and only time in my life. For several years after I'd have nightmares about taking that final exam. This was very bad. I had to pass calculus in order to get my B.S. degree in chemistry. I got an A in inorganic qualitative analysis and philosophical apologetics and B's and C's for my other grades. I had to work hard and spend a lot of time in the Chemistry lab to get good grades.

The only extra-curricular thing I did was to attend wrestling matches and basketball games. The wrestling team especially was unbelievable. In a match with Notre Dame I saw Simmon's, our heavyweight, pick up his opponent and body slam him to the mat. I invited Lois to come out for the Homecoming football game that fall of '49. I did not date any coeds. The girls that were attractive were all taken by some other guy, mostly the athletes. The other handicap to me was the Wheaton pledge, that forbid us to go to movies and theatres. I did not support this, although I observed it during the school year. The other no-no's were dancing, which I'd never learned to do, smoking, which I'd given up, and drinking alcohol, which I'd never done. There was no pledge against "Necking." Non-Wheaton men could take women on dates to movies, dances, etc, and then do some necking. Wheaton men could get to the necking a lot sooner and also that was a lot cheaper entertainment. That didn't make a lot of sense to me then, and now the College has come out of that strait jacket and only forbids smoking and drinking.

During the winter months I went home nearly every week-end to play basketball on our church team and then I'd go over to see Lois. (See addendum: Unusual dates with Lois) Our team was called the SWEDES. Many of the people from our church came to the games to cheer us on with such cheers as: Lutfisk and Pepperkaka, Tak ska da hah, Emerald Avenue Baptist, Rah, Rah, Rah. Our team won the "Y" league nearly every year.

Two of the players on our team were the Dischinger brothers who were Lutherans and didn't have a team. We persuaded them to come to our church during the Basketball season so they would qualify to play on our team. They both ended up going to Bethel College and Seminary and became ministers. This is one of the main reasons I have always been a supporter of churches having sports teams, because I've seen how athletics can be used to draw young people to come church. I've found in my life that most of the men who are my life long friends are those I teamed with on the baseball diamond or the basketball court. When we get together it's like we've never been apart. Many of them were members of our wedding party, and I of theirs. We've laughed and cried together in times of joy and sorrow and defeat. I remember running a good fast break and then running back up the court slapping each other on the butt, and hugging each other when celebrating a victory. Most all of my good men friends hug each other when we meet.

During February of '50 Wheaton College had a spiritual revival that started during one evening of the week-long Bible conference. One after another students, and some faculty got to their feet and confessed sin in their lives and asked for forgiveness from the students', faculty and God. When I got to Pierce Chapel the next morning the service had been going on for 14 hours with singing of hymns and prayer interspersed with testimonies and confessions. I was overwhelmed by thinking of my own partial following of Jesus Christ and how unhappy I was about that. We were asked to stand and sing the hymn, *Have Thine Own Way Lord* I got through the first verse and started the second. "Have thine own way Lord, have thine own way. Search me and try me master today" I physically choked up and could sing no more. I sat down and sobbed, and in the privacy of my heart I confessed that I'd been a poor follower of one who was my Savior but not my Lord. I'd recently read Bonhoeffers: *Cost of Disscipleship,* in which he'd written something to the effect that when Christ calls people to be His disciple he asks them to die to themselves. I turned over my life to Him at that time; it has made all the difference. As an immediate result I went home to our church with another fellow member of our church and we gave our testimonies at the Sunday evening service. That started the same type of revival in our church. The Spirit of God also brought to my remembrance that a few years earlier I had abetted the stealing of several baseballs from the Mages store. I went to that store and confessed to the man at the Register what I had done years ago and gave him ten dollars. He was shocked and overwhelmed that I wanted to make this right with him. He said this was the first time this had ever happened in his 10 years of business.

Two major events took place in the summer of 1950. On June 25th North Korea invaded South Korea which started the Korean War. The U.S. sent troops to repel the invasion. Several of my friends were drafted into the army and a couple of them went to Korea. My draft board told me I would be given a deferment unless I dropped out of college or graduated.

Ever since our house had been robbed in 1947, my parents had felt that the neighborhood was not as safe as it had been. Dad described our neighbor on the north, Mr. Riley, as "lace curtain Irish" and our new neighbor, Mr. Dempsey, across the alley, who insisted on burning the contents of his garbage can several times a week, as "shanty Irish" Dad had told Mr Dempsey many times that Mom and he were upset to have the smell of burning garbage coming in our windows. Their pleas were all to no avail. So they decided to move to Beverly Hills a classy neighborhood on the southwest side of Chicago. My Uncle Albin had a lot at 10015 Oakley that he would build on if they so desired.

Our church was relocating to 99th and Western, our home would be only two blocks away. My folks contracted with him to build a six room house with a screened in back porch. The house was constructed of stone and a variegated red brick. It contianed 1340 square feet and had a full basement and an attached garage. Dad had a back yard five times larger than he'd had on Champlain and no alley for neighbors to burn trash. In the move, I threw out or lost most of my baseball cards and other pictures, and somehow lost all my War Gum cards and Superman and Batman comic books that would be worth quite a bit of money today. We moved into our new home in August. There was one bad thing for my dad; with no alley in back there were no horses to supply him with fertilizer for his roses. But horse -drawn wagons were being replaced by trucks anyway, so fertilizer would have to be purchased.

In summer school I again took calculus. Dr. Brant had only six in the class and three of the others were like me. We had flunked the course and were back to at least get a passing grade so we could get our degrees in either chemistry or physics. With the four of us she taught the subject in a tutorial style. She also spent a lot of her time with each of us on our assigned work. I thank God for her, as I was able to pass the course with a grade of C.

During that summer I read C. S. Lewis'*Mere Christanity* and *Screwtape Letters*, Law's *A Serious Call to a Devout and Holy Life*, These books had a great influence on my life.

In my junior year the major courses taken were: organic chemistry, scientific German, Shakespeare, which was taught by one of the best professors and popular teachers at the college, Other courses that I took were; Basic Christian Doctrine, and Organic Qualitative Analysis. I was thankful to God that I was through with math.

I joined a Red Cross Service group that went every Monday night to the largest veterans hospital in the nation, Hines Hospital. The veteran's were injured in World Wars I and II, and most were Para and Quadriplegics. We'd spend time with one or two of them, and try to help them do whatever they wanted. Some of them had lost part or all the limbs of their bodies. Many were very bitter and were hard to help. It was hard to blame them. How would I have faced living in a wheel chair or laying on a gurney for the rest of my life? What was wonderful and inspiring to see were many of the

WW I vets and their wives, now 30 years after they were injured, holding hands with their spouse as they visited. They had never been home together nor been able to be intimate with each other, yet the love was there. It gave special meaning to me to see how many had taken the vow seriously to "live together in sickness and health as long you both shall live." LOVE AND DEDICATION personified. This service experience was a great learning experience for me.

That summer I again worked in Chicago, running duplicating machines for the commerce department. I learned to do a job well that I had no interest in doing the rest of my life. It was a boring, routine job. As a benefit I got two day's vacation even though it was a temporary summer job, and 10 hours sick leave which I never took.

In my senior year the only chemistry classes that I had to take were Physical Chemistry, which I found difficult because of the math involved, and instrumental analysis. I got a C in physical chemistry and a B in Instrumental Analysis. My Christian faith was deepened when I took a course in Philosophical Apologetics taught by Dr. Ken Kantzer, a brilliant teacher with his doctorate from Harvard. (He went on to be president of Trinity Seminary and Editor of Christianity Today.) In my last semester I had classes only three days a week. My roommate and I decided toward the end of September that we should get a TV to watch the World Series. We went to Muntz TV and splurged on a 10-inch set. I was on the roof getting ready to attach the wires to the TV antenna when Bobby Thomson hit the dramatic home run that won the N.L. pennant for the N.Y. Giants. How's that for timing?

In the Summer of '51 Lois and I dated often and I was thinking of proposing to her at Christmas time. In early September her father, Elmer, had a serious heart attack. That event really affected Lois as she was their only daughter. Her brother was married and had two boys. Being the only child at home she felt responsible to help her parents, who owned a nine- flat apartment building they lived in and managed. We continued dating into the fall and she came out to Wheaton for the homecoming game. In mid November on my way to chapel I picked up my mail and there was a letter from her; it was a "Dear Paul" letter. In it she said that she felt it was necessary for us to end our relationship, because she did not see how her aging parents could get along without her help. I was crushed. There was no other girl I was interested in but Lois. But despite my plea to continue our relationship she would not change her decision. That ended my courtship of Lois. I stored away her 5x7 high school graduation picture on which she had penned, "To Paul, With ALL my Love." In the summer of '53, she married a sailor, Robert Odman, and moved to Atlantic City, N.J. They had four daughters and lived most of their life in Bloomington, Illinois. (In a Christmas letter I received in 2006, Robert reported that Lois had passed away in the fall of 2005. They were married over 53 years. Now, I can say I have nothing but good memories of Lois, my first love, and I'm happy that she married a good man. I couldn't have said that in 1952.)

In May of 1952, I graduated with a B.S. degree in chemistry and was glad school days had ended. I had spent most of my time studying or in the chemistry labs and had not made any lasting relationships with any of my classmates. I did not look forward to going into the army and was not sure anyone would hire a 1A male who had graduated with only average grades.

Two Memorable Dates with Lois

From 1948 to 1951 Lois and I went a few times each summer to see a play at the Maxinkukee Playhouse in Culver Indiana. The driving distance from our cottage to the playhouse was about 11 miles. The play we attended on this occasion was: *Dial M for Murder.* If you've seen this play you'll remember it being very suspenseful. One scene, when the murder takes place, has the audience screaming, as well as the two actors. After the play we had some ice cream and started home on Rt. 10, a lonely country road, where we had our own scary experience. Suddenly, we spotted a group of four to six people and two cars in the road. As we slowed and got closer we saw a body lying on the road and getting even closer saw it was a woman's body. They waved for us to stop. I told Lois this looked like a set-up to get us to stop and that if we did stop we might be harmed. She agreed with my decision. Fortunately, the left shoulder was open and we speeded up as we went by. We agreed we would not tell our parents about this unless something came out about it on the radio or the newspaper. I'm glad we did not stop at that scene. Lois and I often talked about that event. A few weeks later I reported this happening to the police, they told me we had made the right decision in not stopping.

In February of '51 I came home from Wheaton to play basketball on the church team and after to go out with Lois. I was almost to Lois's home when I had a most memorable auto accident. Lois lived in a flat building that her parents owned at 7124 Clyde Ave. The whole block consisted of three- story apartment buildings that made the street a shaded canyon during the winter months. It was a narrow one-way street for south bound traffic. A number of snowfalls had made it a road with two icy ruts. To park your car presented two problems: parking spaces were scarce and to get your car out of the ruts took considerable driving skill. I drove my parents' car heading east on 71st Street. This street is a major street on the South Side of Chicago. The street is bisected by the Ill. Central R.R., the east bound lanes are on the south side of the tracks, the west bound lanes are on the north side of the R.R. tracks. (I hope I haven't confused you completely on the street layout, but it's important for you to picture it in order to understand what happened on this memorable night.) A few seconds after I turned off 71st and headed south on Clyde a car turned off 72nd and headed toward me. I flashed my headlights to let the driver know it was heading the wrong way, but it kept on coming. I saw an opening by a fire plug and tried to get out of the way of the other car as it was now blowing its horn for me to get out of the way. I cut the steering wheel to the right and got the front wheels out of the rut, but one of my back wheels got stuck.

The other car kept on coming and didn't stop until it smashed into my driver's side door. I pushed myself to the passenger's side, got out and went to talk to the driver who had hit me. He, a very big African–American, rolled down his window and told me to get out of his way, for he was in a hurry. From the fumes coming out of his window and his slurred speech I could tell he was drunk. I told him of unlawful things he had done and that we would have to call the police to report this accident he had caused. He hauled out his wallet and gave it to me. I looked at his cards and saw that he was a union steward at Inland Steel in South Chicago. As I didn't have a pencil, I kept his drivers' license when I handed him back his wallet. He kept telling me he had insurance and not to worry about the large dent in my door. Then he began to curse me and told me that if I didn't get out of his way he'd ram my car so he could get on his way. As a 140 pounder, I reasoned that I might sustain serious injury by trying to physically restrain this 200- pound man, As no one was around to assist me I told him to back up a few feet so I could acquiesce to his request. By rocking the car, I got out of the rut and pulled out of his way. Before I could get out of the car he sped as fast as he could to 71st Street and drove west on the east bound lanes. I ran after him and heard many horns honking and then the sound of a crash. When I got to the corner, I saw that he had decided to get out of the way of the on-coming cars by jumping the curb and driving over the railroad tracks. The rear bumper of his car was hung up on the curb, and one of the front wheels was smack dab against the railroad track. While he staggered around his car, he asked many who were now gathered to help him push his car off the track. Our advice to him was to call a tow truck and the police quickly before a train came along. Luckily for him, a bar owner called the police and a tow truck, which came quickly and towed the badly damaged car away. Because it was late Saturday night and trains were on a reduced schedule, no trains came before his car was towed away.

My friend then said he would take the bus home. I suggested that he wait for the police to arrive because of his accident with my car. He went to the bus stop and took the next westbound bus away from the scene. About a half hour had passed and the police had not showed up. I went into the bar and asked if I might call my girl friend and let her know where I was and what had happened. He refused my request and said I should run over to her apartment and he would tell the police I'd be back in a few minutes. I did this. Lois, who was all ready to go out, went with me back to the bar. The police showed up about an hour after they were called. After they had written up their report on the accident on 71st, they drove over to see my car and write up their report on my accident. I told them that the perpetrator had left the scene and gave the police his driver's license. They gave me a copy of the report and assured me that this guy would, "have the book thrown at him." They then informed me that I was parked illegally by a fire hydrant and that if I didn't move it immediately they'd give me a ticket. I remembered this the next time I was asked to contribute to the Policeman's Benevolent Association.

Lois and I went to the ice cream parlor for about an hour. Because neither of us was in the mood to go to the 79thSt beach to watch the Submarine races, I got her home about midnight.

The union steward's lawyer got two continuances on his client's case. They finally gave him a six-month suspension of his driver's license, but no money for us to pay for the damage to my parents car. They had $50 deductible collision for that type of accident, which they had to pay for that reprobate's actions. There ain't no justice!

My Debt to Wheaton College

At Wheaton College I experienced the joy of learning in many areas. My Christian faith was buttressed when I took Philosophical Apologetics taught by Dr. Ken Kantzer. We studied the writings of St. Augustine, Pascal, Chesterton and especially CS Lewis, these became guidebooks on why and what I believed. I also was deeply impressed by the lives of the professors and students who lived exemplary Christian lives. The life and actions of Dr. Edman, our President, stamped all of our lives.

It was important that I had good instruction in my field of major study, Chemistry, as it enabled me to get a job after I finished college. It would have served me well to have taken some courses in business as I later spent most of my career in sales and marketing. But at that time I had no idea that my gifts were in that area.

I solidified my love for Classical music by taking music appreciation. Dr. Simpson taught Shakespeare in a way that made it live. The course in nineteenth century literature of authors Austen, Dickens, Tolstoy, and Dostoyevsky and others led me to read more of their writings after I left school. Because of the times I'd lived through, WW II, and the upcoming 100th anniversary of the U.S. Civil War, I was inspired in a U.S. History class to become a life long student of both those wars. In short, my education inspired me to learn by reading, listening, and travel for the rest of my life.

Most importantly, Wheaton College was the place where I gave my complete allegiance to Jesus Christ as my Lord and Savior. I still sing with conviction the Wheaton College Hymn. "May the mind of Christ my Savior, live in me from day to day, by his love and power controlling all I do and say. May the word of God dwell richly in my heart from hour to hour, so that all may see I triumph, only through his power. May the peace of God my father, rule my heart in everything, that I may be calm to comfort sick and sorrowing. May the love of Jesus fill me as the waters fill the sea. Him exulting, self- abasing this is victory. May I run the race before me, strong and brave to meet the foe, looking only unto Jesus as I onward go. May His beauty rest upon me as I seek the lost to win, and may they forget the channel, seeing only Him."

Chapter 5

My Welcome to the Real World

In May and June I had about a dozen job interviews, with a variety of companies, in the Chicago area: Swift, Armour, Sherwin-Williams, and a number of oil companies. They all said they would hire me if I were not 1A in my Draft classification. The last company I met with was Shell Oil, which was located in the Board of Trade building in downtown Chicago. They also told me to come back and reapply when my military service was over.

I took the elevator down to the ground floor. The Board of Trade building was, at that time the largest corporate office building in Chicago. I went over to the corporation address board and looked down the listings. When I got down to the V's, I saw Victor Chemical Works. I'd never heard of the company. As I had no other companies to call on, I thought, "What have I to lose?, lets see if they will accept a cold call and grant me an interview." The receptionist greeted me, and I asked if I could see someone to interview for a job, and gave her my resume. She said, "You have good timing. The Board of Directors meeting is about to break up, and the Director of Research might have time to see you." She also told me that she was pretty sure the company was seeking a chemist. I did not wait for long. Dr. Willard Woodstock came out of the meeting and set up a date for me to come to their Chicago Heights plant. I went there two days later and met with Dr. Russell Bell and Roger Wreath. When the interview ended, I was offered a job as a Quality Control Chemist with a starting salary of $315 a month.

They informed me that their main products were Phosphorus and Phosphate Chemicals and they believed they could get me a occupational deferment from military service. Their personnel department would set up an appointment with my draft board to plead my case. Wow!! I joined Victor Chemical on July 14, 1952, (Bastille Day). My times of storming corporate barricades were over.

Harry Hopsicker was the personnel manager for the plant. He set up a date for us to meet with my Draft Board to request a change in my draft classification. The meeting took place on an evening later in July. Harry told them that our company was a major supplier of phosphorus to the defense industries that manufactured phosphorus bombs and artillery shells and that phosphorus was also used to make a variety of other explosives. Mr. Peterson, he said, plays an important part in the war effort, and I was just as valuable in the war effort as a soldier on the front lines. I felt like standing and taking a bow. Nobody ever had referred to me in such glowing terms. I wished my sixth grade teacher had been there to hear his oration.

The board chairman told us they would consider our request and get back to us within ten days with their decision. As we left the meeting I asked Harry how he thought the meeting had gone. He said," I think our chances are very good. I've had five wins in a row on these cases, and aside from that the chairman of the board who asked the questions is my uncle!!!" Harry and his uncle, in the course of the meeting, had shown no sign of their relationship. In a few days my draft classification was changed and I had no more chance of being drafted as long as I was employed by Victor Chemical Works.

When I started my job I did not have a car. Fortunately, I found four other men who carpooled each day from 103rd and Halsted St.

My parents allowed me to drive their car once or twice a week. The men took turns driving on the other days. On the days when I didn't drive I'd take the 103rd street bus to Halsted St. to meet them at 7:15am. On the days I drove, my last stop would be to put a dollars worth of gas in the tank. The price of a gallon of gas was 16 cents. My Folks requested that now that I was working I should help pay for my room and board. The amount settled on was $90 a month.

My job as a Control Chemist was to make sure our products met our specifications and those of our customers. After a while it was quite a routine job, as on most days I ran the same tests over and over again.

Less than two months into that job, I and two new chemical engineers were assigned to strike duty at our Silver Bow, Montana phosphorus plant. We drove out there on the Labor Day weekend and worked ten hours a day at many jobs that were assigned by the plant manager. We were housed at a hotel in the city of Butte and drove 15 miles to the plant. Butte was a rough and ready mining town. Its main employer was the Anaconda Copper Company, which had the largest open pit mine in the world. As the strike wore on the days got colder. We got snow in early October. As we three employees from Chicago Heights were not partying types we did not get involved in the drinking, gambling and wenching during the night hours in Butte. Our life was eat, sleep and work.

As Christmas approached we had worked over110 straight days since Labor Day. We drew straws to select who would take Christmas Day off. We did not ask the plant manager to ok our plan. The manager was a retired Colonel in the army Chemical Corps who was always addressed as Colonel Hays. Dave Chapman won the straw vote and took Christmas day off. On the 26th when the colonel saw Dave he asked him; "Were you sick yesterday?" "No," Dave said, "but since we haven't had a day off since Labor Day we thought we at least had the right to odd man so one of us could take Christmas Day off." The Colonel answered, "That's the trouble with young America. All they want to do is play." That was the last straw for the three of us. We called the plant manager at Chicago Heights and told him we were driving back to Chicago on New Year's Day with or without a job. We'd done our turn doing 110 straight days without a day off and felt we needed to be relieved by other persons from Victor's other plants. None of us were rebuked or punished for our action. The company agreed with us. In April the strike was settled, and I never had to do strike duty again. We three guys formed a good bond. We joshed each other many times by saying, "All you want to do is play."

Victor Chemical Works had three Phosphorus plants and five other plants that used the Phosphorus to make Phosphates. At the plant I was known as Pete or POP, my initials. The plant's products were made by reacting POP bonds with salts of Sodium, Calcium and Potassium, to make a variety of Phosphate products. I was involved in testing them and later, for most of my working life, selling and marketing them.

At church I sang in the choir and occasionally filled in for a bass or baritone in our excellent men's quartet. I also taught a fourth grade boys' Sunday School class. The attention and behavior of those boys reflected my behavior twelve years earlier. What goes around comes around.

In 1953 I bought my first car, a sky blue and white, hard top, Bel-Air Chevrolet, for $2,750. It was a beauty and a good girl attractor. I wish I still had it. I had a "neckers knob" put on the steering wheel, which enabled me to drive with one hand that freed the other arm to hug the girl beside me.

Much of my social life consisted of singing in choirs. From 1952 to 1962 I sang in the bass section in presentations of Handel's Messiah under the direction of my good friend, Bob Iler. I also participated in three choral workshops led by the great chorale conductor Robert Shaw. He had the ability to lift every singer to a new level. I went with Joan Kamm, a classmate at Wheaton, to hear him conduct his Chorale, in of all places, the Wheaton Alumni Gymnasium. The major work was a Mass of Schubert. A couple of months later we went to Orchestra Hall to hear him lead the Chorale in Bach's B minor Mass. At each performance, he spent himself so physically and emotionally that the podium's front part was bathed with perspiration which had dropped from his face.

One Sunday I took a girl to a Schubert Leider concert at Orchestra Hall sung by Irmgard Siegfried. Our seats were in the balcony, not the greatest seats for a song recital. As we looked at the program we saw the songs were to be related to the four seasons. She came on stage wearing a sea green gown with a white stole and sang five songs related to the winter of the calendar and season of life. Her next group of four songs had to do with spring and youth, she wore a dark green stole when performing them. At intermission I suggested to the girl that we be bold and go down and take two of the four seats that were unoccupied in the front row. She agreed to take the chance that we might be publicly embarrassed if an usher challenged our sitting there. Fortunately for us this did not happen. We were sitting not more than 30 feet from the artist. She came out after intermission bedecked with an orange stole and sang songs of the autumn's beauty and that season of our lives. Then for the last series, summer, she wore a sky blue stole. At the close of the concert she received a standing ovation and sang a couple of encores.

At that concert I experienced an epiphany. Before she started singing the song that was to be performed she would spend as much time as was necessary to take on the persona that was needed to pour her total being into that song. Sometimes her countenance would brighten, sometimes you almost expected her to break into tears before she opened her mouth. When ready, she'd nod to the accompanist and the recital would continue. That night I and many others found out what a large gap there is between a performer and an artist. It was the most memorable concert of my life. Several years later at a guitar concert given by Pepe Romero at Wolsey Hall,

Yale University, I had an experience that came close to matching it. As an Encore, Romero played Tarrega's, *Recuerdos de laAlhambra* As the final note was fading away, the audience of over 1,500 gave him the ultimate gesture of appreciation by collectively letting out a collective gasp of breath.

The fifties in America were probably the most treasured years for most of my friends. Dwight Eisenhower was elected president in 1952 and served until 1960. Who can forget Ike's smile! During his watch a truce was achieved in July of 1953 that ended the Korean War. He spearheaded the building of our superhighways that made all of America more accessible to our citizens. In that decade most of my friends found the person that became their life partner, families were started, and first homes purchased. Early in that decade Senators' Kefauver and McCarthy made names for themselves, by holding public Senate hearings on the Mafia and supposed Communist infiltration in our government. These investigations were extensively covered on TV in black and white. Television was now in nearly every home, as prices dropped to affordable levels for most everyone. "Giant", 16- inch screens were available. Programs featuring stars such as Bob Hope, Milton Beryl, Jackie Gleason, Groucho Marx and Ed Sullivan were on weekly. The favorite program for most was I Love Lucy. These programs along with telecasts of baseball and football games started many on the road to becoming couch potatoes. Billy Graham started his televised mass evangelism rallies.

All was not good, however. the beat generation led by Timothy Leary and Hugh Hefner with his propagation of the Playboy Philosophy, started, in my opinion, our country on a downward spiral which has led us into deep moral decline.

In July four buddies and I went on a western trip in my new car. The group consisted of my brother Will, Ken Bell, Bob Reynolds, Dick Hedman and I. We visited the barren Badlands of South Dakota and made a long stop at Mt. Rushmore. The next stop was Yellowstone, where we settled in at the falls area. Our plan was to tour it and then go down to the Grand Tetons where we would hike a couple days in those beautiful mountains and then go to climbing school. After seeing the northern loop of the park, we got up early the next morning. Three of them, Will, Bob and Ken, decided to go down the stairs to the foot of the spectacular lower falls. When they decided to come back up they made a big mistake by climbing the steep canyon wall, which consisted of crumbly rock. About two hundred feet up, the rock under Bob's foot gave way and he slid and fell all the way down to the river bank. Ken and Will came back and reported that Park Rangers were bringing Bob up on a stretcher and would be taking him to the hospital in Monmouth Springs. We followed the ambulance to the hospital. Bob was in shock when we saw him and was found to have severe injuries to his legs, hands and buttocks. He was hospitalized for several days and then released with one leg in a cast and on crutches. It's a miracle he wasn't killed by that fall. Needless to say, that mishap caused us to change our plans drastically. For the rest of the trip Bob sat in the back seat of the car with his leg in the laps of two buddies.

We did go down to the Tetons for a couple days, and I talked to the people at the Exum School of Mountaineering about coming out to attend the school for a couple of days. We went to Salt Lake and toured the Mormon Tabernacle and went to the Great Salt Lake and floated on its surface. The trip ended in Springfield, Ill. There we saw Lincoln's home and tomb. On the trip we had driven 4,500 miles.

In the fall I was invited by my Uncle Albin to go to a Union League club meeting and heard Sir Edmund Hillary speak of his conquest of Mt. Everest. At that meeting I met a couple of members of the Chicago Mountaineering Club who invited me to join their climbing parties at Devil's Lake, Wisconsin. The next couple of years I climbed with them there and also at the Mississippi Palisades.

Early in 1954 my best friend Bill Almer was discharged from the Army and we took a trip to Glacier National Park and the

Canadian Rockies. We enjoyed driving and hiking in Glacier, and especially enjoyed driving on "The Going to the Sun Highway." In the Canadian Rockies we traveled to Banff, then up the highway all the way to Jasper. We saw, The Valley of the Ten Peaks, Lake Louise, the Colombian Ice Fields, Yoho and Athabaska Falls. On our way back to Chicago, near Valentine, Nebraska, we came upon the worst accident we'd ever seen. On Route 20, two cars collided head on, minutes before we came on the scene. Five people were in one car and six in the other. Five people died in that crash, and the others were severely injured. Bodies were lying all over the road when we arrived. On the trip we drove 5,270 miles.

In July of 1955 I made a trip to the Tetons and went to the climbing school. In five days I learned proper climbing technique, rappelling, and how to use pitons, carabiners and ropes to assist in climbing. After the classes I climbed the Grand Teton and Mt. Teewinot, with Willi Unsoeld as our guide.

In 1956 my brother got discharged from the army, and we were invited by our cousins Larry and Debby to spend a few days with them in Ft. Lauderdale. On the way down we stopped to see the water ski show at Cypress Gardens and the Bok Singing Tower. On the day Will and I arrived at my cousin's house, Debby had spent a major part of her day preparing a gourmet feast for us. It featured rack of lamb with mint jelly, fresh asparagus, potatoes, and for dessert, lemon cream pie. When we had nearly cleaned our plate, Debby asked if we wanted seconds. Will reached for the mashed potatoes, in doing so his shirt sleeve caught his stemmed water glass and it toppled over, most of the water filling Debby's dinner plate but a good amount also spilled on the table cloth. Larry said we'd better check to make sure no water had gone between the table pads to the table top. After we'd moved a few dishes and utensils we lifted the table cloth to inspect. Unfortunately my water glass which was nearly full fell right onto the lemon cream pie, ruining it.

It was such a disaster that all we could do was laugh until our sides ached. It should have been filmed for posterity. To try to make it right we apologized and told them that we'd take them to dinner the next night at Stone Crab Joe's in Miami. We had already obtained tickets to take them to see, Agatha Christies' *The Mouse Trap*. That evening was the highlight of our trip. The next morning Debbie made Swedish pancakes for our breakfast. We were enjoying them when I knocked the nearly full bottle of Maple syrup off the table onto the tile floor, where it smashed into hundreds of pieces. We carefully picked up all the glass pieces we could see. I then mopped the floor three times to get the syrup off the floor. When the floor looked dry, we walked on it. We heard, "grich, grich", as our shoes stuck to the floor. So I mopped it twice again. The morning we left the floor was still sticky and went "grich, grich" when we walked on it. The forbearance of my cousins was tremendous toward fumbling cousins from hell.

They took us on a boat tour of the canals of their city, and on Saturday, Larry took us to Hollywood Park where we saw the classic horse race between Swaps and Nashua. We called them when we got home to Chicago and thanked them for all they had done to help us have a wonderful trip. I had to ask them if they still had a sticky kitchen floor. The answer was in the affirmative. I was not invited back to their home until I was married and had a wife to housebreak me. On the trip we drove 3,590 miles.

As neither of my parents had traveled west of the Dakota's, I invited them to take a trip with me to the northwest. We started on the trip in early June of '56 and headed first to South Dakota. God's hand of protection was surely on us as we approached Rochester, Minnesota, on two lane Rt.14. We were going up a hill, and as we approached the top, a couple hundred feet ahead, two semis, side by side, came over the crest of the hill. We were going about 60 miles an hour. My only option was to get off the road, going onto the right shoulder. I shouted a short prayer. "God save us." Within a couple of seconds both semis sped by us. The shoulder of the road was firm and I softly braked to a stop. Sweat poured out of me and my heart must have beat at 200 beats a minutes. We sat parked there for at least ten minutes while we recovered from shock. God answered my short prayer and brought us through that near death experience.

We went to Clark, S.D. and saw the one- room homestead house where my dad lived in the 1880s. I can't imagine how tough a life that must have been. We stopped at Mt. Rushmore and then drove two days to visit the serene Crater Lake, and then up the rocky coast of Oregon to Portland to see what my dad wanted to see, their famous Rose Gardens. Driving along the Columbia River we viewed the high, thin Multnomah Falls and then went on to Bonneville Dam and the fish ladder, where we saw salmon leaping up the fish ladder to spawn. We then turned west again toward Seattle.

I wanted to approach Seattle from the east and cross the floating bridge into the city. At the last exit before the bridge we saw a sign that informed us that we should check our gas before we got on the 10- mile bridge, where stopping was not allowed. The gas gauge was down near empty so Mom suggested we get gas. I said I felt we had enough and proceeded to cross the bridge. Two- thirds of the way across the car sputtered and died. There was no place to pull off so I got out of the car and waved the next car down. Fortunately he stopped and told me to hop in, he told me that if the police came I would be hit with a $50 fine for running out of gas. At the end of the bridge ramp there was a garage. I ran in and started to tell my sad tale when one of the people put a red two gallon can in my hand and went out with me to fill it. While doing this, he asked loudly if any of his customers were about to go east on the bridge, and would they be willing to take me back to my car. One man said hop in. I paid the attendant $2 and we took off. I'm thankful it was early Saturday morning so that traffic was light. I believe I was back to the car in 20 minutes and did not get a ticket and fine. Mom and dad didn't say a word. There was no need to do so. But I wondered what they said about their college-educated son, when I left them alone for those tense minutes.

When we got to Mt. Rainier it was covered with clouds. We drove up in the clouds a couple thousand feet and then turned and came down. We were disappointed as others have been before of being on the mountain but never seeing the summit. We took a ferry to Victoria, B.C., and walked through the spectacular Butchart Gardens. This was the highlight of the trip for them. We drove back to Chicago in three days. I was very happy to take them on this trip after all the wonderful things they had done for me. On this trip we drove 6,270 miles.

Victor Chemical asked me to take two Saturday morning classes at Illinois Inst. Of Technology: Statistical Quality Control, and after that a course that helped me get a promotion to the Tech Service Laboratory. It was a course in Microscopy. I learned how to identify foreign contaminants that might be in various products. One Saturday Dr. McCrone took us on an investigation. An elderly lady was suing a landlord because of all the dust that was in her apartment. The landlord asked Dr. McCrone to come and take samples of the dust to determine its make-up. After taking samples, we went back to the lab. It was determined that 80 percent of the dust was her skin!! She was shedding most of it in her bed and easy chair. In the Tech Service lab I found satisfaction in working with customers in developing new and better products that used phosphates.

One of the great benefits the Company offered the salaried employees was a family style lunch. Four Italian ladies prepared wonderful meals, including desserts, for 25 cents. There was quite a bit of grumbling when the price was raised to 40 cents in1956. We had lots of fried chicken, lasagna and spaghetti. About 80 of us sat around 10 tables and talked shop and mostly sports. There were 8 to 10 women who ate with us at a separate table so that helped to keep the profanity to a minimum. At one of these lunches our Director of Research, Dr. Art Toy, who was a native- born Chinese, asked a fellow resident of Park Forest; "Is that sung a da beech bartender running for school board again?" Herb answered, "Yes."

Art asked, "Do you think he'll win? Herb answered, "He hasn't got a Chinaman's chance." Art answered, "This Chinaman's got a chance." Poor Herb. If the floor could have opened and swallowed him he would have welcomed it. That meal ended with a deathly silence. Herb took an engineering job with another company within a year.

At work I buddied around with several other Cub and Bear fans. In that era of baseball, nearly all teams played double-headers on Sunday afternoon. We'd go to three or four of these each season. In the Fifties and early Sixties the Cubs as a team were awful but they had some great players: Ernie Banks, Billy Williams and Ron Santo to name several. The most thrilling game I ever attended was the first game of a double header played May 15 1960, when Don Cardwell pitched a no- hitter for the Cubs against the Cardinals. The last batter for the Cards hit a sinking line drive to left field. "Moose" Moryn made a shoestring catch to end the game. I still have my rain check from that game.

Six of us shared three season tickets for the Bear games. In those years each team played a 12 game schedule, so we each saw half of their home games. Their defense usually was what won their games. Mike Ditka and Johnny Morris were their best offensive players.

In 1958, I was promoted to the Product Development Lab and became the company's expert on detergent and toothpaste formulations. The main companies I had contact with were P&G, Colgate, and Calgon. I worked a lot with P&G and Colgate chemists as they formulated the first fluoride toothpastes.

Chapter 6

Girls, Girls, Girls

After a few months of recovering from the end of my first serious affair of the heart with Lois, I began dating again. Usually during the date we did some eating. We went to drive-ins where young girls came to our parked car on roller skates and took our order. After a short time they would skate back to the car balancing a tray which they attached to the side window. She would take the money and skate off to another car. It's amazing that I don't ever remember seeing one of those burger-bearers fall. From there we'd go to the drive-in movie where we'd pay the entrance attendant and then find a vacant parking spot next to a post with a corded speaker that you attached to the inside of the side window. In that era you could go on a date and never leave your car. I, at least for propriety, always went to the front door to greet the girl and walked her to that door when our evening together ended. My buddies and I all thought that you should expect to kiss the girl goodnight after three dates.

A Drive in Movie was an especially good place to be on a cold night, as the girl was more apt to get closer to you to keep warm. Unfortunately for me, one night the girl asked me to run the engine and turn the heater on for a few minutes. A few minutes later I said, "Something smells." I looked down and noticed her shoes were off and her feet were on the heater vent. That was my last date with her.

A great place to go in the summer was to the Grant Park band shell to hear the symphony concerts. You could sit on benches or recline on a blanket and enjoy the music and the company of your date. Sometimes we'd put together a picnic basket, and that added to the pleasure. I'll never forget the night when Chicago's Mayor Daley gave opening remarks at the first concert of the season: "The Chicago orchestra is one of the greatest sympathy orchestras in the world," he said. That statement went into the lexicon of priceless statements that our mayor made. My favorite of all was made during a press conference the day after some of his police had beat up rioters during the Democratic Convention. He was asked to comment on their rough tactics and said: "The police were not there to cause disorder but to preserve it!!! At one of these concerts my date and I sat on a bench, and a pleasant young man was sitting next to me. We had a good conversation with him before the concert and during the intermission. She urged me to give him a Christian tract. I told her I would feel awkward doing that and refused. From then on to the end of our date she was very cold to me. As I walked her to her home's door I said, "Good night, Virginia." Her name was not Virginia, Oops!

I asked a girl to go with me to an Assembly of God tent meeting where I would be singing in a quartet. It was a hot August evening. Our church quartet was asked to sing a number of rousing Gospel songs at the meeting. I was substituting for our baritone, Bill Brown and Dick Hedman was filling in for the second tenor. The leader of the singing asked people to stand and give a two or three word testimony. This I thought was rather bizarre, but people began to stand and say hymn titles such as: *Jesus Saves, Blessed Assurance, Holy, Holy Holy.* Our quartet was seated on the dais facing the audience. Dick whispered to me, "I'll stand and say "from Greenlands," and you stand and say, "icy mountains," a rather obscure Hymn. Before I could reply he stood and spoke his bit and motioned for me to stand and say mine. I did not do so. This was embarrassing to all concerned and confused the song leader. We sang, *'Joshua Fit the Battle of Jerico,* and *Dry Bone* s that night, and then came down to sit in the audience. The girl I dated was a Lutheran, who said, as we discussed the service on the way home, that she felt the whole experience was weird. I told her I agreed, and that was not the way I practiced the worship of God. I did not take her to any more tent meetings.

Janet was a wonderful girl who was in much demand as a Marimbist. I dated her a few times before she asked me to go to one of her concerts. When I went to pick her up she was in the middle of disassembling the instrument and invited me to help, which I did. We then put it into the back seat of the car and trunk and drove to the restaurant where she was to perform. We brought all the parts into the banquet hall and reassembled it. I got a free dinner that night, and after she gave her performance we reversed the process of dissembling and finally got it put back together in her living room at about midnight. We had several other dates when we went out to eat or to a movie, but they were interspersed with me being caddy for the Marimba. I soon decided that if I ever married her I would have to spend too much of my life tending to her and the Marimba, and I wasn't interested in being a bigamist.

Because it's normal for a man in his twenties to have hopping hormones, I had two dream girls in those years. Both of them were born in the year of my birth: Audrey Hepburn and Grace Kelly. My favorite films of theirs were: *Roman Holiday* and *Sabrina* for Audrey, and *Rear Window* and and *To Catch a Thief* for Grace. If, in my fantasy dream life I'd had to choose between Grace's classic beauty and Audrey's soulful eyes, I'd have chosen Audrey. Oh, that I could have been Gregory Peck in *Roman Holiday.* I'd never have let her go back to the boring life of being a dutiful princess.

One summer I dated a girl named Nancy. She had a summer job in our plant office. Her father was secretary-treasurer of Victor Chemical Works. We dated quite a bit, and she spent a couple of weekends with our family at Bass Lake. We had a couple of fun dates when we went to Second City to see Mike Nichols and Elaine May do their marvelous improvised skits. She was a tall blonde girl, 5'10, and had finished her junior year at DePauw University in Greencastle, Indiana. I drove her back to school when the summer was over. When I called her at Thanksgiving, she told me she had just become engaged and planned to get married in June.

There was a girl clerk in the storeroom, who let me know that she wanted to date me. She called me, and also wrote me such steamy letters that I was surprised the envelope stayed sealed. She was 21 and divorced, smoked, and had a filthy mouth. This was before the days of being fired for sexual harassment. Finally, Victor fired her because she was spending more time chasing men than doing her job.

My favorite restaurant to go to on dinner dates was George Diamonds' Steak House in Chicago's loop. I nearly always ordered the Rib Eye steak and Baked Potato, along with a salad that consisted of a quarter head of lettuce, with a choice of three dressings. I've since learned that this restaurant, which held so many wonderful memories was destroyed by fire in 2006. That's sad.

In those years I dated two other girls. I had a deep love for each of them. Unfortunately for me, neither of these great girls had a similar feeling toward me. One of the relationships ended with a mistaken identity phone call, and the other with a kiss at the front door that was motherly. In God's timing, they married wonderful men and raised great families. They and their husbands are still good friends of mine. We never know where life might take us, but God had a plan for my life which didn't include these ladies. And then there was Lee!!

Alida Fern Anderson

The Early Years

Lee, as she was known to all, was born on February 18th 1938, to Carl and Florence Anderson. She was given the first name of her maternal grandmother, Alida Erickson. She was Carl and Florence's second child, Allan was born in 1936. Carl was a mild mannered man who worked for the Commonwealth Edison Company. In the following years four more siblings were born: Sherwood, Keith, Elizabeth (Lisa) and Victor (Vic).

One of Lee's early jobs was shepherding her younger brothers and sisters. I am indebted to them for supplying me most of the information I am now reporting.

They all remembered her as a kind, nurturing sister who looked out for them and contributed much to their early learning. Woody reported how she patiently taught him to tie his shoes. He said she was a saint. Keith remembered running home from kindergarten so she could take him to Bible Club. A few years later she taught him to ride her 26" Schwinn bike and did not complain when he put some scratches on it, sideswiping a wire fence. Keith said, "over the years I observed that Lee was hard working and took on tasks like playing the violin and was sincere in pursuing her Christian growth. One not so good memory was when Lee and I were driving along a busy Chicago street, in Paul's '56 Chevy. Each of us was looking for a florist shop. Suddenly the car in front of us stopped. Although Lee slammed on the brakes, it wasn't soon enough and we rear ended the car. Thankfully the wedding of Paul and Lee still happened. Her enduring legacy in my life was her suggestion that I, "take out that nice Joan Tatge on my graduation night instead of those trollops that you go out with." Joan had assisted Lee in a vacation Bible school the summer before and had liked what she had seen in Joan. Joan was also impressed with Lee. I will always be grateful for Lee's endorsement of her."

Her brothers all mentioned her feistiness. I'm sure that came because she had to compete with her 4 brothers. That trait came forward when she gave herself a hair cut at age three. (Much of that hair was saved, and a glassine envelope of it was given to me by her mother when I married Lee.) Woody remembered coming home one afternoon when Lee was a teenager to find her wrestling with one of Keith's buddies, Gene Brunzell.

Lee attended Esmond Elementary school when they lived at 11011 Church St. In the early fifties the family moved to a large two- story house on the corner of 107th and Bell Avenue. She enjoyed swimming in the summertime in the Kennedy Park pool. In October 1952, she started taking violin lessons from Esther Jacobson and at the church Christmas party that year played *Silent Nigh*t.

I now quote some of the entries from her diary which were entered in 1952 and 53. "On August 13th I was riding my bike on 111th St. A car door opened, and I ran into it. I was taken to the Roseland Hospital where I stayed a day and two nights. My left eye was cut, and it swelled enormously and closed. My right leg swelled all down my thigh. X-rays were taken but were all negative. After my purple eye opened, there was a red splotch, which was a blood clot. It looked horrid!! My left and right eye were both black. The red spot went away after about one month. I still have my black eyes though. One thing the scar is hidden under my eye brow. I forgot to mention in that that summer I went off the boys' high dive board."

"On Christmas Eve we watched, "A Christmas Carol" and "Alice in Wonderland" on TV. On New Year's Eve we went to Joliet to be with the Johnson family. After dinner I went and played my violin for Mrs. Chapman and Naomi. On Jan. 2nd watched Ozzie and Harriet, Mama and Henry Aldrich. Made brownies and got my first pair of Saddle Shoes. My favorite friends are Barb and Bev Bowman and my cousins, Caryl and Barb Lund. Jan 4th went to Camp Fire girls to assist Mom."

"Jan. 5th The boring days are here again-hated Geometry- a terrible day. I'm playing in the school orchestra and was named second chair. Went to Orchestra Hall- Esther took me – heard Micha Elman- played four encores. Keith went to a party at his Sunday School teacher's home. Paul Peterson drove up, he said he had a wonderful time. Jan 10th I went to Esther's for my lesson, and she said I had a very good lesson. My tone was good and true. Jan 12th, my Sunday school teacher, May Nelson, gave me a glow in the dark plaque, which says, Jesus Never Fails. Jan 20th we went to the Assembly Hall and watched the inauguration of President "Ike". Jan 22nd today we went shopping and I got my first pair of high heels for Jerry's wedding. Jan 24th went up to Michigan for Jerry's wedding."

In the next three years much of her time was spent with the Hi-C Chorale in which she played her violin and sang alto. A highlight of her graduation from Morgan Park High School came in 1955, when she performed with the Chorale in a concert they gave at Orchestra Hall.

A month later we met at Bass Lake.

Chapter 7

Then there was Lee

My first remembrance of Alida Anderson dates from Christmas Sunday 1952. I was sitting in the balcony of our church. The winter sun was streaming through the south window of the church and a young girl came out of the choir room door, stood in a shaft of sunlight, and unaccompanied, played Silent Night on the violin. I was touched by her playing and how beautiful her brown hair shone in the light. She was 14 years old, and I had just had my 23rd birthday. After church I remarked to my mother about her. My mother told me that she had known her mother, Florence, since 1920, and Lee was one of her six children. Several people had remarked that Lee was a tremendous help to her mother.

On the last Saturday of July, 1955, I invited all post high school young people in our church to come for a day of fun and games at our cottage at Bass Lake. Lee came to it, and It didn't take me long to notice that she was a very pretty girl. I talked to her and found that she was planning to go to Grant Hospital on Chicago's north side and begin nurse's training come September. When I came home, I called her and asked if she would like to go with me to a Grant Park concert on Wednesday night. She said yes, and I picked her up in my new '56, green and white, Bel Air Chevy hardtop, and drove to the concert. I clearly remember that she wore a blue and white dress, white shoes, and wrist high white gloves. But most of all what I noticed most were her beautiful, expressive eyes and eyebrows and slightly pouty lips that invited kissing. We talked a lot that evening about our love for Classical music, and I told her how much I enjoyed her violin playing. She was now playing often in our Sunday morning worship service. She told me her favorite composers were Beethoven and Rachmaninoff, and I said mine were Mozart and Schubert.

Several days before she entered the nursing school we again went to a concert in the park. She offered to make picnic supper, and I brought a blanket and the sodas. She prepared a chicken salad. We had a great evening, and that night we exchanged our first kiss.

The first months of her training were intense. She could go out only one night a week and had to be in by ten pm. She could go home only on Thanksgiving and from Christmas to New Year's. Several of the students who could not take this discipline dropped out before the capping ceremony in February.

When Lee came home at Christmas time I spent quite a bit time with her. Spending time with her also meant going to church with her where she again played the offertory on the violin. She played Beethoven's Romance #2 for the Sunday offertory between Christmas and New Year's. I'll never forget mother Anderson's remark to me during that joyous season; "I'm glad Lee's dating an older man, now she'll know how to be treated when she dates men who are her age!!" When I told Lee what her mother had said, she said; "Don't worry, you're young enough for me."

By the time I went to Florida in March with brother Will, I knew I wanted to marry her. In the summer of '56 she said she had two dreams: That she would marry me and that she would be able to finish her nurse's training and become a nurse. She would not be graduating until June of '58. I put a lot of miles on the Chevy, driving to the school a couple times a week. It was 17 miles away, and on the fastest route there were 24 stop lights and 8 stop signs to slow my progress in getting to her. The girl I met at the end of the drive was well worth it.

We spent many hours walking in, and enjoying Chicago's Lincoln Park and its' Zoo, and the Lincoln Park Beach. We loved going to the Chicago Symphony and singing and worshipping together at several churches and our home church. She had an excellent alto voice, and we loved to harmonize when we sang. While at the Art Institute we agreed that Renoir was our favorite artist.

We had one terrifying experience while parked one night at the Lincoln Park lagoon. We were engaged in serious necking when two policemen, one on each side of the car, surprised us by shining their flashlights on us. They asked us to get out of the car. Lee was taken to the squad car, and I was told to get back in my car and was confronted by the other officer. They accused us of having sex. We both denied it. The other officer, with Lee, said she would be reported to the Nursing School, which would probably lead to her dismissal. The policeman with me said I would be reported to my employer. When Lee returned to my car she was in tears. They then said to me that they would not report us if we gave them $100. I had read about crooked cops doing this kind of shakedown, now I was experiencing it. I showed them that I only had $25. They said they would take that, but they wanted me to come back the next night to the same spot and give them $75 more, or they would follow through on their threats.

After I dropped Lee off at the Hospital, I went to the Lincoln Park Police Station and told the desk sergeant what had happened. I told him I would be willing to go back to the park the following night so they could set up a sting to catch these officers taking a bribe. He dissuaded me from doing that. He gave many reasons and advised me not to frequent that area again. Nothing ever came of the threats the crooked cops had made, but it was a miserable memory for Lee and I, seeing the police at their worst.

A favorite place for us to park was out on the point of the city's lake shore, where the Planetarium stands. From there we had a spectacular view of the city lights and skyline. We also watched a lot of submarine races from there. In October of '57 we went into the Planetarium and got a close view of Sputnik, the first satellite that the Russians launched into space. We went back to the car on that clear night and watched the speck in the sky as it streaked by.

On Thanksgiving Day, 1956, I was invited by the Andersons for dinner. After dinner Lee and I met with her parents, and I asked their permission to marry Lee. Her father, Carl, readily agreed; Mother Florence said that she thought Lee was too young and inexperienced to make that decision. Lee would be 19 in less than three months. After some further discussion in which we agreed to wait until Lee graduated to get married, Florence agreed. Lee and I told them we would like to be married in September of 1958. I gave Lee her diamond on Christmas Eve. From my experience, I would not recommend such a long an engagement. It is too hard for a couple to put off consummating their relationship until the wedding date when they are committed to each other and have many opportunities to give expression to those desires.

In the summer of 1957 I took a 10 day trip to visit Civil War battlefields and other historic sites in Pennsylvania, Maryland Washington, D.C and Virginia. It was a round trip of, 2,628 miles.

I did not enjoy it as much as I should have as I was separated from my love.

After our engagement, my closest uncle, who was a contractor, said he would be pleased to build us a house in Oak Lawn, where he was building a new development of two to four bedroom brick homes. He offered us a lot on a cul-de-sac that would give us more privacy. He would schedule the house to be finished a month before our wedding so we could get our painting done and furnishings in and be ready to move in after the wedding. We selected a three bedroom model having an area of 1,100 sq. ft. with a full basement. The price was $19,715. We decided to have a variegated red brick and stone front on the house. They started building the house in March of '58.

What a thrill it was to go out to the building site and see our house going up. I took many pictures of it. My favorite picture was of Lee sitting in the bath tub of the unfinished bathroom. My uncle was very generous in giving us extras such as a solid concrete driveway and a dishwasher.

With the good came the unpleasant task of planning the wedding with Florence, my mother-in-law to be. My future father-in–law Carl, was a quiet man who for the most part, seemingly, had little to say in the running of the family. He worked at Commonwealth Edison. In order to earn more money to support the family of eight he worked the night shift. Consequently, when Lee and I discussed the wedding plans with Florence, he was usually not there.

Our former neighbor on Champlain Avenue was the chief pastry chef at the Palmer House in Chicago. He said he would be pleased to gift us with our wedding cake. The only other matter that was settled and agreed to was to limit the guest list to 300. When we came to discuss the number in the wedding party, we decided on a bridal party of 10. This met Mrs. Anderson's approval as long as I had Lee's two older brothers in that group. This would not be right, I said, because I had several close friends I wanted to be my groomsmen. I felt it was a real victory when she agreed that my brother should be best man. Wow!! On other nights we discussed the wedding gown. Lee wanted to buy it. Mother wanted to make it. Mother made up her invitation list of 200 leaving our family with only 100 to invite. On the night we discussed this, her father was present. Lee, her father and I agreed this was not fair, but she would not back down. Lee left the table in tears and her father left also, leaving me alone with my future mother-in-law. After a couple of minutes passed I told her I was very upset, that she was turning what should be the happiest day of Lee's and my life into a nightmare. It was becoming her wedding not ours. She was running the whole show. I told her I was respectful of their prerogative to have a major say on our wedding plans, but once we were married if she tried to run Lee's life then like she now was, she would not be welcomed in our home. That was the nadir of my relationship with my mother-in-law.

When the wedding gown was not finished a week before the wedding, Lee, I, and my Uncle Albin and Aunt Elvira went to a bridal store. After Lee picked out a gown, Uncle Albin paid them to put it on hold in case we would need it in a few days. Fortunately, Florence did finish the gown four days before the wedding.

On the 27th of September 1958, Lee and I were married in the Salem Baptist Church. It was a beautiful fall day. The highlight of the wedding celebration was the cake, which was encircled with a rainbow of spun sugar lace. Then my best friend Bill Almer gave the best toast I've ever heard at a wedding. I'm so glad it was at ours. It had great bits of seriousness. and there were times when we were doubled over with laughter. After the reception, we left on our honeymoon. We didn't have to go far to our new home at 9940 Cook Ave. I had the joy of carrying Lee over the threshold and laying her gently on our bed.

On Sunday morning we set out for New England on our honeymoon trip that Lee and I had planned. We arrived at the Tally-Ho motel in North Kingsville, Ohio, shortly after sunset and checked in. When I signed the register, "Paul Peterson", the owner asked, "Who's your lady friend?" I'm sure I blushed as I explained that we had been married the night before. He put us at ease by telling me that I wasn't the first new husband to do that. I was glad when we got a room as far as possible from busy Route 20. The motel was not air conditioned, so after we were in the room a few minutes I opened the back window. We immediately heard a rumble and the crash of a bowling ball hitting the pins! A bowling alley was right in back of the motel. After about an hour, the room had cooled down so we closed the window which shut out the noise. We went to sleep. Late at night I got up and opened the window. At around seven o'clock we were awakened by the sound of mooing cows and the barnyard smell that came in with the breeze. A cattle truck had pulled into the alley in back of us. We had plenty of incentive to get up and get on our way to Niagara Falls.

Lee accumulated memorabilia from the places we stopped on our trip, things such as brightly colored leaves and stones from streams and ocean shore. We visited Lake Placid, Lake Champlain, rustic covered bridges in Vermont and New Hampshire, Franconia Notch, the Old Man of the Mountain (before his face fell off), Mt. Washington, and the Rock of Ages granite quarry. We hiked up Mt Mansfield, and explored the rocky coast of Maine: Bar Harbor, Acadia National Park, Portland, and Kennebunkport. Along the way we had several Lobster dinners, then we went to Lake Winnipesaukee, Mt Manadnock, Brattleboro, and Albany. The whole trip was a journey of 3,510 miles. We were gone 14 days and spent the astronomical sum of $329.17. The average price of our room for each night was $8.75. We also enjoyed testing quite a few mattresses as we got to KNOW each other.

When we got home mom and dad invited us over for dinner. After dinner, they gave us a check for $5,000. When I started paying them room and board in July of '52, they opened a savings account into which all my payments were deposited. What a gift!! That was about my yearly salary at that time. We applied all of their gift to reduce our mortgage. Was I ever blessed to have parents like them!

HOW TO GET HIGH IN YOUR FIRST YEAR OF MARRIAGE

Driving back from our fall honeymoon in New England we started talking about where to spend next year's vacation. Lee suggested going to either Bermuda; a romantic spa in the Poconos; or the Greenbrier. I said. "You chose where we'd honeymoon, I'd like to plan our next trip and show you the glories of the West." I suggested we tour The Black Hills, Yellowstone, and the Grand Tetons, where I would do some climbing. She asked me why I wanted to climb mountains. I said, "It stretches my body and soul and that allows me to learn that I can do something difficult that may be beyond my present ability. I should dare to dream dreams about things that may be beyond me."

In our courting days, I had foregone many weekends of climbing with members of the Chicago Mountaineering Club at the Mississippi Palisades or Devils Lake, Wisconsin, scaling rock bastions to improve my strength and climbing technique. Before I met Lee and was enchanted away from athletic endeavors in order to win her heart, I had gone to the Exum School in the Tetons to learn proper climbing technique. I was taught by Dr. Willi Unsoeld, who would soon be the first American to climb Mt. Everest by the west ridge. That training school experience was now five years old. Willi encouraged me in his Christmas letters to come back and climb the "Grand" with him. He thought I had the perfect body for climbing, (almost six feet tall and 140 pounds.) He described me as a wiry spider. That was better than the 99 pound weakling that others thought I resembled. I knew that if I didn't climb it soon, I never would. I was out of shape partly because on many nights, when instead of playing basketball, Lee and I parked on Chicago's lake front.

Some weeks later we discussed mountain climbing again. She had seen my pictures of the Tetons and climbing. She said, "If you're going to climb, I'm going with you, I'm not going to sit in a cabin three to four days while you climb." I was taken aback to say the least and made some unkind comments about her physical condition and the improbability of her being able to do a climb of this difficulty. I went on, "you'd have to sleep one night on the mountain with only a tarpaulin and sleeping bag cushioning you." In addition, there were no "comfort stations" on the mountain. She would probably be the only women with four or five men. When nature called she'd need to alert us of the fact, then move a short distance away to squat while the rest of us turned our backs, while she got rid of you know what, which many times, would be blown to who knows where. If someone did this in high wind conditions, you'd best keep your eyes and mouth closed. This did not dissuade her, and she gave me an, "I'll show you" look.

As Christmas approached she asked me to give her a pair of climbing boots and a "Y" membership as presents as she wanted to be fit to climb. We made imprints of her feet to assure her of getting a proper fit, and sent an order off. During the holidays I talked to several of her family and nursing classmates and told them of her intentions to climb. Most of them said they were not surprised. She had participated with them in rough housing and could give as good as she got. Was this the girl I'd married? She seemed to me to be an "Audrey Hepburn type" lady" who wore white gloves and broad brimmed hats on Sundays.

She got the boots and most days walked the five mile round trip to the hospital, where she worked as an O.B. nurse. She worked out at the "Y" and was soon doing sit ups and push ups in our living room. I was amazed at her determination to prove to me and herself that she could do the two day climb. I called Willi and told him we were coming the first week of July with the goal to climb the Grand Teton, and requested him to be our guide. He said we should both go to the 2 day school, and he would judge whether we could do the climb.

We drove out and got to the school on the first of July. At the school we were taught how to use pitons and carabiners, to tie a bowline knot, to rappel down a fifty- foot cliff, the importance of three point contact, belaying techniques, climbing commands, and what to do if altitude sickness or frost bite hit us. (He was concerned about this as we had not spent the suggested conditioning week at high altitude.) We took a long trek loaded up with full gear, and were taught to walk slightly bent at the waist to more easily neutralize the pitch we were ascending. This also helped us to concentrate on our breathing in order to get as much oxygen as possible into our blood. This would be important in avoiding altitude sickness above 10,000 feet. Willi judged we could do the climb but because of deep snow on the "Owen" route, a grade three climb, we would have to take the tougher route, the "Exum," a grade four climb. This meant we would have to be "roped up" 25% of the time once we got above 11,000 feet.

On July sixth our group of five climbers left our camp on Jenny Lake and in a couple of hours started up the draw between the Middle and Grand Teton. At 10,000 feet we got into a lot of loose rock (scree) and snow. We used our ice axes to pick our way up. As the sun began to set we arrived at the middle saddle between the mountains. In six hours we had climbed 5,000 feet. From here, at 11,644 feet the Grand rose spectacularly up on our right. For the main part of our supper, Willie asked us all for our cans of soup. which he then dumped into the cooking pot, a mixture of tomato, chicken, mushroom and oxtail and onion. With our cheese and crackers, food never tasted better. Willi talked some about what the next day's climb would entail. We put a tarp on the snow, unrolled our sleeping bags onto it, and crawled in while pulling another tarp over us. Willi then secured this tarp with some large rocks. At 3:30am he greeted us with a cup of cocoa. We got up and had breakfast. By the first light we started for the summit. We needed to get there by noon in order to get back down to the climbing camp by nightfall.

As we made our way to the upper saddle, our first technical difficulty was the "Belly Around," which is a seven foot high semi-circular outcropping of rock. We roped up and belayed Willi, as he, using a large crack, pulled himself, sliding on his belly, to the next ledge 15 feet away. He then pounded in a piton; attached a carabiner, and put the rope thru it, pulled in the slack, and one by one we bellied over to his side. We had a great incentive to hold on as a chasm of 300 feet was below us! As we turned a corner we caught sight of our next challenge, "Wall Street," a narrow ledge midway up on a shear rock face of 1,500 feet. Willi led the way. After about 150 feet he stopped and pounded in another piton. Following the same procedure used on the "Belly Around," he let out enough rope to allow himself to jump across a 5 foot gap on the ledge. His and our fate was linked to each other by a bond of rope. He made it look like he was playing Hop Scotch. Then he got set to belay and invited Lee to Jump across. As she was about to go a strong wind gust blew her out away from the wall. Willi pulled the rope taut, forcing her back. He praised her for not screaming. He claimed later that she never even blinked. Then the remaining three of us, with Willi belaying, jumped to the other side. After ascending several rock chimneys, we got to the most difficult part of the ascent called the "Friction Pitch." I'll quote the climbers guide.

"It is thought to be the most difficult part of the "Exum Route." It is a 150 foot lead with no protection for the leader. Climb about 15 feet somewhat right of center, then traverse left up on knobs and friction to two large black knobs and friction for perhaps 30 feet, then the rock becomes easier to climb as one climbs to the belaying spot."

Thank God for Willi, who, without any belaying support from above frictioned up to to a broad ledge. This was by far my biggest challenge of the climb. I reached up at full stretch and found a knob for my three middle fingers and breathed a sigh of relief. When he had the rope secured he told me to climb as he kept the rope taut. For an endless moment everything was concentrated on the outcome of my shift of body weight, one calculated decision to move, upon which the outcome of my entire climb, if not my life depended. One by one we, with Willi's guidance got up to the ledge. Without him we amateurs would not have made it because of icy conditions on this pitch. At this point we all got our cameras out and took pictures as each one came over the ledge. From here we climbed up a sharp ridge known as 'The Horse," and climbed the last 120 feet to the summit.

On the peak Lee and I embraced and looked west into Idaho and rest of the world, then east to Jenny Lake, where we had camped the previous morning. We stood in quiet and reflected as we realized that we had done something that had tested the limits of our bodies and souls. I told Lee how astonished I was of her achievement and how proud I was of her, and how glad I was that she was my wife.

On top we took more pictures, signed the register, and started our descent at about 1pm. To get down to the upper saddle we tied two ropes together and free rappelled 120 feet. What a thrill! Willi yodeled as each of us jumped off and slid down, regulating our rate of descent by the ropes friction across our shoulder and arms. When we came to a snow covered glacier we got down on our haunches and, still roped together, glissaded down several hundred feet. Willi told us to look ahead to the lead person on the rope and if he disappeared we were to dig in our ice axes to brake. There was always the possibility that a snow bridge over a crack in the glacier would collapse and we would fall into the glacier. The only mishap on our slide came to our German team member, who slid on his butt a few times. At places the snow was rough and he tore off one side of the seat of his pants, exposing a snow burned, half moon to us. A short while after we got off the snow, Lee became sick and the rest of the way down had occasional dry heaves. Willi said that it was probably altitude sickness. We got back to camp at about nine and had some soup, which Lee was able to keep down. Willi gave us certificates commemorating our conquest of the Grand. We formed a circle and sang Auld Lang Syne and went to bed, two days later we started driving back to Chicago. (On this trip we drove 3,300 miles. We spent $420. The cost of the school and the climb was $180.)

As I had surprised Lee suggesting we go West on our next vacation, somewhere in Nebraska, she surprised me when she softly said, "I think I might be pregnant, maybe that's why I got sick." When she went back to the hospital a few days later her suspicion was confirmed. On February 29, 1960, she went into labor. Fortunately, for our son, David, she delayed delivering until March first.

Lee gave several talks and showed slides of our climb. I was especially proud of her achievement. For the next 11 years we had no more discussions about where we would take a long vacation. I took a new job in Manhattan, we moved three times, and Lee delivered two more sons. When David was twelve, our family took a three week trip west. In the Tetons we looked up at the summit of the Grand where Dave, as a two to three month fetus, had been carried by his mother. If you believe that prenatal experience affects a child, then it explains why he achieved as an athlete. At Ludlowe High School he set records in the mile and two mile run. He was All State in track and cross country, and got an athletic scholarship to Virginia Tech. There he ran distance and cross country for four years. In 1982, he set a new Virginia Intercollegiate record in the 5,000 meter (3.1mile) race with a time of 14:04. He and my oldest grandson, now 17 years old, have climbed to the highest point in each of seven states. (Atta Boy, Dave and Matt, only 43 more to go.)

(In 1963 Willi and doctor Tom Hornbein climbed the west ridge of Everest to the summit. The first time this route had ever been tried. Because of darkness they had to bivouac at 28,000 ft. without oxygen. He lost nine toes to frostbite. That didn't stop him. In 1978 he died with a student when they were caught in an avalanche on Mt. Rainer. In'54 and '58 I spent not more than five days with him in the Tetons but in that short time he made a tremendous impression on my life. How I wish I'd spent more time with him! A great man.)

Chapter 8

Fatherhood, Mourning and Uprootings

Lee and I returned from our honeymoon, and she immediately was employed by Little Company Hospital as an obstetrical nurse. It was great that she began working in O.B. for within a year she would need to pick a doctor to guide her through her pregnancy. When that time came, she picked Dr. Fallon. Her judgment on doctors was vindicated when he was promoted to head the department. She worked there until January 1, 1960, when she retired to prepare for our son's birth.

In the next months I spent most of my spare time landscaping, painting and adding personal touches to our home. Now that Lee had dental insurance she decided to get some much delayed work done. I suggested that she use my dentist and she agreed to try him. He had grown up a block away from our house in a large Italian family. I'd played ball with several of his younger brothers and had been a patient of his since he set up his practice. He was married and had a son. Lee was happy that he had evening hours on Tuesday and Thursday as she was working full time. Lee remarked that there were a few other women who were there waiting when she left. She said he was always joking while he worked. No dental assistant was there in the evening. One night when she was the last patient he asked her if she'd like to go out with him for a drink and a little dancing. She told him she did not want to, and he said he knew that and was only kidding. When Lee told me this I said he always was a joker and to take it as that. Lee, however, wasn't sure he was kidding and decided she would make her future appointments for Saturday mornings.

A few weeks later on a Fall Saturday morning, Lee went to see him for an 11 am appointment. I was in the basement when I heard Lee come into the house. She was crying and calling for me. I came up the stairs and as she took off her coat I could see she was wearing the blue bib that dentists put on the patient before they start to work. I hugged her and asked her what had happened. After a while, she calmed down enough to tell me.

When she got to the clinic no one was there except him. He told her that she was his last patient, and he had let his assistant leave early as she wanted to do some Christmas shopping. He laid her back in the chair and put the bib on. In an instant he was on her. She struggled to get free and kneed him hard in the groin. He slid off her and she stepped over him, grabbed her coat and fled home. I could not believe this had happened.

In the mid- afternoon Lee was calm enough to discuss what we should do about this attack. I called him that evening, and told him I was ashamed of him and incensed by his attack on my wife. We would never see him again, nor would we pay him for the dental work he had done. The only thing stopping me from reporting him to the police and the ADA was the effect that would have on his own family's reputation and the shame this would bring to him and my wife in revealing it. All he said back to me was, "I'm sorry"!! I never saw or heard from him again.

On a happier note, that fall of '59 the White Sox won the American League Pennant and played the Los Angeles Dodgers in the World Series. My Uncle Albin got tickets for the games and took me to the first and sixth game at Comiskey Park. The Dodgers won the series in six games.

That same fall, a small group of couples decided to get together once a month for fellowship and study to deepen our faith. Over the next few years we studied the Bible and read great Christian Classics such as; *The Cost of Discipleship. Mere Christianity, The Screwtape Letters, Augustines Confessions*, and many others. We also set a goal to memorize a key Bible passage and hymn every month. Elmer Johnson and Willard Erickson led our group, and I sometimes filled in when they were out of town. For Lee and I this was a great time of learning and bonding with life- long friends. In the next five years our couples group at church needed that strength as one of the wives, Dorothy Erickson, and two husbands, Ted Roseen and Bob Beaver, died while in their thirties, each leaving several children with a single parent.

One Halloween about 20 couples were at a Halloween party at the Warren Fredericks' home. We had enjoyed a potluck supper and went down to their finished basement to play games. One of our group went upstairs and found that a candle had burned down and set the top of the piano on fire. She shouted for help and quickly all came up from the basement and put out the fire before it spread. This was a lesson to us all that candles should be put out before one leaves a room. A few minutes later the fire would have been out of control, and as there were no exit doors to the outside from the basement, we could have all died. God again spared our lives.

In 1959, Victor Chemical Works was bought by Stauffer Chemical Company, and at that time I was asked to take a position as a Technical Sales Representative working out of the downtown office at 155 N. Wacker Drive. This was a job that would require a lot of travel. My main job was to work with customers in developing new products for them and our company. It was a challenging and exciting opportunity. I still spent about a quarter of my time at the Chicago Hts lab, another quarter traveling to work with customers, and half of my time in the office. I got a good raise in salary, which was much appreciated as Lee was soon to leave her job to prepare for the arrival of our first child.

On March first at about seven in the morning, Lee jumped out of bed and dashed to the bathroom. When she came back she had a bath towel between her legs and announced that her water had broken. I had the natural reaction for a first time father —panic— and started to get dressed. Lee tried to calm me down by assuring me that we had plenty of time, as she had not even felt a spasm of labor. Nevertheless, I got showered and dressed so I would be ready to go when she said so. Right then I told her I was happy I'd married a nurse. We ate breakfast and then drove to Little Company of Mary Hospital. A few hours later she delivered our first son: David Bradley Peterson.

Dr. Fallon came to the fathers' waiting room and escorted me to the nursery, where the doctor directed one of the nurses to bring my son to the window. What I saw was a red, wrinkled baby who was crying loudly. My first question to Dr. Fallon was, "Is he normal?" He assured me that he was, except for a minor hernia, which would be easily repaired in a couple of months.

When summer came, we spent a couple of weeks of our vacation and nearly every week end at Bass Lake. Dave was now the fourth generation to enjoy our place there. I got a plan to build a 16' X 26' foot garage and the building permits to do it. Because this was my first experience in building, I decided to get my uncle's firm to pour the foundation slab and put the base 2x4s down so that the building would be square at the start. I spent every Saturday and most evenings after work on this job in the fall with the goal of completing it by winter. By the end of October, I had the framing and wallboard done and was ready to put the shingles on the roof.

My next door neighbor, Paul, was a roofer and he offered to help me with that job. On Friday night I helped him lay down the tar paper, and then he showed me how to put on a row of shingles. The next morning I started on the second row. In the next couple of hours I saw Paul out of the corner of my eye checking my progress. By noon I had 6-8 rows put down. After lunch I started again.

Suddenly I felt and heard a ladder being put up on the other side of the roof. I walked up to the peak and observed Paul at the top of the ladder with a couple bundles of shingles on his shoulder. I protested weakly that I didn't need his help, but to no avail. He finished that side in about an hour. He then came over to my side where I was now about half done and started working. His method of dispensing nails was from his mouth. He seemed to spit them between his fingers and as soon as the nail touched the surface the hammer was on its way down to ram it home. He was a virtuoso at his trade. I think he had to show me what a true roofing artist could do. I thanked him and embarrassed him by offering to pay him for his labor. He refused my offer, but we found other ways in the next few years to show our appreciation of a great neighbor. I had my uncle's men put up the overhead door and I put the side door up before Thanksgiving. During the winter I put on the cedar shake siding, and in the spring painted it battleship grey with white trim and put a red wood gable on the front.

In the course of this building project, I only injured myself once. One evening I was sawing a board when the saw hit a knot, jumped out of the groove, and cut me seriously across the back of my left thumb. I came into the house through the back door dripping blood across the floor to the kitchen sink where Lee was working. I turned on the faucet to wash the wound. Lee examined it and said, "You'll have to go to the hospital emergency room and get that stitched up." She estimated it would take 8 to 10 stitches. She gave me a dish towel to wrap around it so I wouldn't drip any more blood on her floor. I asked if she'd drive me to the hospital. She gave me one of her wonderful raised eyebrow looks and said, "Look, I have to put David to bed, and besides you drove with one hand the whole time we were dating and I'm sure you still have that skill." When I married a nurse I expected to get back rubs and TLC. Lee brought me back to the real world. Every time I look at that scarred thumb I remember that evening.

In September of that year at age 30, I took my first flight from Chicago to Pittsburgh- a flight of 414 miles. I was to meet with research people at Calgon with regard to, a new automatic dishwashing compound which I had developed in our laboratory. Since that flight I have taken 1,372 flights (thru 2010,) and flown one million fifty- four thousand miles. With all that flying I had only three, "white knucklers". On a flight to Des Moines in a Convair, a two engine plane, I was seated next to our Midwest sales manager. He had the window seat. We were to have a business lunch with a customer in Des Moines. He said to me," I don't think we'll make our lunch date," as he pointed to the starboard engine, which was on fire! The Captain told us not to be alarmed, they were shutting down that engine and hitting it with CO2. He also assured us that they could fly with only one engine, but we would be making an emergency landing in Dubuque. We landed perfectly but did miss the lunch date. The second thrill flight came on a landing at LaGuardia when there was zero visibility until we were right over the runway. Our pilot "Pancaked" onto the runway, bounced several times, and then used maximum reverse thrust in order to not overshoot the runway. As we exited the plane, a passenger's knock on the cockpit door caused the crew to open it. The passenger shouted in, "Captain, you and my underwear know what a lousy landing that was." Most of the passengers agreed with that statement and applauded it. The scariest flight of all came at the end of a "red eye" flight from San Francisco to JFK. We were landing on a clear day and were in the final landing approach when the pilot put on maximum power and banked sharply to the left. I was seated at a window and looked down to the wing tip that was only a couple hundred feet off the ground. The plane shuddered as the pilot struggled to gain altitude. We finally did gain altitude and leveled off. The Captain came on and with a shaky voice told us that he had to do what he did because another plane had taxied onto our runway and the alternative for us would have been to crash into that plane. Thank God we had a great pilot that day. It's odd I never heard or read anything about this in the press. I never told Lee about this close call as I didn't want her to worry about me when I flew.

One other first was achieved when I was given a $400/month expense account. What a plus that was!! At the end of my career that account was up to $1,500/month. When I retired it was hard to learn to live without that crutch.

Decimating news came to our family when my mother was found to have colon cancer. She had surgery to remove part of the colon and then chemotherapy, which was then in its infancy. She suffered much from these treatments. The doctor did not offer much hope and she became weaker and lost weight.

When we went to Bass Lake that summer I got a Sears book on wiring a house and set out to rewire the cottage which my parents had purchased from my recently deceased grandmother's estate. The main problem with the cottage was a lack of outlets and wall switches. The lighting fixtures in the bedrooms and kitchen were activated by a pull chain. When we came into those rooms at night, we had to flail our arms around in order to find the pull chain. Meanwhile you tried not to trip or stumble over something on the floor or knock something off a dresser.

I went up into the attic via a trap door and started the job of re-wiring. The temperature was up near 100 degrees. I only had my under shorts on and was sitting astride a couple of ceiling rafters, feeding four lines of BX cable into a junction box. It took me quite a long time to do this job. When I got up, one of my legs was asleep and it collapsed! I fell and came through the living room ceiling. Lee was holding David, who let out a scream as I made my entrance in a surprising loud manner. I skinned up my legs and ribs as I fell thru the rafters, but fortunately was able to catch myself by my elbows with my body from trunk down exposed for Lee and Dave to see. Lee was laughing hysterically at the sight. I told her to get the step ladder so I could get down but she wanted to get her camera to take a picture. I told her in no uncertain terms, "Forget that", for in a few minutes I'd drop to the floor as my strength was giving out. I directly ordered her to get the ladder, which she did. I climbed down exhausted and stretched out on the floor. This mishap led me to also become an expert in replacing ceiling wall board. That's a job I wouldn't wish on anyone.

That October the U.S., Russia and the world held its breath when Russia sent missiles to Cuba and threatened us with nuclear war. President Kennedy countered with a naval blockade of Cuba. I remember walking through Chicago's loop and seeing TVs in many store windows broadcasting this event. On several days I wondered if I would ever see my family again. Fortunately, the Russian premier, Khrushchev blinked and was forced to withdraw the missiles which were only 100 miles from the U.S.

I was not at all happy when I had to spoon feed Dave his baby food. Sometimes I'd put a spoonful of Oat Meal or Apricots in his mouth and he'd spit back two, which I'd have to wipe off his face. One day after many attempts to get him to stop this practice, I lost it and flipped a whole spoonful of food in his face. His eyes opened wide in fright and a startled look came on his face, closely followed with a blood curdling scream. After that episode our relationship improved when I fed him.

Lee was unhappy with me when she'd come home and detect the unpleasant odor of a dirty diaper in the house. I said I didn't smell anything and said my sense of smell was probably not as good as hers since it had been at least partly impair by chemicals that I inhaled over the years. She didn't buy my copout.

We got Dave a potty chair and when he'd get that strained look on his face I'd quickly pull his pants down and sit him on it, but I was usually too late. One day he gave me a wonderful surprise when he came to me with the potty bowl containing a brown lump. I gave him a big cheer and hug and he proudly showed it to Lee when she came home. That presentation made Lee very happy as it saved her from washing many diapers.

On Memorial Day, May 30, 1963, our second son Glenn Stuart, was born at Little Company of Mary Hospital. Dave was a Peterson; Glenn was born with brown hair and more resembled the Anderson side of the family. Shortly after this we added another member to our family, Sandy, a sheltie collie mix. I remembered how important my dog, Sharp, had been in my early years and enjoyed seeing Dave lead her around at Bass Lake on a leash. In late summer we had Glenn dedicated during a church service. Glenn had consumed a bottle of formula just before we went up to the altar for the ceremony. As I carried him I had his head on my shoulder and patted his back as the dedication vows were made. When the rite was completed I walked back up the aisle where I was told by the head usher that with my patting, Glenn had baptized the back of my suit with a considerable amount of his recently ingested bottle. I don't know of any friends that ever suffered this indignity and I think it ironic that this son became a minister of the Gospel.

At about the same time I was offered a promotion which would move me to Stauffers' headquarters in NYC. I would be the company's tech sales and service representative in the New England and Atlantic states. I would also get a 50% raise.

I was 33, and in order to look older I decided to grow a mustache. At various times I would be asked to show I.D. when we'd go to a bar. This was embarrassing to a father of 2 sons. That change worked. I was never again asked to show proof of age.

Although this was a significant promotion to corporate headquarters on Madison Avenue in New York, I had several reservations in taking the position I'd lived in Chicago all my life and loved the city. There was also Bass Lake. All of Lee's and my friends and most of our relatives lived near us. Most of all, my mother was dying of cancer and my father had just turned 80. Additionally, after several visits to Manhattan I did not like what I saw. To me it was too big, dirty and unfriendly. But in spite of that we made the decision to move. I loved the work I was doing and the company, and was challenged by the job and the opportunity for further promotion, and most of all, I had the blessing of my parents to do so.

The company gave Lee and me, two, three- day trips to do house hunting. On our second trip we decided we'd get more for our money in the northern suburbs of New Jersey than we would in Ct. In early September we bought a house in Upper Montclair, NJ for $22,800 and sold our home in Oak Lawn, Ill. for $24,000. Our new home was less than 200 feet from the bus stop for the bus to the Port Authority bus terminal in NYC. We felt the house could be easily sold if things did not work out for us in the East.

We moved in on a Monday morning and immediately discovered that we had bought a house on one of Montclair's busiest streets. We'd never noticed that when we'd been shown the house on a peaceful summer Sunday morning. I knew it was on a major bus route to NYC, but we didn't know the grammar school was just around the corner with its school buses. Last but not least the Montclair Teacher's College, a major commuter's school, was a half mile down the road. Fortunately for us, the house had a deep back yard that was completely fenced in so there was no need for our boys to play out front of the house near the street. The house at 802 Valley Road was a two- story Cape Cod with a full basement and a one car attached garage. On the first floor was an L shaped Living/ dining room with a fire place and kitchen with a small pantry, a half bath and a small porch. Upstairs were three bedrooms and a full bath. The house had a big exhaust fan in the attic which cooled the house quickly when the door to the screened porch was opened. We bought our first air conditioner for our master bedroom but didn't use it more than 8 to10 days a summer. That Thanksgiving weekend my Mom and Dad, Uncle Albin and Aunt Elvira and Brother Will and wife Eunice came to spend the holiday weekend with us. Unfortunately for us and the rest of the country, we spent it watching JFK's funeral.

Before I left Chicago, I had told my buddies at the plant to sell my regular season '63 Bear tickets, but if the Bears got to the NFL Championship I wanted to get in on the drawing to get one of the three tickets for the game. My name was drawn from the hat and I flew to Chicago to see the game against the N.Y. Giants whose stars were Y.A. Tittle and Frank Gifford. The Bears were quarterbacked by Bill Wade with Johnnie Morris at running back and a guy named Ditka at tight end. The temperature at game time, 1 pm, was 10 above zero. Icicles on the upper deck of Wrigley Field were dripping on us, but who cared!! The Bears won in a battle of great defenses, 14 to10. Richie Pettibone ended the Giants' last scoring drive when he intercepted a Tittle pass in the end zone. I finally got to see one of my Chicago teams win a World Championship!

That Christmas we flew home to Chicago with our sons for what was to be our last Christmas with mother. On New Year's Eve Lee and I went to NYC to see the ball drop in Times Square. We had dinner and then gathered with the thousands to await the big event. We saw it drop, cheered the incoming year and headed home. We were creeping along in merging traffic that fed into the Lincoln tunnel. In our line a man stood with what looked like a short rope. He'd try to talk to each driver, some of whom would roll down their window. When he came to our car I rolled down the window and heard his tale of woe. He was holding a broken fan belt that had broken on his car. He said he had no money and needed six dollars more to buy one. He asked if I'd buy a tunnel toll ticket for $2 so he could get the needed funds to replace the belt and get home. I gave him $2, and he gave me the toll ticket. When I got to the toll booth, I gave the attendant the ticket. She said, "Where's your ticket book?" I said, "I don't have one," and started to explain my purchase of the ticket. She told me I'd been taken. The ticket was a counterfeit. She told me to hurry up and give her $3. "Next time, buy a book and let the attendant detach it." She told me she'd sell me a book of 10 tickets for $20. I said no thanks and drove off steaming. I'd celebrated New Year's, being taken in by a New York con artist. We never went into the city again on New Year's Eve.

My brother Will and his wife moved into my folks home in order to give them both the care that they needed. Dad was 81 and mom was 66. She had undergone further surgery, and now had to cope with a colostomy bag. She had lost a lot of weight and had little strength to do anything. Will and Eunice gave our folks the care that they needed and never asked for my help. They were starting their own family. Their daughter Lisa had been born in '63.

In July, we came back to Chicago and took Mom and Dad to Bass Lake. My most precious memory of that summer was seeing my mother rocking on the big swing with her grandsons Dave and Glenn and then telling her that she would be a grandmother again around the first of the year.

Mom did not live to see Craig. She died in the fall of '64 at the age of 66. I was in Chicago on business the second week of September. I stayed over to see Mom on Saturday before flying back to N.J. She looked terrible, having lost a lot more weight since I'd seen her in July. She was skeletal and wan in appearance. It took all the strength she had to lift a glass of water to her lips. As the time approached for me to leave, she said, "Paul, I can't understand why Jesus lets me suffer like this. I want to die." I had no answer for her. She then asked me to pray that Jesus would take her home to be with Him so her suffering would end. I did so. It was the most difficult prayer I'd ever prayed.

I kissed her goodbye and flew to Newark Airport, rented a car, and drove home. At the door Lee greeted me with a hug and tears. She told me that Mother had died an hour ago. After a night of troubled sleep we got the boys dressed and we packed up to fly to Chicago for her funeral. On the way to the airport I turned on WQXR and in a few minutes heard a pianist play Schubert's Impromptu #3 in G. It went to my soul and provided balm for my grief. In a few years I would hear it played again on the darkest night of my life.

Chapter 9

Getting Settled in New Jersey

After attending several area churches we decided to become members of Brookdale Baptist Church. Lee and I joined the choir and struck up a great friendship with the choir director and his wife, Paul and Rae Liljestrand. Paul had been trained at Julliard, one of the top schools in the country for musicians. He is a gifted pianist, organist, composer and choir director. Paul taught us to be better singers. The Choir was not my only service opportunity at the church, I also served on the mission board.

We also joined the Montclair Chorale, a chorus that did many of the works of the great composers. The director of the chorus had been a member of the Robert Shaw Chorale. Our participation in the Chorale enhanced our love of singing and music.

We were very surprised in May of '64, when our doctor found that Lee was pregnant. Because Lee was RH negative and I was RH positive, we had been advised by our doctor, not to have any more children as there could be problems if we did. We took his advice and took precautions to avoid another pregnancy.

In the fall Lee began to have several physical problems, the worst being painful varicose veins in both legs. In the last two months of her pregnancy she wore support hose and had to have help getting upstairs. By Christmas the pain got so bad we had to put a bed in the living room for her to sleep on. In January when the obstetrician told her the baby could come at any time, and she was a week overdue, she decided to speed things up by taking Castor Oil to induce labor. It worked mightily. On January 15th when Craig Stephen Peterson exited Lee's body, so did a lot of other very unpleasant stuff. This did not please the doctor and nurses in attendance, and they let her know it. Lee took their rebukes in return for getting Craig out and being relieved of most of her pain. In May she went back to the hospital to have her varicose veins stripped and also had her tubes tied.

That summer we again spent a couple of weeks at Bass Lake. My dad was now 82 and had lost much of his urge to live since mom's death. His days at the lake were spent pitching horse shoes against himself, or sleeping or listening to his Cubs lose another game. His love for the Cubs continued, but the allegiance didn't demand much. It is difficult to dash hope when there is none.

As my dad desired to stay in Chicago most of the care of Dad fell to Eunice and Will. With their young children, they needed to have more room and their own home, and so Dad agreed to live with them. Our family home in Beverly Hills was sold and he moved to their new home in Glen Ellyn, III in 1966.

We had now lived in Upper Montclair for three years and had made friends in the town and in our church. I liked my job and was able to cope with the travel, but now with three sons we needed more room. Dave was ready for Kindergarten and we wanted him to go to the school in our district. In September we were shown a house at 580 Highland that we fell in love with and that was within walking distance of Bradford School. It sat on a 80 x 180 foot lot which had a 90 foot elevation. The street level area was eight feet wide and was bounded by a four- foot high stone wall. In front of and on top of the wall were seasonal perennials, and from the wall there was another rise to the two- story house with several gables. At the top of the driveway on the left side of the house was a two car garage and to the right, a gently sloping lawn to a stone patio, built into the 50 foot high rock face. The owner had constructed a 40 ft waterfall on part of the rock face that cascaded down a rock course into a pool that was on the back yard level. A sump pump in the pool re-circulated the water to the top of the fall. The house had a stone front. The back was shingled and painted grey, the roof was slate. The interior of the house contained 2,200 sq. ft. A spiral staircase ascended from the front entrance hall to the second floor, which had three bedrooms and two full baths, and a small sewing room off the master bedroom. Also on that floor were numerous nooks and closets, which added to the uniqueness of the house. On the first floor there were a living room and dining room, kitchen, half bath and study. There was also a full basement that had a paneled rec room with a fire place On the back of the house was a screened porch which looked out on a small, beautifully landscaped back yard, the raised patio and the waterfall. The house sat near the top of what was called First Mountain, and overlooked the campus of Montclair State College. In the distance was the New York skyline, clearly visible when our trees shed their leaves. It was the most beautiful and unique home we ever owned.

We moved into the house in November, 1966. The house cost $39,500. Unfortunately, for me, the real estate market was soft at that time, and for two years I had to rent our Valley Road house. The first year it was rented to a young couple, wonderful tenants who paid their rent on time and called only twice when minor repairs had to be made. They left the house as clean as they found it.

My tenant the next year was a middle age single parent with a teen age son and a dog and cat. She was a computer programmer for Hoffman-LaRoche Pharmaceuticals. She called me often with problems. She even called me twice when a light bulb burned out. I gave her only a six month lease as I wanted to put the house on the market on July 1, 68. When she moved out in mid-June I went over to clean it up prior to putting it on the market. I had cut the grass and raked up the leaves so the outside was presentable, but inside it was a pig pen. It reeked of cigarette smoke. The countertops in the kitchen had burn marks from her cigarettes. When I went down in the basement there were a couple hundred stamped out cigarette butts on the floor. I had to repaint her bedroom because of the smell and cigarette tar on the walls. There was dog and cat fur all over. When I went out on the glassed- in porch I was nearly overcome with the odor. There stood a garment moving box full of cat and dog droppings on newspaper that she had covered the porch floor with and periodically changed. She must have left the animals out there all day when she was at work as they had also clawed the porch doors so badly that I had to have them replaced. The animals had also chewed or clawed to pieces the porch furniture. That was my only experience with renters. I had seen the best and the worst. She, by mail, asked me to send her the escrow check she had given me at the beginning of her lease. I called her at work and told her I was going to use that money to repair the damage her pets had done. She did not ask me again for the money. In September '68 the house sold for $25,000

In Montclair there was an excellent store that sold Stamp and Coin supplies. I had not done anything with my stamp collection since I was in grammar school. Dad tried to keep my interest alive in collecting by getting first day covers of every stamp issued by the U.S. These envelopes I kept in a couple of shoe boxes. He also collected plate blocks and sheets of the commemorative stamps. I bought albums and put the stamps and covers in them and started collecting seriously. I found in N.Y.C. auction firms where I could buy some of the rarer stamps that I needed to add to my collection. In addition to U.S. stamps, I started collecting the countries of Canada, Australia, New Zealand and nearly all of Western Europe. I started investing in some high value U.S. stamps costing over $500 each. Now at 81, I still collect the stamps of the U.S. Austria, Germany, and the Scandinavian countries of Norway, Sweden and Denmark. Stamp collecting has been a lifelong hobby that has given me a lot of joy and has also helped me learn much about the countries that have issued the stamps.

In May of 1966, I was promoted to the position of Product Manager of Detergent Phosphates, which accounted for $40 million of Stauffer sales. My biggest customer was Proctor & Gamble, followed by Colgate, Calgon, and Economics Laboratories. My main competitors were Monsanto and FMC Corporation. My travel time was cut somewhat by this promotion, but I was still out of the office about a third of the time.

Some of the few things that made travel interesting in the late sixties were the freebies that the various car rental companies used to get business. I was told by Lee to rent National Cars because they gave S & H green stamps. When I'd rent a car for a week I'd get thousands of them. When I turned the car in, the green stamp machine would spit out a strip, 5 stamps wide, that was at times over 100 feet long. Several times when I came home after Lee had gone to bed I'd start at the front door and play the strip out until it reached her in bed. After a long warm kiss, I'd give her the end of the strip and let her reel them in. Several times she rewarded me wonderfully for my generosity.

Our corporate headquarters moved to the Westvaco building on Park Avenue, next to the Waldorf Hotel. I still took the Decamp bus into the city via the Lincoln tunnel and the Port Authority Bus Terminal. I was now 36 years old. Lee's cooking had helped me put on 25 pounds, so I now weighed 165lbs. Even with that added weight I didn't take up a lot of room on the bus seat. That being the case, it led a man who was obese to seek out where I was sitting when he got on the bus. He'd sit next to me and take two-thirds of the seat. I'd duck down when he'd get on hoping he wouldn't see me, but more times than not he'd find me. He'd open his N.Y. Times, and put an elbow in my ribs, and after a few minutes he'd fall asleep. When that happened, he'd spread his legs and I'd be wedged between him and the side of the bus. Without being obvious I'd try to get my elbow into his flab to get him to move over, but it was of no use. Finally, one day I'd had enough and I gave him a solid elbow, squeezed over him and stood in the aisle. He looked at me with a surprised look and asked what was wrong. I told him I was tired of wearing him and he could now spread out and go to sleep. He looked hurt and said, "I'm not aware that I was crowding you." Fortunately, that episode stopped him from ever sitting next to me again.

The buses on Wednesday evening were crowded with the blue-haired ladies who had taken in a Broadway matinee performance. They usually came in with a girlfriend. So if you were in front or back of them, you'd be the victim of their incessant chatter and giggles. On one of these trips two ladies were trying to impress each other and as many commuters as they could with a litany of their world travels. Finally, one said; "You know Agnes what was the most fun trip we ever took together?" "No, what was it?" Her seatmate asked. "When you called me and said, Lets fly to Bermuda for Lunch." I felt like getting up and bowing. Who could top that?

One of the cultural benefits I enjoyed when I was in the city on Wednesdays was to go to St Bartholomew's to hear the noon organ recitals. After attending several of them I began to wish that I had learned to play the piano better when I had taken lessons as a kid. A few days later when I was with Paul Liljestrand, I told him I'd like to start taking piano lessons. He said a lot of adults get that urge but nine out of ten give up after a short time. But, he said, "You read music well and I can get you a self teaching piano lesson book. If you work your way through it and still then want to go on, I'll suggest a teacher for you." He found a teacher for me who gave lessons on Saturday or evenings. That started me on learning to play the piano which I had given up on twenty- five years earlier. Because of my travels and job responsibilities I would take her last lesson on Tuesday night or on Saturday morning, if I'd had enough time to prepare and practice my lesson. I took lessons from her for several years and enjoyed playing for myself and Lee.

After Mother died in 1964, we'd still go to Bass Lake for at least two weeks each summer. Dad would join us for most of our time there. My generous Uncle Albin bought us two boats, first a Boston

Whaler with a 25 HP engine which he later traded in for a V- hulled boat with a 50 HP engine. Lee, Dave and I learned to water ski, and I even learned to slalom on one ski.

One Saturday evening, when Dave was seven, he ran into our cottage after he had just been swimming and slipped. In the fall his ear hit with full force on the edge of a coffee table. The ear was cut clear through, as if by a scissor, and bled profusely. We wrapped a diaper around it and sped to the E.R. at the Knox hospital. When the doctor saw it he jokingly asked if we might just want to leave it as a sign of ownership! (Farmers often notched their livestock ears to do just that.) We said we'd rather not, and he sewed Dave up.

We came home to Chicago every Christmas either to Lee's home on Bell Ave. or my brother Will's in Glen Ellyn. We had a Dodge station wagon. It was prior to the days when by law underage children had to be strapped into car seats. The back seat of the car was put down, making a platform on which we put a foam rubber cover. I'd come home at 3pm and take a nap. We'd have supper at 5:30pm, get the boys in their flannel pj's, wrap a blanket around them, and stretch them out in the back of the wagon. After an all night drive, we'd get to Chicago by mid- morning the next day. We did this until 1970. That year even with Lee driving for an hour or two, I almost fell asleep at the wheel and decided that at age 40, I should not endanger the family by driving all night.

In 1966, we took a five- day trip, with Paul and Rae Liljestrand to Williamsburg and then to Jefferson's Monticello. The next year, we went with them went to Expo '67 in Montreal. The Canadian government had funded building temporary housing for guests coming from all over the world to this world's fair. These were four-story wooden buildings which had only the bare necessities. Our room was on the first floor. One night it rained hard and we were awakened by the sound of water dripping on a puddle on the carpet, luckily not on our bed. The people on the fourth floor must have been swimming.

Back home in New Jersey our neighbors the Nelson's had two children that were close to the ages of our Glenn and Craig. They played well together and felt free to go into each other's house. One day Craig went into the Nelson's house looking for his playmates. He could not find them on the first floor so went up to the second. He heard someone in the bathroom and opened the door. He surprised Mrs Nelson, who was just stepping out of the tub. As she grabbed for a towel, Craig asked, "Mrs. Nelson do you have any cookies?" It may have been that summer that we celebrated the fourth of July in the Nelson's back yard. At one point we adults got into the fenced off play area and locked our children out so that we could have some peace. Our children were not quiet types.

1968 was not a good year for the U.S., Hippies, Flower children and druggies gathered at Woodstock to do all kinds of degrading things. Bobby Kennedy was shot to death in a hotel kitchen, and Martin Luther King was shot and killed on a Memphis motel deck. The Vietnam War was being protested all over the country and the Democratic Convention in Chicago was punctuated by rioting. In November, Richard Nixon was elected president. Another Kennedy, Senator Ted Kennedy, disgraced himself and his family when he drove off a bridge on Chappaquiddick and a girlfriend drowned. A very bright spot for our country and the world came about in July '69 when we saw Neil Armstrong land on the moon and plant our flag.

That same year, after Lee's youngest brother, Vic had graduated from high school, Lee's parents retired to Pentwater, Michigan. My father's health deteriorated due to Lewy Body disease which causes severe dementia. My brother Will, and his wife Eunice had much to cope with in caring for him. Some examples: He'd take the train to Chicago and then not remember how to get back home. They would have to go to Chicago to get him. When he'd stay with us for a couple of weeks in New Jersey, he'd go to the bathroom, lift the cover on the clothes hamper thinking it was the toilet and urinate on the clothes. One evening he asked me why I'd let people kill all the squirrels on our property. One morning he came down stairs in his pajamas, handed me a dollar and asked me to go out and pay the Halsted Street bus driver for his all night bus ride. It did no good to tell him he was in New Jersey and that Halsted Street was in Chicago. I went out, walked around the house, came back in and told him I'd paid the bus driver. He thanked me for doing that. What a sad thing it was to see my wonderful Father's life ending in this way.

In the fall of 1968, Lee and I celebrated our tenth wedding anniversary over the Columbus Day weekend at Brookdale on the Lake in the Pocanos. This was one of many romantic retreats in that area. We had a one room cabin with a heart shaped bath tub for two. It had a small Kitchenette in one corner, a fireplace with a large sheepskin rug in front of it in the sitting area, and a canopied, four-poster bed in another corner. We went there each Columbus Day weekend, from 1968 thru 1972. We hiked, canoed, read and spent much time re-kindling our romance on those weekends. After we married, it was the only place she played her violin, and it was just for me. She'd play Beethoven's Romance #2, Liebestraum, Grieg songs and our special song which we'd sing to each other, "It's Magic" –"You sigh the song begins, you speak and I hear violins, it's 'magic. The stars desert the skies and rush to nestle in your eyes, it's magic. Without a golden wand or mystic charms, fantastic things begin when I am in your arms. When we walk hand in hand the world becomes a wonderland, it's magic. How else can I explain the rainbow when there is no rain, it's magic. Why do I tell myself, these things that happen are all really true, when in my heart I know the magic is my love for you" (Friends, they don't write them like that anymore.)

In late October my friend Paul got pneumonia and was confined to his home. When you live in the northeast, one of the annual tasks that must be done in the fall is the raking of leaves. Paul had been unable to do this, so I asked my son Dave if he'd like to go with me to the Liljestrands' on a Saturday and do that job. He agreed to do so. What joy Dave and I had doing that for our friend. Paul never ceased to thank me for that small act of kindness. As a bonus, Dave also got joy from what we did, and it helped to make him the man he is today.

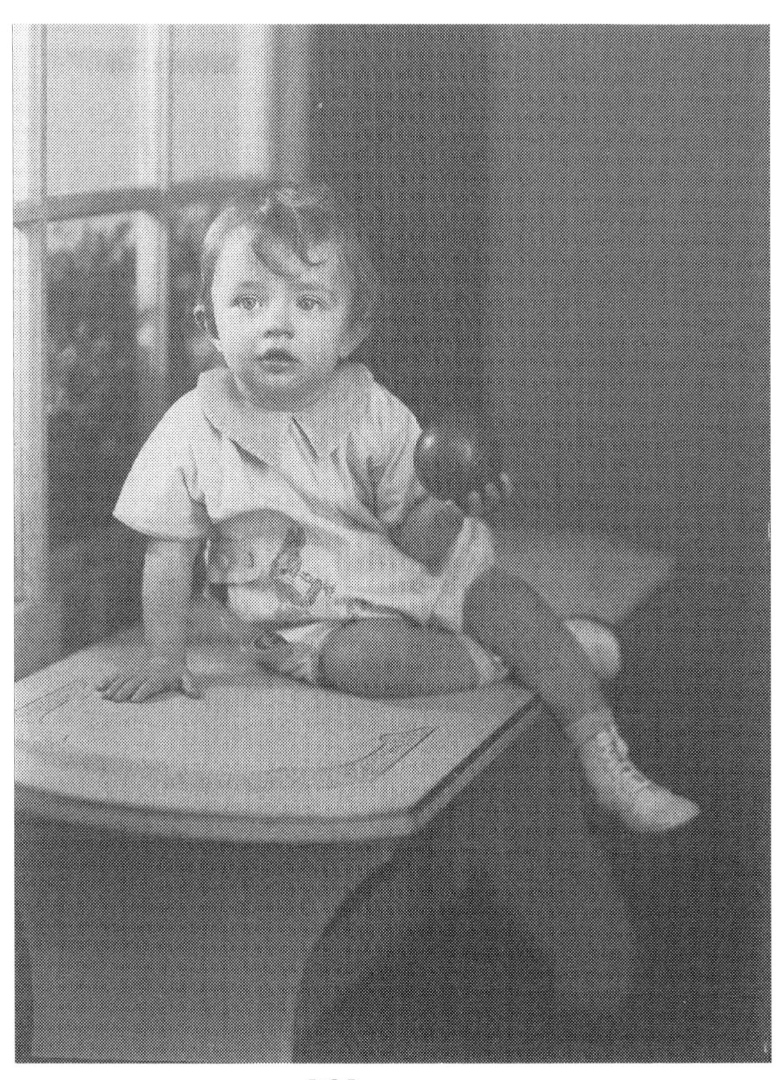

POP at age one

Alice and Oscar Peterson with sons Paul age 7, Willard age 4

Will and Paul with dog Sharp, 1940

High School graduate 1948

Fiance, beloved wife Lee, graduate nurse, May 1958

Lee and Paul's wedding September 1958

Our family 1967, Sons David 7, Glenn 4, Craig 2

Boy's in Streak-O-Lite wagon at Bass Lake 1970

Chapter 10

A Chance Meeting, Shadowlands, A Life Changing Vacation

In the summer of 1969, a second cousin of Lee's, Carolyn Friske, wrote Lee, and said that she would be attending a summer school class at Rutgers University for two weeks on the subject of alcoholism. She asked if we might be willing to take her in on the middle weekend as the school closed on Friday. Lee asked if that was ok with me, I said that's fine because I had to drive Dave up to a boy's camp that Saturday and I wouldn't get back until late in the day.

She came and when I got home late in the afternoon I was re-introduced to Carolyn, I had met her in summers past at Erickson family reunion. On Sunday we went to church. I remember that she sang the tenor line on a couple of hymns and blended well with my baritone and Lee's alto voice. We had dinner at home and she left to go back to Rutgers in the evening. Lee asked me what I thought of Carolyn. I said that she was a winner and I couldn't understand why she wasn't married.

In the summer of 1969 my Cubs were in first place. Dad, I, and the boys all drove to Chicago to see them play. They lost that game and had a horrible September. The hated Mets beat them out in the pennant race and won the World Series. That gave me added scar tissue on my Cub blue heart. At this time Glenn and Dave also made their commitment to be life long Cub rooters. Craig was rebellious and became an Oriole fan. The boys also started collecting baseball cards. I made a deal with them. Every Sunday the Sunday School gave them a Bible verse to memorize. I'd ask them to recite the verse as we drove to Church. If they knew it, I would stop and buy them each a pack of Topps cards. Each pack had ten cards and that wonderful pink bubble gum, all for a dime. In a short time I was also hooked on collecting them. I really needed another hobby.

As we left Bass Lake that summer Dave took with him, without our knowledge, a new pet. It was revealed to us when a large bull frog jumped out of the container Dave had. This greatly excited our dog Sandy who began barking and making lunges to catch it as it jumped around in the car. It also got Lee's attention as she hated any kind of slimy creatures. I decided it would be prudent to pull over and attend to this frog before it caused us to have an accident or a serious family fight. I can't remember if we liberated the frog there or gave in to Dave to take it back to New Jersey. At any rate it didn't remain with our family much longer. At about this same time Dave asked us if he could have a gerbil. We agreed that he could have only one and we wanted to make sure that it was a male. Dave got it and the cage that he ran around in. A couple of days later Dave brought us the cage to show us two little gerbils that had been born. My dislike for gerbils was intensified when one night the cage fell and the gerbils got out. I think our dog Sandy dispatched one of them, but one escaped and we spent a few days trying to find it. We finally found that it had squeezed into the area behind our paneled wall in the basement. It was a lot of fun taking the paneling down in order to get what I now called the varmint. I don't know what we did to placate Dave to convince him that we didn't have room in our heart or home for rodents, but we disposed of it.

In the fall of 1969, Stauffer Chemical announced that they had purchased a 60 acre dairy farm and planned to build their corporate headquarters on that land. They hoped to move there in the summer of 1972. This was upsetting to both Lee and me as it meant that we would have to move. This was especially dismaying to Lee as she had only made a few friends in New Jersey and knew no one in Connecticut. We also received the bad news that her father Carl, had suffered a stroke and was walking using a cane.

In 1970, Lee began to experience times of deep depression. This came to a crisis time after we'd spent another week at Brookdale in the Pocano's. I woke up in the middle of the night and discovered that Lee was not in bed. I saw under the closet door that the light was on. I opened it and found her sitting on the floor, packing her suitcase. I asked her what she was doing. She said, "I'm leaving you because I'm a terrible wife and mother." I spent the next few hours telling her how much I loved her and what a wonderful mother she was to our boys. At the end, we agreed to seek counsel about her depression problem.

We first went to our pastor, who gave us much help. Lee had been given little sex education by her mother, and what little there was happened to be negative. She was taught that all men wanted from a woman was sex, and a wife's duty was to endure it, that sex was not enjoyable and, if it was, it was sinful. Lee stated that she loved sex and even lusted for me and then afterward felt guilty about it. Our pastor said lust is an intense desire and if it's directed toward one's mate there is nothing wrong about it because that's what God intended when he said we should be one flesh. He later wrote; "It takes a great love to fuse two people together, one flesh, without inhibition. That may be why sexual love is so intertwined with thoughts that it's sinful. That's certainly wrong thinking." Pastor Anderson also advised us to go to our Dr Francis to try to find if there was something medically that could be a cause for Lee's depression.

Doctor Francis was a wonderful doctor and friend. In addition he was a member of our church and a good Bible teacher. After examination and tests it was found that her depression stemmed mainly from a problem in Lee's brain that could be treated with a Lithium drug.(It was found later on that at least one other of Lee's siblings had the same problem.) We also went to a marriage counselor where we worked out several problems we had in our marriage. Unfortunately, she also got some bad advice from well meaning but mistaken lady friends who advised her to take this or that pill. Worst of all, she was told by a few that Christians should not be depressed, and if they were it was because there was sin in their lives. May God forgive those who gave her this advice. Lee desired with all her heart to be a follower of Jesus Christ.

In February of 1971, Lee's father Carl died, and we went to Michigan for the funeral. We then stayed for a few days to help Florence sort through his things. I have been a Pepsi lover all my life and at that time drank two to three cans a day. Florence would not allow any cola drinks in her refrigerator, so to have them available I hid them in the snow in front of the house. When it snowed again, I had trouble finding most of them. Vic later reported that his mom was surprised when the spring thaw came and she found Pepsi cans on the lawn.

In the Summer of that year we spent what were to be our last days at Bass Lake. My father died on October seventh of cardiac arrhythmia six months short of his ninetieth birthday. Dad died in DuPage Hospital. That was a blessing as he had never wanted to go to a nursing home. I thank God for Eunice and Will, who gave him all the care they could in his last dementia- filled years. Lee and I shared only a fraction of his care. He was buried next to my mother in Oak Hill Cemetery. Dad left us an estate of $57,572 that was divided between my brother and I. Will, was not interested in keeping the Bass Lake property, and I could not justify owning it when we lived 800 miles away. We put it up for sale. The cottage sold for $19,500. Part of me died when we did that.

In October, Craig had an accident learning to ride a two wheeled bike. He was speeding down our street one afternoon and turned back to wave proudly to us when he slammed into the back of a parked VW. His face met the back of the car resulting in serious cuts. He still has the scar to remind him of that episode.

At this time Lee and I decided we needed to start taking vacations that would allow our sons to see the beauty of our United States. Because I was now a 20 year employee of Stauffer, I was eligible for four week's vacation. We promised the boys that when they were12 they could choose where we would take a two to three week vacation in the U.S. We would help them plan the trip and make the necessary reservations. Dave was eligible for this in 1972. I thought for sure that Dave's choice would be to go to Disney World in Florida, which had opened in 1971. What a great surprise it was when he chose for the major part of his trip to go on a raft trip with me through the Grand Canyon. We'd also tour the states of Utah, Wyoming, Colorado and end at Mount Rushmore. We spent many hours together making plans, reading, researching, and finally making reservations for the trip.

We went to Pentwater for Christmas and then to Bass Lake, where we rented a U-Haul to take furniture and priceless mementos from the cottage where I had spent cumulatively, almost five of the happiest years of my life. With a full trailer and the boys in the back of the wagon we set out for home. At Cleveland it started to snow and it kept getting worse. When we got to the Pennsylvania Turnpike we were told all trailers were banned on the turnpike, and we were advised to go north to Rt. 80 as it might be open and motels could possibly have rooms available. We did so but after stopping at several filled motels we gave up on getting a room and decided to drive all night. At that time Rt.80 was not completed, and at several places we had to get off and take secondary roads as we headed east. It kept snowing and blowing and we saw very little traffic on the road. We stopped for gas once and kept on plowing through snow drifting across the highway When we got to Hazelton, we needed to take a break. It was about five in the morning. I got off the highway and went to a gas station which was jammed with people. After some conversation, we learned that a tractor trailer had jack- knifed on the east bound entrance ramp to 80, and no one could get back on it. We also learned that the hi-way that we had driven on had been officially closed since midnight!! No wonder the traffic was so light!

A young man approached me and asked what our destination was. I told him Montclair, N. J. He said he could get us there if we would drop him off in East Stroudsburg on the New Jersey border. He said he knew the back roads that the ski resorts kept open, and he'd be our guide to get out of the "mad house" we were trapped in. We took him up on his offer and he climbed in with his gear and he did get us through to N.J. Sometimes you have to take a chance and trust someone to help you. He is part of the story of the "hairiest" drive of our life. We got home at sunrise. We'd been on the road for twenty hours.

In February of '72, we took a couple of trips up to Connecticut to look for a house that would be within ten miles of our company's new headquarters in Westport. When we began comparing similar four bedroom houses, we considered several factors along with the price of the house. We found that generally, a 2,000 square foot house in Westport cost thirty thousand dollars more than the same size house in Fairfield. Also the real estate taxes were about a third higher in Westport. Driving time to work would be ten minutes more from Fairfield and would be on local streets. We decided to live in Fairfield. In June we bought a four bedroom house, located at 300 Gilbert Hwy. (The highway was two blocks long with a dead end), The house sat on a two acre lot. The lot had an acre and a half of woods that were mainly oaks, beeches, and dogwoods. There were 28 trees that I could not reach around and one Oak that was 16 feet in circumference. The house was a two story colonial with a floor area of 2,100 sq. ft. Downstairs it had a living and dining room, kitchen, den with a fire place, and a half bath. Upstairs there were four bedrooms and two baths. It had a full attic and basement and an attached two car garage off the den. We bought the house for $67,500 and sold our beloved home in Upper Montclair for $52,000.

On Memorial Day weekend I went up to Fairfield to paint a few rooms while Lee and the boys started packing up their things that we would move. A couple of months before I had contacted a couple of church organizations to get their recommendations on churches in Fairfield County, and from their suggestions we'd narrowed it down to three. One was Black Rock Congregational in Fairfield, which I went to on that Sunday morning. I entered into and enjoyed everything in the worship service which was very similar to what we had in New Jersey. We stood to receive the benediction, and as soon as that ended I was tapped on the shoulder by a man in the pew behind me. As I turned he said; "My name is Josephson, and I don't believe I've met you." I said; "My name is Paul Peterson and I'm visiting from New Jersey." I then told him what I was doing in Connecticut, and he asked me if I had any plans for dinner. I said no, and he promptly invited me to dinner at his house. I met his wife Bee, his son and several daughters. In our conversation I learned he was a partner in an insurance agency and the mission board chairman at the church. We talked a lot about our children, and his girls told me a lot about what activities they were involved with at the church. I told him that we would be greatly influenced in choosing a church where our boys could meet new friends. He and his wife told me a lot of how the church operated, and they invited me to call them at any time if I had additional questions. Lee and I never considered joining any other church once we'd made our move.

In late June we moved into our new home and my new office in Stauffer's corporate headquarters. My office was on the second floor and looked out on a magnificent Copper Beech, with a trunk that was 22 feet in circumference with a large masonry dairy barn behind it.

We had barely had time to move in when we set off on Dave's birthday trip to the west. This is David's accounting of the trip that was recorded in a scrap book that he gave me.

"On the 22nd of July 1972, we started on our trip west. It took us 14 and a half hours to get to Uncle Will's house. The next day we drove to Omaha. We visited Uncle Allan one day. The next day we drove to Berthoud. The next day we saw beautiful Rocky Mountain Nat'l Park. Then we flew to Flagstaff, but on the way we got off at Farmington, New Mexico. The next day we took a bus to the Grand Canyon and took pictures. The next day we hiked down and began our river trip. The next day we got a hole in the raft, 2nd we went to a swimming hole with a 90 ft waterfall, and another swimming hole where you could jump 10 feet into the water. 3rd stood under a 70 ft. waterfall. Hiked into a side canyon. Went over to Havasu creek, beautiful. 4th went over Lava Falls, I got sick, Fifth, I got better, Dad got sick, 6th crossed Lake Mead. Bob drove us to Las Vegas. Saw Zion the next day. Saw Bryce the next day. went to S.L.C. Went floating in the Great Salt Lake. Drove around the Tetons, Went swimming in Jackson Lake. Took a 10 mile hike saw 4 Moose. Went to Yellowstone saw many interesting things. Drove to Rapid City. Saw Crazy Horse. Went to Pentwater for two days. We arrived home on the 19th of August." He gave me this scrapbook full of folder picture and souvenirs for my birthday with these words: "To my father on his 43rd birthday 12-20-72. Thank you for my chance to pick where I wanted to go. Thank you for a wonderful trip out west. I am the only boy I know of whose father lets him have a trip for a birthday present. Thank you for an unforgettable 12th year. I now say thank you Dad for all the times I haven't in the past. Your son, David."

Was it worth it!!! (I'm shedding tears as I copied this from his scrapbook.) That trip started a relationship with my eldest son that has been beautiful beyond belief. That raft trip was of great value aside from the adventure of it. That was his first time to experience being for days with people who were strangers, some of whom had a lifestyle and values that were foreign to our own. For example, there were two couples on that trip whose main worry was that they would run out of Vodka before they got off the raft at Lake Mead. He also, as did I, found out what you have to do when you're in the middle of a wild river and have to cope with nausea and/or the runs.

On the raft trip I did not do something that I've regretted for most of my life. Dave always wore a sailors' hat. One morning as we were pushing the raft off the sandbar, the hat blew off and sank quickly in the brown swirling water. Dave immediately got tears in his eyes because of the loss of his hat. I was trying to comfort him when one of the Vodka drinking men, went over the side, went under the water, and in no time came up holding Dave's hat. Why didn't I do what our raft mate had done? I asked Dave's forgiveness then and since that time. He's always said, "Dad there's nothing to forgive."

That fall Dave started junior high school at Tomlinson and Glenn and Craig went to Timothy Dwight grammar school. It was the first time any of them had to take a bus to school. Glenn was quickly recognized by his teacher to be her top student, and she loved his infectious laugh. Lee got involved in being a nature guide when classes took field trips to the Mill River and surrounding woods, and she enjoyed doing that. She and I immediately joined the church choir and she made good friendships with Joanne Veth, Carolyn Robertson and Joanne Peterson.

I was selected to be the company's representative to the Soap & Detergent Association which met once a month to discuss how we might work together to grow our businesses and fight the environmentalists demands that we remove phosphates from detergents. In January of '73, the SDA had a five day convention at the Waldorf that Lee and I attended. We did a lot of entertaining of customers and their wives. I was in charge of the hospitality suite, not something that Lee or I enjoyed.

In October I was able to find a piano teacher and began taking evening lessons usually every other week. I was now beginning to play, only for Lee's entertainment, some Chopin; waltzes and nocturnes; Mendelssohn; *Songs Without Words* and Schubert and Schumann pieces. Lee's favorites were *Traumere*i, and the popular, "*Send in the Clowns*," and "*Climb Eyery Mountain*," her favorite hymn," *Fairest Lord Jesus"* and our song, "*It's Magic*"

Chapter 11

My Darkest Day

The early 17th Century poet and clergyman John Donne in his last sermon said: "It is the exaltation of misery to fall from a near hope of happiness."

In April 1973, Lee and I had spent nine months in Connecticut with our sons David, Glenn and Craig who were 13, 9 and 8 years old. We loved our new home, and our dog Sandy had all kinds of room to run in the woods. I was happy in my job as a Marketing Manager and glad to have a 20 minute commute to work. I was making over $21,000 a year. We had great neighbors to the north of us, the DaSilvas, and the Nichols across the street. We were getting involved in the life of our new church, Black Rock Congregational, and were in the membership class. Lee and I sang in the choir, and the boys had made new friends in the neighborhood, schools and church.

Lee was especially excited because her only sister Lisa had recently moved to Concord, N.H., and was only three hours away. We planned to drive up there on Friday, April sixth and spend the weekend with her, Jon, and their new daughter.

On Wednesday evening we went to bed fairly early. Lee was excited about the trip on Friday, and as she wanted to sleep well that night had a glass of wine before she got in bed. Dr. Francis had advised her to do this when she needed a good night's sleep. As I kissed her goodnight, I kiddingly said, "So you're hitting the bottle again." She then gave me a bigger kiss, rolled over, and went to sleep.

As I was leaving for work the next morning, we kissed good-bye and she asked me to leave $10 so she could fill the station wagon's tank with gas, thus speeding up our trip to Concord. I laid a ten dollar bill on the kitchen table and went to work.

As soon as I got to my office the phone rang. I picked it up and spoke to a very unhappy, Bob Heinze, the raw material purchasing manager at P&G. They had received an 80-ton rail car of sodium tripolyphosphate that was contaminated with red roofing shingle granules. Fortunately, they had not unloaded the car into their storage silo, which would have been a major disaster. We had to get them a replacement shipment quickly in order to keep their "Tide" line running. He wanted my assurance that this would not happen again. It was one of the ten worst days of my working life. I spent until 6:30 that evening investigating the problem shipment and expediting our Chicago Heights plants effort to ship them four bulk trucks that day in order to assure them of supply.

As I drove home I rolled the car window down. It was a bright sunny day and the forsythia was coming into blossom. I got home at about seven. The boys met me as I pulled up to the garage. They reported that they were locked out of the house and the hidden key was missing. Lee had always been there to greet them when they came home from school and were as surprised as I was to find her gone. I had not had a chance to call her, as I usually did, and she had not said that she was going anywhere except to get the car gassed up.

I got my key out and with the boys went into the house calling her name. Silence! As we searched the house, we noticed that every room was cleaned up, immaculate, but there was no sign of or message from her. In the kitchen I immediately noticed that the ten dollar bill was right where I'd left it. I sent the boys out to the neighbors to see if she was with them or ask them if they had seen her. While they were doing that, I made a more thorough search of the house including closets and under beds. When I got to our main coat closet I looked to see if one of her coats was missing. There on the floor I saw her purse. Everything was in it including her wallet and keys. With that discovery I got dry mouth and a feeling of dread came over me. When the boys came back with a negative report, I called my neighbors and asked if they could take the boys in while I made calls for counsel and advice. All I could think, was Lee's been kidnapped. I first called Pastor Allaby at his home. He advised me to call the local hospitals and the police and report a missing person to them, which I did.

Pastor Allaby came within twenty minutes, and we again searched the house starting in the basement. When we had finished the search on the second floor, he asked if we had an attic and if I'd searched it. I said yes we did, but because access to the attic was made by pulling down a retractable staircase, I had not considered that as a place she could be. When you went up to the attic, you left the stairs in place for your return. He said, "Let's go up."

I went up first. The attic was dark and I pulled the chain on the light fixture that was directly above the stair opening. Pastor followed me up. I looked ahead to the shorter south end of the attic and saw nothing amiss. When I turned around, Pastor Allaby, with tears in his eyes grabbed me and said; "Paul, I'm sorry." As I looked over his shoulder to the far side of the attic, there I saw, hanging from the ridge-pole of the roof, the body of my wife. I felt like someone had hit me in the stomach and again my mouth went dry. Spasms of sobs shook my body as he helped me down the stairs and then to the living room where I collapsed into a chair. If Pastor had not been with me, I don't know what I might have done. When? Why? How? Who did it? All came out of my mouth as my brain reeled.

In a few minutes the police arrived. Pastor took them up to the attic and then came down to be with me. The police did their investigation and called the medical examiner. He came and did his examination and then asked me a number of questions. He asked what undertaker should be called to take Lee's body. As I had never given any thought to that possibility, I asked pastor to make that decision for me. I called my neighbor and told them what had happened and that I would like my sons to stay there over night. They said ok, and I told them I'd be over in a little while with their sleeping bags. The medical examiner asked me what medications Lee took, and I led him to the kitchen where Lee kept her pills. When he examined the bottle with her Lithium pills he said that she should have run out of those pills in January. She had not been taking them as prescribed. Why didn't I track that? Mainly I assumed she was taking them because she had not had a serious bout of depression since we'd moved to Connecticut.

All my ambitions and plans for the future came crashing down. I asked the eternal, "Why?" IF ONLY thoughts swept continuously through my brain. What was I to do with my three sons whom I had fathered but had left mainly for Lee to bring up? How could I keep the job I loved which required me to travel nationwide?

I walked across the street and gathered with my sons and cried. I told them that some people die of heart attacks and others because of something that goes wrong in the brain. This attack in her brain had caused her to end her own life. I can't begin to imagine how this was understood by them. They asked no questions. We had a four way hug for a long time and cried together, and then I helped them into their sleeping bags and told them we'd talk more when they came home in the morning.

Many people were called in the next hours as I gave them the terrible news. Her mother insisted that Lee must have been murdered. Her sister in New Hampshire, who we were to be with the next night, said that they would come down to be with us in the morning. Her other siblings could hardly believe what I told them. All made plans to come to lend me their support. I thought of my recently deceased parents and was consoled by the fact that they would not have to mourn the loss of Lee, whom they loved so dearly. Uncle Albin and Aunt Elvira were stunned by the news. He gave a Bible verse that reminded me of what I should rely on in the days ahead: Isaiah 41: 10, "Fear thou not for I am with thee. Be not dismayed for I am thy God. I will strengthen thee, I will help thee, I will uphold thee with my righteous right hand." I repeated that verse many times in the months ahead.

I called Calvary Baptist Church in NYC and left a message to have my best friend, Paul Liljestrand, call me when his choir rehearsal was over. When he called, he asked me if I had any one with me. I answered that Pastor Allaby was with me, but he would soon be leaving. Paul said, "I'll drive home to New Jersey and get Rae, and we'll be there by midnight." He was true to his word and arrived just as Pastor was leaving. He, Rae and I got into a three- way hug that lasted for minutes. After that we exchanged a few words of love for Lee and then expressed our love for each other. He went to the piano. I could not believe it, he started playing the Schubert Impromptu in G flat, the same piece that I had heard on the radio when my mother had died. I had never told Paul of that experience. That piece of music went straight to my soul. I believe God led Paul to play that piece of music. I don't believe it was a coincidence. Paul and Rae stayed with me until Jon and Lisa arrived at noon on Friday. That's why Paul is my best friend. He came the night when I needed him to hold me together. I don't think we talked more than ten minutes in that hour before we went to bed, but our hearts communicated. That meant everything.

The boys came home. Jon, Lisa and their daughter Jennifer, took care of them. In the afternoon detectives came over to do further investigating. I told them that I was not certain that she had not been murdered. Lee had never given me any sign that she was thinking of taking her life. The thought of one doing that repelled her. A year earlier my Cousin Adele's 17- year- old son had taken his life. This is an excerpt from the letter Lee wrote to Adele at that time. Adele sent me this letter within her own letter of condolence to me.

"Dear Jack and Adele, We just heard this past weekend of your son's passing. Needless to say we were stunned. Our prayer for you is that you might know and feel God's comfort and love in this dark time of your life. At times such as these, we wish to be of help, but must content ourselves in fervent prayer on your behalf and let the Lord be your help and strength. Your Cousin, Lee."

Lee did not leave a suicide note. We had reservations to go to Bermuda in May to celebrate our 15th anniversary. On Monday she bought two outfits and modeled them for me. On Tuesday she had finished a pants suit she had been making and was wearing it when I came home. She bought a plant that she was going to give to Lisa when we got to N.H. that weekend. That evening she went to a women's meeting at church and came home to tell me of the talk she'd heard on flowers mentioned in the Bible. The night before she died she and I finished re-upholstering a small chair, and she fried chicken and refrigerated it. It was to be our supper as we traveled on Friday night to New Hampshire. Flats of seedlings, which she looked forward to planting in a few weeks, were on the window sills in the den.

Because of her normal behavior in her final days, I asked the detective to prove the case that it was a suicide. They showed me photos of her left hand that was severely bruised in the thumb area. They believed the bruises were caused by the hammer she used to pound in the spikes that were together in the ridge pole. I asked, "How did she get the attic stairs up from the second floor?" They showed me the blue and yellow plastic rope she had used. They tied it to the lower hinged section and pulled it up into the attic. They believed that she died around noon. At that time there would have been enough light coming from the attic ventilator windows for her to see as she completed her terrible act. Thirty-eight years later, I still can't believe how her mind could have worked so logically and efficiently to cover her tracks in making it hard for me and the boys to find her. Lee was 5'6" tall, so she had to bend her knees in order to get her full weight on her neck and effect her strangulation. How desperate she had to be, to die such a horrible death!

I called Dr. Francis on Saturday and gave him the sad news. When I told him she had not been taking the Lithium pills, he expressed surprise that she had not shown any signs of depression. When it finally came, it must have been overwhelming.

On Friday many men from the church came over or called me conveying their sympathy and offering support. Choir members brought over casseroles, fried chicken, fruit and vegetables. Family members helped me as I picked out a casket and made funeral arrangements. The boys' teachers at school and the church offered their support. God, in the next few days gave me the strength to give the boys further detail on their mothers' illness and death. I asked them to think of what a wonderful mother she was and how much she loved them. I was amazed that they seemingly recovered much faster than I did.

Lee's funeral was on Monday. I stayed home on Tuesday and helped her siblings as they bundled up her clothing and personal items and took them to Good Will. Then they left, except for Lee's mother, who stayed on to help me and the boys.

I found this written in Lee's Bible, "The grace of final perseverance is that quality of patience which is always equal to passing moment, because it is rooted in the eternal order over which the passing moment has no power,". In the fly leaf of her Bible she had written; I Thess. 4:16-18. We shall meet our loved ones again. What a comfort to <u>know</u> that all of us who believe in the Lord Jesus will see her again, even more beautiful than she was in this life. On a separate page she had this poem.

"So I am waiting quietly, everyday
Whenever the sun shines brightly, I rise and say,
Surely it is the shining of his face.
And I look into the gates of his high places, beyond the sea
For I know he is coming shortly to summon me
And when a shadow falls across the window of my room
Where I am working at my appointed task
I lift my head to watch the door and ask
if he has come, and the angel answers.
Only a few more shadows and he will come.
Even so Lord Jesus come! Come quickly."

Chapter 12

A Life in Suspension

After the shock and the life Lee and I had shared was over, I lost the desire to do much of anything. Lee and I shared our lives. Each of us planned our lives around the other. I had no desire to do the things that we enjoyed doing together. I never played the piano again. As much as I love music, I couldn't bear it. Most times when I played, she'd sit on the piano bench beside me. My audience was gone. She was not there to share it. It is easy to understand why people who lose their mate give up living themselves. What reason is there to keep up one's appearance, health, or the house, when no one is there who cares? My lover was gone; my life was empty.

There is no such thing as death for a Christian; the body dies, but the spirit goes to Heaven to live eternally with God. The ones that experience devastation are those who loved that person and have to live on without the one who made their life complete. I could search the universe and not find her, feel her touch, or hear her voice. Many times in the first few months I reached out in my sleep for her and wakened to the reality of being alone, and dissolved in tears until blessed sleep came again. I felt not only the absence of her presence, but deeper still the presence of her absence. A poem of the Victorian Era Poet, Christina Rossetti, echoed in my soul.

I have no wit, no words, no tears,
My heart within in me like a stone,
Is numbed too much for hopes or fears.
Look right, look left, I dwell alone.
I lift my eyes, but dimmed with grief,
No everlasting hills I see:
My life is in the falling leaf:
O, Jesus quicken me.

My life is like a faded leaf,
My harvest dwindled to a husk.
Truly my life is void and brief,
and tedious in the barren dusk
My life is like a frozen thing
No bud or greenness can I see.
Yet rise it shall- the sap of spring
O Jesus rise in me.

My life is like a broken bowl,
A broken bowl that cannot hold
One drop of water for my soul,
or cordial in the searching cold
Cast in the fire the perished thing,
Melt and remold it, till it be,
A royal cup for him my king,
O Jesus drink of me.

Because Lee died of unnatural causes, I felt the embarrassment of many who avoided me, rather than grope for words of comfort or put me through giving them a recital on the details of her death. How valued were those that did come and allowed me to share with them as they listened. Sharing my loss with them was great therapy for me. I didn't feel like starting anything new. Before Lee's passing, I never had enough time. Now time dragged on. Fortunately, several good friends urged me to take up tennis. One of these men, Ray Whittles had a clay court on his property and invited me over to get started playing the game. I went to the Westport Tennis Club and took ten lessons, and several great new friends invited me to play doubles with them. Ray invited me to bring my friends at Stauffer over to use his courts, and that enabled me to make many long lasting friendships that centered around the game of tennis. I never got to be a very good player, but I came to love playing. It was one of the things that helped me come out of my grief.

All of Lee's and my social life involved other couples. Now I was single. Even though most all the husbands reached out to me, I was left out of all those gatherings that involved couples. That was understandable, but really hurt. I was thankful for the families who occasionally had me and the boys over for a meal.

Then there was the hardest thing to try to understand. I know Lee loved me and our sons. Didn't she think about how her act would upset our lives? My only answer is that, in her desperation, all thoughts of us who loved her so deeply, were blocked out of her mind, or else she wouldn't have taken her life.

The understanding and acceptance that my sons showed regarding their mother's passing were beyond belief. They seemed to have a short period of mourning. I believe that God gave them this protection. David, at 13, who Lee always thought was the least in need of her love, took her loss very deeply and seriously. He became a man and took and accepted more responsibility than I ever expected. I had to make him feel less responsible so he wouldn't be robbed of the joys of his teen years. The boy's simple faith in God's love for Lee and themselves, helped confirm my own belief in God's goodness and sovereignty. What priceless notes they gave me on Fathers' Day, regarding their love for me and their mother. My sons were my dearest treasure and gave me my reason to live.

At the time of Lee's passing I would have said God was my top priority in life, family next, then my job and church last. But really my job was the top priority. Now God became my #1. Many Bible verses came back to my mind to strengthen my faith in Him. Deut. 31: 6: "I shall never leave you or forsake you." Jer.29: 11,12: "For I know the plans I have for you—" and as I quoted before Isa. 41: 10, went through my mind many times each day. Hymns such as, "*Great is Thy Faithfulnes*', "*It is Well With my Soul*" and "*My Soul Has Found a Resting Place*" filled my empty shell. To many who asked; How are you doing? I'd say, "Terrible, but God's doing wonders." I never was angry at God and understood that he loved me and had a purpose for me.

My second priority became my sons. An older couple from church came to me and said that if I wished, they would come to our house every day at three, when the boys came home from school, and stay until I got home from work. They were known to everyone in the church as Mom and Pop Sulik. I was overwhelmed by that offer and accepted it. They did this until I found two housekeepers. Mady Roux, who came on Monday and Friday and Mary Keblish, who worked Tuesday thru Thursday. They started working in mid- May. Until then, the boys and I tried our best to keep the house as best we could. Until the housekeepers started working, our evening dinner was provided by the choir members of the church. Nearly every meal I got instructed me to put it in the oven for an hour at 350 degrees. One day I got a box containing a casserole with brown beans and cut up hot dogs. I put it in the oven at 350 and went into the den to read the newspaper. After sometime I detected the smell of burning plastic. I rushed to the oven, opened the door and saw that the plastic casserole was melting into the oven tray. I turned off the oven, put on insulated gloves, and pulled the now half melted vessel out, along with the tray to which it was now attached. I carried it to the back door and set it on the back stairs. While it was cooling I looked in the box and saw the electric cord that was to be used to warm the casserole. A couple of weeks later, I went to the church as choir practice was ending to return all the dishes they had brought us. When I pulled the "Daliesque," plastic cooker from the bag; Doryce Smelter gasped! It was hers. The gasps quickly turned to uproarious laughter as I presented her with a new electric crock pot.

When I'd come home some days, Dave was cutting the grass. On another day he'd tell me that the next afternoon he would be doing a dark load of wash and asked me if I had anything to contribute. Every Saturday we'd draw straws as to what rooms we'd have to clean. One Saturday, Glenn's assignment was the kitchen. On Sunday morning when I came down for breakfast I couldn't find where he'd put the sugar bowl. I yelled up the staircase, "Glenn, where's the sugar bowl?" Because Glenn was a sports trivia buff, the quick answer came back, "New Orleans!!" God knew we needed to laugh. In those first few months, we developed a bond of trust that was a miracle.

Two months after Lee died, I decided to join the church that had poured out their love to me and the boys. I left the house after supper telling the boys I would be home around nine. There was a large group in the membership class and all of us told the story of our faith journey to the pastors and elders of the church. The meeting lasted much longer than I expected, and I did not get home until after ten. When I came home, my neighbor who had kept the boys on the night Lee died came running up the driveway with my sons who were all crying. They rushed to me and hugged me. When I had not come home by nine, they all started thinking something horrible had happened to me so they panicked and went over to my neighbor. I apologized to them and my neighbor, and promised my sons that I would never be so thoughtless of them again. That night we made a rule that lasted all through their high school years. When we went out, we would tell each other what time we would expect to be home. If we got delayed, we would call home at the time we were expected and set a new time of arrival. With rare exception we observed that agreement.

Two days after the funeral all the family members left, and I went back to work. I hadn't been working more than an hour when the number two man in our division, Jack Kennedy, VP of Sales and Marketing, knocked and came into my office and again expressed his condolences and his shock that I was at work. He said that I was entitled to ten days off due to the death of a spouse, and he wanted me to know nothing was more important than my family. I told him the boys were in school and the family members had gone home so the best place I could be was at work rather than sit home and cry. I remember his next words as the most wonderful that I ever heard in my career. He said, "Paul I value and respect you highly and I know you have to travel a lot. Until you get to the place where you have somebody at home at night to be with your boys, if you have to see customers, I'll make the trips for you." In the coming years I had several offers to go to work for other companies. However, because of the quality of my company, and the people I worked with, I never considered any of those offers. Sad to say, I don't think you'll find many companies like that today.

Chapter 13

Remembrances of Lee

After Lee's death, I received many letters in which friends expressed condolences, gave expression of their grief, and shared remembrances of her. The following are some quotes from those letters. From a neighbor of my mom and dad, Naomi Goggin : "I'll always remember your mother. She used to tell me about Lee, how good Lee was to her at all times, and how happy she was to have her as a daughter-in-law." Lee adored my mother, learned a lot about cooking from her and especially my favorite foods. Lee's, kidney veal chops, creamed green bean and onion casserole, goulash, and Apricot Dream dessert were duplicates of my mother's. Mom made her three knit dresses which fit Lee's figure perfectly. She also taught Lee to knit.

From a sister-in-law of Lee's: "I am glad that you have a belief in God that offers you such consolation and strength. I know it has been harder for me to accept Lee's death without such faith. I think of her often and still feel my own bitterness that one of the most loving, kind, and giving people that I ever knew died as she did."

From great friends in Chicago, Roy and Rose Sandstrom: "We will always remember Lee completely devoted and in love with you and the boys. She was without guile or pretense and a joy to be with."

Cathy, a youth worker at Black Rock Congregational Church;" I really enjoyed getting to know Lee by sitting beside her in choir. One Wednesday I realized that those three well behaved boys in church were hers. I realized that when David joined Jr. Hi Chorale, and I told her how much I enjoyed and appreciated him and his attitude and willingness to do whatever was asked of him. I told her that I thought that this was a direct reflection back to her, that her children were so well behaved." What others saw, Lee most times did not see in herself.

Karen Buck, at BRCC, who Lee trusted and confided in: "Many of us loved Lee and wanted to reach out to her, but all of a sudden there was no more time. That has been one of the hardest things for me."

Joanne a friend at Brookdale Baptist in N.J.: "When Pastor Anderson suggested prayer partners, Lee and I "buddied up". Out of it grew the kind of relationship one would have with a college roommate if they really hit it off. I went through the kind of depression you mentioned with her. I had experienced something like it in the late 50s. So I knew what she was experiencing. I saved all of her letters which were full of her plans and details of her spiritual growth. She mentioned doing battle with Satan in her February letter, but no abnormal preoccupation with it was evident. She longed for victory over self. She was worried about you eating too much popcorn. We who were fortunate to really know Lee will hold untiringly onto that love."

From Mary Jo, her bridesmaid: "Lee will always be, to me, the dear sweet, beautiful girl I knew and loved and spent part of my life with when we were in nurse's training. We were like sisters those three years. Please use the enclosed money for a missionary project Lee was interested in."

From J.R. Kellerman, a missionary to Ethiopia: "We want to thank you for your very generous gift to buy a wash machine for the

Leprosarium in memory of your dear wife." From Sophie Jenista, a missionary in the Philippines: "God will not forget Lee's labor of love in sending boxes of books and literature for the Jenista student center project."

From the Sillman's, neighbors in Oak Lawn: "Lee was a beautiful woman. Bill and I often mentioned how beautiful she was, and seemed so self- assured" They were right on their judgment of her beauty but not on her being self assured.

Lois and Ray Riley, lead singers in the Montclair Chorale in N.J: "We will always remember Lee as a person of inner as well as outward beauty. She had many talents and much to give. She was aware and responsive to people outside herself. It is hard to imagine that Lee is gone; and to believe such a gentle, giving person would have ended her life."

In May, I went back to New Jersey for a performance of the Faure Requim that was sung by the Montclair chorale in her honor. I cried through most of the performance.

Alan and Barbara Bachman, missionaries in Brazil: "We loved Lee and still do. She was a beautiful testimony to the love of Christ. We will miss her sweet letters and fellowship."

Joy Shaw, director of Mill River Guides, a wetlands study group in Fairfield: "I know of no person of Lee's special quality of loveliness and deep inner grace."

Deloris Parillo, a missionary to Morroco who was home on furlough: "When I had a day with her in January '71 she shared many of the hang ups you spoke of in your letter-not a good mother-not a good Christian- not a good wife."

Carol Weeks, my cousin: "Her interests were so varied, she enjoyed water skiing as well as the wonders of nature and the beauty of music- all of life."

Her closest friend told me at her memorial service, that she doubted that Lee would ever have been able to be happy and carefree again. If her condition had become worse, she would have been a different person than you and the boys knew and loved. She is free now, and we're left with wonderful memories of her beauty and life.

Lee had the most beautiful and expressive eyes I have ever seen. The graduating class from Grant Hospital in 1958 had this legacy from Lee. "I Alida Anderson, will my expressive eyes and eyebrows to Margie Byam." The only person I ever saw who could match her eyes was Audrey Hepburn. That's why she is my favorite actress. Lee's eyes were the window to her soul. Our sons and her brothers also knew by her look that they better not go farther in what they were saying or pursuing. I had the pleasure of swimming in those eyes during our marriage. She was the cover girl on the information catalog for the Grant Hospital Nursing School for several years. This poem of Lord Byron described her well.

> She walks in Beauty, like the night of cloudless climes and starry skies;
> and all that's best of dark and bright meet in her aspect and her eyes:
> Thus mellowed to that tender light which heaven to gaudy day denies.
>
> One shade the more, one ray the less, Had half impaired the nameless grace
> Which waves in every raven tress, or softly lightens o'er her face;
> Where thoughts serenely sweet express How pure, how dear their dwelling place.
>
> And on that cheek, and o'er that brow, So soft, so calm, yet eloquent.

> The smiles that win, the tints that glow, But tell of days in goodness spent,
> A mind at peace with all below, A heart whose love is innocent!

She was a lady. We seldom went to church, dinner or concerts without her wearing gloves and a hat. I loved to see her wearing broad brimmed hats that framed her face so beautifully. I was so proud to be with her. On the other hand she could be feisty and ready for a challenge. You should have been with us when we climbed the Grand Teton, or when she played volleyball or water skied, you would have seen a strong competitor.

She and I were both introverts, we took our time making friends. When Lee had a dinner party, she preferred to seat no more than six to eight. We disliked cocktail parties and avoided them as much as possible. Our friendships were close and deep. We loved to skinny dip at Bass Lake on warm summer nights, and lie on a sheep skin in front of our fire place on cold winter nights. We both loved to listen to Classical Adagios when we worked, read or became one.

She and I had a strong desire to grow spiritually and read many Christian Classics of C.S. Lewis and Bonhoeffer. She especially loved to read missionary biographies. She corresponded with half a dozen women missionaries. We prayed together for them and helped support them financially. Lee's favorite hymn was, "Fairest Lord Jesus." I still get choked up every time I sing it.

The boys could not have had a better mother. She taught them manners, and they obeyed her. She and I agreed on giving discipline and backed each other up on family decisions. Because I was away on business much of the time, she was the provider of much of the love and the support ours sons received. She did a beautiful job.

I sang this song to her many times. It comes from Bernstein's, "*Wonderful Town*" and is titled: "A Quiet Girl." It so aptly described her.

> I love a quiet girl, I love a gentle girl
> Warm as sunlight, soft, soft as snow.
> Her smile a tender smile, her voice a velvet voice
>
> Sweet as music, soft as snow
> When she is near me, the world's in repose,
> We need no words, she sees, she knows.
> But where is my quiet girl, where is my gentle girl
> Where is that special girl, who is soft, soft as snow.
> Somewhere, Somewhere, my quiet girl.

The Somewhere for my quiet girl is heaven where she is with her beautiful Savior, and I have the blessed hope of seeing her again someday soon.

Chapter 14

A Miracle

In May, Lee's mother called me from Michigan and offered to have the boys come and stay with her at Pentmater for the months of July and August. I accepted her kind offer. Before we left, I talked with Mary Keblish, who the boys liked, and asked her to come back in September as our housekeeper three days a week. She agreed to do so. I did not ask Mady Roux to return as the boys did not like her.

We drove to Michigan on the July 4th weekend and I stayed with the boys in Pentwater for two weeks. During this time away from my job and friends I was extremely lonely and spent quite a bit of time with Lee's uncle Will, who was 12 years older than I. We had been together many times in Chicago, as we went to the same church. In the early sixties his wife Dorthy had died of breast cancer, leaving him with their three girls. Within a year another good friend of mine Bob, with whom I'd played basketball, died of a rare intestinal disease, leaving his wife Joyce, with two boys and a girl. A couple of years later Will and Joyce married and now had six children. They lived in Chicago but spent most of the summer in Pentwater at their summer home, which was a half a mile from Lake Michigan. As they had gone through the same experience I was going through, we talked much about our journey through a terrible time.

On a Friday evening as the sun was setting, Will and I took a long walk on the beach. He asked if I'd given any thought to remarrying. I said that even though I was still in deep mourning, I realized that for me and the boys it would be good for me to find a woman who would be a good life companion for me and a mother to the boys. He asked if I had any women in mind that I might consider. I named a couple of single women I knew in the past, but the one I was most interested in was a relative of his and Lee's, who had visited us a few years ago when we lived in New Jersey, Carolyn Friske. I asked if he knew if she was still single. He said, "I know she is still single. I don't know if she's romantically involved, but if I were you she'd be my first choice. Oh, incidentally, I saw her yesterday with a couple of girlfriends, and they're staying here over the weekend for an art festival. She said she'd see me in church on Sunday. I'm sure if you go to church on Sunday you'll see her."

Because Pentwater is a summer resort town, most churches have two services in the months of July and August. The Baptist Church had a service at 8:30 which I went to hoping to meet Carolyn. She did not attend that service. I stayed for the 9:45 Sunday school. She did not attend. I hung around the front of the church to see if she would attend the 11:00 AM service, but my wait was in vain. I went back to Florence's home and had lunch with my boys and then decided to go to the beach. I grabbed a beach towel and a book and walked down to the beach looking for the woman I'd seen and admired five years earlier.

In a few minutes I spotted her with her two friends, and I tried to saunter up casually to their spot of beach. She looked up and recognized me, and after introducing her friends, Nan and Nellie Barr, asked me if I'd like a cup of coffee. I am not a coffee drinker! I love tea, but I'm not dumb! So I said I'd like to have a cup, which she poured. She also made room so I could sit down with them. I couldn't help remembering that my first acquaintance with Lee was made at a lake with her in beach attire.

I can't remember much of our conversation other than catching up with what we'd both been doing, and mentioning that my sons would be staying with Grandmother Anderson for the summer, and that I'd be back in August to call on Amway. I told Carolyn that I'd like to have dinner with her on my return visit. She asked how I was handling my loss of Lee and expressed her condolences. I wrote her in mid- July and asked her to have dinner with me on August third at Safees' restaurant. She accepted, and said she would get tickets for a play for later that evening.

I picked her up at her apartment. She was very attractive and perfectly attired in a pastel colored dress. We had a good dinner and saw what we agreed was the worst play either of us had ever seen: *The House of Blue Leaves.* It had been 18 years since I'd held any ladies arm other than Lee's. I was afraid to hold hers as she might think I was being forward and not a gentleman. I felt like a teenager on my first date.

Later in August after we'd talked a number of times on the phone, she wrote me and asked what my middle initial O stood for and she was pleased to know it stood for Oscar, my Swedish descended fathers' first name. Her letter later that month was addressed, "Dear Paul Oscar." She said the weekend of the 22nd of September was open if I wanted to take her to Chicago to meet my brother and his family. At the same time I could meet good friend of hers who lived in Rolling Meadows. She could stay with her friend, and I would stay with my brother Will in Glen Ellyn, Illinois.

I had an appointment to take a sugar refiner to see our bone char plant in Houston on Thursday the 20th of September, and he invited me to the tennis match between Bobby Riggs and Billy Jean King in the Astrodome that evening. So I was able to see Billy Jean close Riggs' big mouth by soundly beating him. It was an enormous boost for the feminist movement in our country.

On Friday I flew to Grand Rapids, changing planes in Chicago. When I arrived in Grand Rapids, Carolyn met me at the airport. Unfortunately, my bag missed the connection in Chicago. We filed the missing baggage claim, and asked them to deliver it to my brother's home, and set off for Chicago. As Carolyn did not want anyone to see us in Grand Rapids, she suggested that we have dinner in Holland, Michigan. When we walked into the restaurant we were greeted by a number of her public health nurse friends. You can imagine how the phones rang over that weekend as her fellow workers gossiped!

When we got to Rolling Meadows, it was quite late. After I had met the Kasen's and Carolyn got settled in, I drove to my brother's home. My suitcase had not arrived by the next morning, but my brother gave me the necessary toiletries and underwear to start the day fresh. I can't remember what we did on Saturday besides visit with Carolyn's friends and my brother's family, but I have a lot of memories of that evening at my brother's. At one point my three year old niece Andrea walked up to Carolyn and said, "I think you should mawey Uncle Paul." I'm eternally grateful to her for that suggestion. That night we sat up until one in the morning when my suitcase finally arrived. United's big problem was that they were trying to deliver my bag to 684 Elm Street in Chicago, which would have been in Lake Michigan. That night on our long second date, we started talking about dreams, goals, and ifs. I drove her back to Grand Rapids Sunday evening. On parting we exchanged our first kiss. I flew home on Cloud Nine.

On the 24th of September she wrote; "Dear Paul, I'm in shock and elated and I was proud to be with you, who looked handsome." Love is blind. I wrote to her on the 27th and expressed my deep feelings and told her she was the person I lived for. We agreed that I would buy her a ticket to fly out to N.Y. on October 19th to meet my sons and friends.

Early in October I went to consult with Pastor Allaby. It was now six months since Lee had left me. I told him I was still mourning her loss, but I'd met a woman who I was in love with, and that I was all mixed up in my emotions. I described Carolyn to him and told him she was coming out to meet the boys and a few friends. I asked him, "Do you think I'm moving too fast? What do you think is a proper interval between Lee's passing and marriage to another? He set me at ease in saying that if God had led me to find a suitable mate, I should not be controlled by what others might think. An important factor would be how the boys would accept her and she them, especially as she had never been a mother. He did say it would probably be good for all concerned to wait to be married until 1974.

On the 14th of October Carolyn wrote;" I'm looking forward to meeting your sons and friends". On the weekend of October 19th we began our third date. She met and spent time with my boys touring around the town and their schools. I then took her to see our corporate headquarters and my office and spent Saturday afternoon with several of our friends. She met and stayed with George and Joanne Veth

That night my best friends' at Stauffer, Herb and Nancy Rieman, invited us and the boys over for a spaghetti dinner. They knew the boys would rather eat in the basement family room where they could watch the World Series between the Mets and A's than sit in the dining room listening to adult talk. They set up a card table for them down stairs. The boys filled their plates and went to the basement. A few minutes later there was a loud crash from below and we all went down to investigate. Glenn was on the floor with red sauce and spaghetti on his shirt and face lying next to a collapsed folding chair. From that spot to the fireplace, on a white shag rug, was a broken plate, spaghetti and red sauce. I asked," What happened? He gave the following explanation: "I was standing on the chair, watching the game, eating my food, when the chair collapsed and threw me backwards." We cleaned up what we could of the mess. I told them to have the rug cleaned and to send me the bill. Glenn apologized. We adults went upstairs and finished our dinner. The Reiman's had a good time getting acquainted with Carolyn. When the ballgame ended, the boys came up and we made an exit as quickly as possible.

The family was never invited back to the Rieman's. Glenn learned that it was not wise to stand on a folding chair, especially when eating. I later paid my buddy, Herb, the money to replace the rug, as the tomato stain could not be totally removed. Although Carolyn did not say anything to Glenn regarding the incident, I wouldn't be surprised if she did not wonder if she should be part of our family.

On Sunday we went to Calvary Baptist in N.Y. to worship. We met Paul and Rae Liljestrand and had dinner with them. In the evening I took Carolyn to La Guardia and she flew home. On October 24th she sent me the message I'd been longing to receive: "Honey, I'm gone!!"

I agreed to come out to meet her family in Algoma on Thanksgiving weekend. Before that weekend, she had to tell her 77-year old widowed mother that she was dating a man who lived in Connecticut, and that she might marry him. She had spent her entire life, except for college years, within a few miles of her mother and saw her, with rare exception, every Sunday. I can't imagine how emotional that meeting must have been. On that weekend I formally proposed to Carolyn. Our fourth date was over. She wrote me a few days later, "I'M YOURS."

When I got back home, I called Carolyn and invited her to come to a business convention in Washington the first weekend in December. It was to be held at the Mayflower hotel, and because I would be entertaining customers I would have a two room suite. I suggested that I would like her to come to occupy the other room and that I would get her a ticket using some of my frequent flyer miles from United. She accepted my invitation, and we enjoyed several days touring the sights when I did not have "Food for Peace" meetings. This was our fifth date. I proposed and she accepted. We set May 18th for our wedding date. She asked me to promise her several things: (1) That she could have her own bank account; (2) That she could have her hair done weekly;(3) That if possible she would be able to make her own decision on where she would spend her later years if I preceded her in death; (4) That we would agree on rules of behavior for the boys and that I would back her up when she set up boundaries for their conduct; and (5) asked that I would be willing to look for another house for us that would not be filled with memories of Lee. I agreed with all her requests and put them in writing when I returned home. What a wise woman I was soon to marry!

In mid-December Lee's mother came to be with us for the Christmas holidays and stayed until the middle of January. On the trip home from La Guardia I told her that I was planning to get married the next spring. When I told her it was her youngest cousin, Carolyn Friske, she was overjoyed as she knew Carolyn and admired her. Whew!! Was I relieved to hear her say that. I knew I'd be much happier with her as a cousin than as a Mother-in law. The next day I told the boys that I was planning to marry Carolyn and they were happy for that news. I asked them not to tell anyone about this until we announced our engagement in January. Dave sent Carolyn a small Connecticut license plate with CAROLYN on it.

I must express my appreciation to Lee's mother for helping take care of my sons during the summer of 1973, and for a month and a half that winter. (The boys were not very happy in the summer when she laid on several disciplines for them to observe, but I'll not get into that but leave it to them, if they wish, to tell their stories.) Her help freed me to court Carolyn, to get back into my professional life, and do the other normal things of life.

Some years later I found that my Mother- in - law was busy at home when the boys and I were gone. One of my hobbies was photography. I'd collected the annual editions of *Photography* magazine in which were a collection of the pictures judged to be the best of the year. I had a complete collection from 1955 to 1973. One day I went to these annuals to try to find a picture of Crater Lake. As I was skimming through the issue I noticed that there were no nude still life photos in the issue I was perusing. This was strange in that at least a half dozen of such photos were normally in each annual. I turned to the back where each photo was shown in miniature giving data on lens, camera and lighting, etc. There I noticed several nude photos and turned back to the page referenced. Those pages were all missing. They had all been cut out close to the binding by what I believe was a razor blade! She had ruined all nineteen issues without my approval. The family protector of morals had acted to make sure her grandchildren would be protected from the filth their father brought into the home. C'est la vie. That was a small price to pay for all the help she gave me in my darkest year. She now rests in peace.

Carolyn and I were now talking to each other every day. I have a precious letter she sent on December tenth, where she signed off, "Your Lover". On December 20th, my birthday, she called. I was a basket case. It was my 44th birthday, and for the first time in my life I did not have a mother or wife beside me on my birthday. I could not forget all the love I had received and the beautiful things they had done to assure me of a beautiful day. I'd spent a good part of that evening in tears. Carolyn called and promised me that when I turned 45, she would give me the greatest party I'd ever had.

I went to Michigan to celebrate New Year's with Carolyn. One of the firsts I had that weekend was to go snowmobiling. I was on the back porch bent over pulling the boots of the suit on with Carolyn's help, when an explosion took place. I jumped about two feet and landed all ensnared in the suit. There stood her brother Carl with his smoking shot gun. He had taken a shot at a rabbit in their yard. He apologized for not giving me a warning, while I swallowed hard to get my heart out of my throat. Carolyn and I did get him to take us for a ride. It was my first and last time to do so. I especially was not happy when on turns we slewed close to several trees. Later that weekend, we went to Glen Ellyn, and spent a couple of nights at my brother's, and went out with Chicago friends.

In mid- January, I went to the Boca Raton Hotel and Club to attend the week long convention of the Soap & Detergent Association. Since I was the low man on the totem pole to attend and my job was to man the hospitality suite for our top executives, their wives and our important customers in the Hotel and Cabana Club. I played tennis every day with customers and one day chartered a boat to take several of them to fish for sailfish. I caught a Bonita that was about 10 inches long, and the mate suggested that I use it as a live bait to attract a sailfish. He did this for me and attached my line to a snap on the outrigger.

About ten minutes later, my line snapped off the outrigger. The line went singing off my reel. The mate came and put a harness on me and sat me in a chair with a holding cup and then coached me on how to reel in the monster that was on my line. The fish leaped from the water numbers of times trying to get off the hook. For the next hour and a half I had one of the greatest sporting thrills of my life in battling this blue-silver fish. My forearms and fingers cramped up at times during our battle, and the mate massaged my arms and poured Gatorade into me.

Finally, I got the fish to the side of the boat, and the captain asked me if I was going to keep it and have it mounted or let it go. I asked what it would cost to have it mounted, and he said to figure $35 a foot and he estimated the fish to be seven feet long. I did the quick math and said I didn't know if I could afford that. One of our party said take it on board. He said, "If you don't want it, I'll lie that I caught it and put it on my office wall." The fish was gaffed and taken on board. As we headed back to shore, all the men advised me to have it mounted. When we arrived at the captain's office he showed me the one he had on the wall. That confirmed my decision to do the same with my over seven foot, 44- pound prize.

That night I called Carolyn and said that a quarter carat of her diamond had turned into a fish. Even so, she said she'd marry me. That didn't stop her from hating the fish that hung in our den and collected dust for 27 years. The fish cost $300 to mount and another $300 to ship it to Connecticut. She didn't like the trophy that I won for catching the largest fish during the convention fishing tournament. The fish did not come with us when we downsized and moved to Florida in 2001.

On the 26th of January Carolyn came to Connecticut to pick out an engagement ring in NYC and to go to a Winter Wonderland church program. At that wonderful party, our engagement was announced, and Carolyn was warmly welcomed by our church family. Many came to her and said she was an answer to their prayers for me and the boys. I was so proud of her as she just glowed the whole weekend. Also that weekend she met our neighbors and met others at our church on Sunday. We also told my sons that we would be getting married in May.

On this weekend Carolyn shared with me that a year ago, six months before we met on the beach, she had lost a man she loved and was planning to marry to pancreatic cancer. She was still mourning that loss when we'd met in July. If I'd met her on the beach a year earlier, she would not have dated me. God's timing was right for both of us.

Carolyn and I had talked about a problem we might have in living in a house that was Lee's and mine. We set a date with a realtor for a weekend early in March to look at houses in the same school district that might suit our needs. I told the boys what Carolyn and I would be doing. They told me they would rather stay where we were. Carolyn flew out, and we looked at four or five houses. We felt none of them matched the one I had. At the end we decided to stay at 300 Gilbert Hwy. and make it "our home." The boys were happy with our decision. I assured Carolyn that the inside of the house was hers and her ideas of decorating in our bedroom and on the first floor would be followed. I told her I had plans to build a deck off the kitchen and a screened porch off the dining room which we could use for entertainment in the warm months of the year.

One night I made a serious error in judgment. While we were having dinner, I asked the boys if, after we were married, they could call Carolyn, Mother. They all started crying, left the table and went to their rooms. If I'd thought before I spoke, I never would have asked them to do what for them was impossible. They only knew one mother. I went to each of them individually and apologized. I told them Carolyn did not expect them to call her mother, but she did want them to give her the respect and obedience they had given their mother. She wanted them to call her Carolyn.

As time passed, I would overhear them telling thier buddies. "I'll ask my mother", when they were talking on the phone. Within a year they addressed her as Mom or Mother. Carolyn's love to them in word and deed, earned her that right.

I drove out to Michigan a few days before the wedding to do several things. Carolyn had a Plymouth that we decided to trade in on a new Dodge. The boyhood buddy of mine, Eldon Palmer, from Bass Lake days, was now the largest Dodge dealer in the state of Indiana. He gave me a great deal on a top of the line demo model, and we went down to Indianapolis to make the deal.

Another day was taken getting my blood test and the marriage license. Carolyn advised me that I could save some money by having the blood test done at the VD clinic that was part of the Board of Health, where she worked. I went to the clinic and after signing in was directed to a small gymnasium that served as the waiting room for the patients. The room had benches on three sides and there were about 40 men waiting to be called and have their blood tested. Most of them were hunched over looking at the floor. They were not a happy bunch, and as I recall I was the only one wearing a tie. My most vivid memory of that room was of the giant poster hanging directly over the exit door. On it was pictured a gigantic house fly and the wording under it read; FLIES SPREAD DISEASE, KEEP YOURS CLOSED. Carolyn had called ahead to let them know that I was coming, so I didn't have to wait long before my name was called. I passed that test with flying colors, and the next day we went to city hall and got the Marriage License.

After eight dates, most of which lasted a few days, we were married on May 18th, 1974, in the Algoma Baptist Church. It was our mutual decision to have a small, family only, wedding and a larger reception for 150 family, friends, and her work associates. The reception was held in the Finial room, which was on the top floor of the Union Bank building in downtown Grand Rapids. Beth Kasen was her maid of honor, and my brother Will was best man. Carolyn's friends, Hap and Margaret Teesdale let us have their trailer on the Muskegon River for our several day honeymoon. We spent a couple of days packing up the largest U-Haul trailer we could get with Carolyn's belongings, and then drove back to Connecticut.

We spent most of the summer getting settled into the house. We got a builder to design a deck. After Dave and I had dug the holes and poured the footings, the builder came over to frame up the deck. Then Dave and I put down the 2x8 decking and the railings. One of the things Carolyn did not want was our sheltie, Sandy, a dog who loved to bark. Being a Michigan farm girl, she firmly believed that dogs did not belong in the house. Her wish to be rid of the dog was granted when 13- year-old Sandy died from an infection one week after Carolyn arrived. Sandy probably died of a broken heart, receiving no love from her mistress. The boys mourned her loss and were not too sure that Carolyn had not had something to do with her demise. That fall, after much pleading from the boys, we got a Golden Retriever, Cindy, which in time Carolyn came to love dearly.

In late September, Carolyn and I took the Sea Venture for a week long honeymoon cruise to Bermuda. After that cruise, the ship was sold and for the next decade plus, was "The Love Boat" that became a TV hit. Bermuda is my favorite Island. We've gone back to it twice. We love the pink sand beaches, pastel houses, and abundant flowers.

As we approached the island, Carolyn and I went up to the promenade deck. I didn't stay there long. I ran all over the ship taking pictures of the hilly Island set on the beautiful variegated blue water, spotted with yacht harbors and the pastel- colored buildings. When we were just about to dock at Hamilton, I looked at the film counter on the camera and it read 42. I'd never got more than 38 pictures on a 36 roll of film, so I went down to the cabin bathroom to check on it. When I opened the camera, I found that I had no film in it. We enjoyed motor biking and taking the buses to various places on the island and took many pictures, but I refused to let Carolyn tell about my missing pictures for many years.

In the first year of our marriage, Carolyn had many friends over for dinner, mostly those who had so wonderfully befriended me in the past year. On one occasion someone complimented Carolyn on her superb cooking. Glenn spoke up, "Dad always marries good cooks." Amen!!

As Carolyn had promised on my previous birthday, she prepared a marvelous Smorgasbord for the 20th of December. She invited 10 couples to come to that party. We had a wonderful time of feasting and fellowship that evening. Carolyn quickly got the reputation among our friends as being the "Hostess with the Mostest."

I knew quickly how wonderfully God had blessed me with a wife who was as beautiful on the inside as she was outwardly. I have marveled all my days with her, at her gift of hospitality and the joy she receives from serving others. I have been made rich beyond measure because of her. Truly, she is, A MIRACLE.

Chapter 15

Bass Lake

Bass Lake is the third largest lake in Indiana, located seven miles south of Knox on U.S. route 35. It is shallow with a treed shoreline of ten miles, about a mile wide, and four miles long, making it a good lake for sailing shallow- keeled boats, and a great lake for boating and water skiing. Years ago the spring-fed lake was a good lake for fishing, and there are still some who fish for perch, bass, pike, crappies, carp and catfish. The majority of people who had cottages on the lake were from the Chicago area, as it was only 75 miles away.

In the early 1900s when cars and roads afforded people the opportunity to get out of the cities for recreation, my grandfather AF and some of his brothers and friends bought property at the lake and built cottages on the northeast shore line. That area was called Swedestown by long- time residents. On the northeast corner of the lake was a little group of stores called Winona: consisting of a general store, Roepstorff's, a bowling alley, a bar, a gas station, and a riding stable. The general store had a great soda fountain. Leaving the town, as you drove up a slight hill, you came to the Swedes' area.

My parents brought me to the lake as an infant in the summer of 1930 to stay at the Caroline cottage, named for my grandmother who everybody called Mussie. From then until 1972, when my dad passed away and the cottage was sold, I spent over 1,700 days there, many of the happiest days of my life.

The cottage sat on the top of a 15- foot hill and was built on a two and a half acre lot. The lot had 150 feet of shoreline. For some unknown reason, A.F built the house right on the north property line, only eight feet from the Mortenson's two story house. The cottage was originally sided by yellow stucco but later wood siding replaced the stucco and it was painted white. It was topped off with a gabled roof. The cottage had three bedrooms, a living room, dining room, and a kitchen with a pantry that housed the well water pump and tank. To get hot water we heated the kettle on the white gasoline range or the wood stove which was in the dining room. There was one bathroom, with a toilet and sink but no shower or bath tub. The cottage's great features' were screened porches: a side porch off my grandmother's bedroom and a front porch that stretched across the entire front of the cottage and fronted the lake with a western panoramic view. There was only one closet, but two bedrooms had steel wardrobes. All the floors were covered with roll linoleum except the living room which was carpeted. The kitchen fronted the road as did a one car garage with a woodshed and two seat outhouse on its south side. Fortunately, the outhouse was seldom used except for emergencies.

Before a couple of laundromats opened in the late forties, our clothes were scrubbed on a washboard that was attached to a galvanized washtub. Soft water came from rain barrels that sat below the downspouts at each corner of the cottage. The cottage was not winterized nor did it have air conditioning or a telephone. A refrigerator was acquired in the late forties. Before that we had an icebox that held up to 100 pounds of ice. We did have three or four rotating fans to cool us on the hottest evenings. The living room had a fireplace. For entertainment we had a couple of radios and 78RPM phonograph. We were blessed not to have TV. Instead of that on rainy days we played card or board games and read books, while the adults sat around the dining room table, drank coffee and laughed and talked. We only watched TV once at Bass Lake. On July 20, 1969, our neighbor's invited us over to see Neil Armstrong step out on the moon. All of our relatives had about the same type of cottages.

When we were at the lake it wasn't all fun and games. Until the fifties, when dad purchased an electric lawn mower, my brother, I and dad cut the grass every couple of weeks with a reel mower that required one-man power.

The milkman came three times a week. He'd take the money and note from the bottle on the back porch and leave the ordered milk. I was often asked to get the milk and put it in the icebox. Before milk was homogenized, the cream would come to the top of the bottle. Sometimes when no one could see me I'd take off the cardboard cap and take a mouthful of cream, add a little water, put the cap back on, shake the bottle, and hope no one would notice my thievery. Boy, was that a treat! It was also my job to let the ice man know how much ice we needed when he'd come at his three day intervals. I'd put a sign in the kitchen window facing the street, that informed him that we needed either a 25, 50, 75 or 100 lbs.- block of ice. Many times I'd go out to the truck as the ice man would chip off a weighed block and get a few shards of ice to suck on.

Down below the hill on the south side of the property was a boathouse that was later enlarged to become a two-story house for my uncle Roy, and then later for my Aunt Judy's family. Up until 1965 we had a rowboat with an ancient 3hp Johnson Sea Horse out board motor. Then my uncle Albin bought us a Boston Whaler with a 25hp engine, and in '69 a V-hulled boat with a 50hp engine. Lee, Dave and I all learned to water ski and really had a lot of fun using that boat.

Each year we'd go to the lake on Memorial Day to cut the grass and clean up the debris from winter. We ended our year there on Veterans' Day, raking up and burning the leaves that had fallen. (I miss that smell of burning leaves in the fall, but admit it's better not to do so because of the environment that we need to protect.) The other job we did at that time was to drain all the water pipes and the toilet to prevent pipes freezing and breaking during the winter.

What kept me wanting to come back to Bass Lake after we'd moved to the east coast in '63? By then I'd seen many more beautiful lakes, such as Crater Lake, Jackson and Jenny Lakes in the Tetons, Lakes Moraine and Louise in the Canadian Rockies and in New York and New Hampshire many mountain lakes which were at their best with the fall colors. I came back mainly because of the memories that I shared with family and loved ones, where on Sunday after church we had fried chicken, mashed potatoes, corn on the cob and apple pie a la mode or a hot fudge sundae at Rupstorff's. On some days I enjoyed a quick nap on the cushioned porch swing, playing ballgames with cousins and friends, or pitching horseshoes with my dad. I remember my mother sitting in a rocker, knitting or crocheting a tablecloth or dress for herself, Lee, or my aunt Elvira, or making a patchwork quilt.

I remembered my aunts and uncles and Mussie sitting on a veranda in the shade of two enormous oak trees on a Sunday afternoon. There would be a lot of laughing and lots of coffee and coffeecake consumed as they fanned themselves and socialized.

In 1986, my Aunt Elvira died. At her funeral reception I asked my cousin Ralph about a time when all we cousins were swimming in the lake and we heard the sound of our parents' laughter coming out to us. I asked Ralph at that time; "Ralph, what do our folks do for fun?" I asked him if he remembered what he'd said at that time. He answered: "I don't remember, but now we're them." How true! What he and I did remember were many bonfires, wienie and marshmallow roasts, fireworks on the fourth of July, and Taps sounding every night from Camp Gridley.

There I first fell in love with a girl named Lee, who became my wife, lover, and mother of my three sons. The boys spent many days of their childhood there. On many hot, steamy summer nights Lee and I would wrap ourselves in a beach towel and go down to the lake and skinny dip. I remember one night when we embraced in chest high water. Lee said, "Honey, look up, the stars are so clear tonight." I preferred to see them as they were reflected in her beautiful eyes.

I could recount many other reasons why Bass Lake meant so much to me, among them, watching hundreds of sunsets from a rocking chair as the crickets started chirping and frogs added their croaks. Bass Lake was part of me and gave me experiences that defined me.

In the early 90's, as Carolyn and I drove to Chicago to visit family and friends, we had some time to spare so I asked Carolyn: "Would you like to see Bass Lake? It's about a half hour away." She said yes, so we took hwy 35 south. The Burma Shave signs were gone. Not much seemed changed as we passed by many farms and finally got off on the road to the lake.

Twenty years had passed since we'd sold our cottage. Many of the cottages had been replaced or remodeled, and when we got to ours place it also had changed. Many of the big trees had been cut down and the house was painted brown. I went to the kitchen door, and rang the bell and then knocked, but there was no answer. We took a chance and walked around the premises. Both screened porches had been glassed in. I expect that the house had also been winterized and was probably used year around. Below the hill the boat and well house and three poplar trees had been removed. Near the beach was a large willow tree that Lee had planted as a rooted branch 35 years earlier. I shed a few tears as my memories came back to her care for that tree.

Carolyn hugged me. I suggested we leave, as bittersweet memories took hold of me. We drove back through the town of Winona as I had done many times before. It had hardly changed. About a half mile down the road we took a right turn off the lake road and headed toward Knox. As I drove over a couple of little hills, at the top of each hill I'd look in the rear view mirror to see the lake recede from my view. Each time I looked I saw less and less of it, and finally, it disappeared. I started sobbing. Carolyn counseled me to pull off the road until I could control my emotions. She patted me as I was overcome by my memories. I mourned not only for what Bass Lake had been, but for all that it had meant in my life but no longer was, and would never be again.

Chapter 16

Conventions, Cars, Church, Children

In January 1975, Carolyn and I went to the Boca Raton Hotel and Club for the annual five day convention of the Soap & Detergent Association. It was to be the first of nine that we attended. I was involved with the organization as we were major manufacturers of sodium and potassium phosphates for the detergent industry. I served as product manager and later as marketing manager of these chemicals. The top officers of Stauffer were at the convention for at least part of the time. This being our first year, I was the ranking junior of our group and had the responsibility of serving them and our customers in our hospitality suite. I was also responsible for booking tee times and tennis courts reservations for them. Being at this convention was a great perk. The hotel was a Mobil five star resort and all expenses were paid, including our house keepers expenses for taking care of our boys in Connecticut. When the convention ended we planned to go down to Ft. Lauderdale and spend a few days with Uncle Albin and Aunt Elvira.

As this was Carolyn's first convention, on the flight to Ft. Lauderdale I gave her a list of our company's attendees and their wives, and she tried to learn their names. At our first gathering she met each of them. When she met our director of research, Dr. Art Toy, he introduced his wife Hui to both of us. Carolyn asked her for the correct pronunciation of her name. She said, "Just say Hawaii and take the Ha off the word." Two days later Carolyn met Hui in the gift shop and said, "Good Morning Lulu." She had taken the Hono off Honolulu. Hui and Carolyn had a big laugh over it.

On another day when Carolyn was on the bus to the Cabana Club, she sat next to a man named Jacobson. He asked, "Are you Paul's wife?" She said "yes." He told her that he was one of my customers. When they got off the bus, Carolyn said," I'm always glad to meet another Swede." He responded by telling her he wasn't a Swede. He was a large dark skinned man, who nearly always had a cigar in his mouth and happened to be Jewish.

The last year we went to Boca I served as the convention chairman. In the 70s and 80s Carolyn and I attended conventions at some of the plushest resorts in America; The Homestead, Greenbrier, and Cloisters, in the south; Camelback, Desert Springs, Vantana Canyon and several hotels in Las Vegas, out west, The Waldorf and Plaza in NY, and The Drake, Palmer House and Continental Plaza in Chicago, to name a few of our favorites.

Our major family trip in '75 was to California. This was Glenn's choice to help celebrate his twelfth birthday. We flew to San Diego and rented a car, making our first stop at the San Diego Zoo and the next day Sea World with Shamu the whale. The next stop was Disneyland and Universal Studios in the LA area. One afternoon a friend took us on a sail on his 50 ft sailboat from Santa Monica south to Dana Point. The next day was spent at Hearst Castle. We had a hard time keeping our eyes on the road as we drove up the coast to Big Sur, Monterey and Carmel. We then headed east to Sequoia Park with the gigantic redwoods, and finally to what I judge to be the most beautiful place in the U.S., Yosemite National Park. We stayed three nights at Curry Village. There we had several breathtaking experiences. When we got up to Inspiration Point, hang gliders were taking off from there and circling the valley between Half Dome and Yosemite Falls.

That night we had quite a different scene. Carolyn and I were asleep on cot beds that were on either side of a big open window. Between us was a table that was about level with the window ledge. I was awakened from my sleep by Carolyn's scream! I saw a person kneeling on the window ledge with most of his body on the table. The person quickly backed out the window, leaped to the ground, and ran off. I'm sure glad the person did not get trapped in the room as he might have harmed us. Several people came to our cabin in response to Carolyn's scream. One was a park ranger who reported that there were a lot of hippies in the park that summer who were subsisting by stealing from the tourists. I was glad we'd put our wallets between the mattress and the bed spring. We closed the open window and locked it, but it took us several hours to get back to sleep.

We ended the trip spending a couple of days in my favorite U.S city, San Francisco. One of the afternoons we went over the Golden Gate Bridge and drove up to Muir Woods in Marin County. We all loved the cable cars, and Carolyn endured a Giant's night game at Candlestick Park, where we nearly froze to death even though we wrapped ourselves in blankets which we'd stripped off our Holiday Inn beds. The last day we spent with friends of Carolyn who showed us some of their favorite spots. We adults had a great dinner at Ernie's, one of my favorite restaurants.

When we got home, I started playing tennis at least twice a week: once each week with a group of guys from work, at my friend Ray Whittle's clay court, and the other group were men from our church who played on Saturday morning at the Trumbull Racquet Club. Once in a while I'd fill in for friends who played at the Westport tennis club, where a man named Blake was the tennis pro. One morning when we got to the club, one of our foursome was missing. Mr Blake was rallying with his 10 year old son on the next court. He asked us if we'd like his son to play with us. We accepted his offer. We played three sets and James changed partners each set. Whoever had James as a partner, won. That 10 year old is the James Blake who is now one of the top US players in tennis. I can say that I had James Blake as a partner when I played tennis in Connecticut.

I had promised Carolyn that we would build a screened in porch on our house. We took action and met with Neil Carley and contracted to build a 16 X 24 ft. porch off the dining room on the south side of the house. Dave and I dug five- four foot deep holes and poured the footings. Neil then came and framed up the porch. When it came time to put down the tongue-and-groove flooring he let Dave and I do that job. Neil finished the rest of the job except for the roofing, and in a few days I put on the final shingle. In the next few summers we spent most of our spare time enjoying it.

In 1984, with the help of a stone mason, we build a small pool and a re-circulating waterfall in front of the screened porch, which added to the beauty of our home. I planted Impatients in the flower bed around the pool and hired a young woman landscaper from our church to plant some evergreens on the sides and in back of the waterfall. I asked her what kind of fertilizer I should uses on them. She recommended horse manure, and said that she could get some for me at no charge from a stable where she worked. As we stood by her pick up truck, she asked me how much I wanted. I said, "Oh, half a truck load will be plenty."

A few days later I heard a large truck in our driveway and went out to investigate. It was a dump truck and I saw Kathy my landscaper sitting on the passenger side. She smiled, waved, jumped out of the truck, and said, "Where do you want us to dump it?" I was stunned as I'd expected to get half a pick up truck load, not a couple of tons, but was too embarrassed to tell her so. I told them to dump it as far off the driveway as possible. It was soon done, and they left me with an eight foot high pile of steaming manure. I was very lucky that Carolyn was working that afternoon. When she got home it was dark, and the wind was blowing away from the house. The next morning when Carolyn went for her walk the wind was blowing from the west. She was greeted with the smell as she walked up the driveway and then saw the pile. When she came in she was not happy. I won't rehash our conversation but I'll just say she was not impressed with what I'd done. Fortunately, it was late fall and people would not open their doors and windows until late spring. Only a couple of them even noticed the pile, and one said it was a nice reminder of his early life as he'd grown up on a farm.

Because we had so many trees on our two acre lot, I bought an 18-inch Stihl chain saw and cut up many downed or dead oaks, beeches and maples. I then bought a wood stove and installed it in the den. Most of my neighbors offered me their downed or dead trees. I cut them up, took the logs home and split the large logs with a sledge hammer and wedges. This produced a lot of firewood. It was great exercise and I loved to do this work. It also cut our heating bill in half. There are few things more beautiful than firewood stacked in perfect rows. My firewood made me happy. It made me feel secure and prepared for whatever the winter would bring. One of the things I've missed most since we've moved to Florida is not having a wood stove, containing a hot fire, which I used to snuggle close to with Carolyn or our wonderful Golden Retriever, Cindy.

One quick lesson Cindy learned was not to chase after skunks. In doing so one day she got sprayed, and I got the great assignment of putting her in the bathtub and washing her down first with tomato juice and then soap. Cindy did not like baths, and several times shook herself. She decorated me and the bathroom twice with red spots, and we used up several quart cans of the juice. Even with this, we left her outside or in the basement for several days to let the smell wear off. She never again got in contact with a skunk. She did love to chase squirrels, which leads me to my next memory.

In the cooler months, Carolyn found the screened porch to be a great place to store her baked goodies. One fall day Carolyn had gone out, and I had occasion to go out on the porch. I immediately saw a squirrel chewing up one of her cakes. While the squirrel ran around the porch, I discovered the spot near the floor where it had clawed its way in. It was running around in terror and jumping from one screen to the next while I swung at it with a canoe paddle. Finally, I hit the varmint and it fell to the floor and met its demise. I carried it out to the woods and put it under a large rock. When Carolyn came home, I led her to the porch to show her what the squirrel had done. What a surprise it was to find another squirrel eating up the crumbs. This time, to complicate the matter, Cindy came out with us and commenced chasing the creature. I told Carolyn to catch Cindy and go into the house so that I could get the squirrel. She did that, and in a few minutes I was able to dispatch it and put it under the same big rock. I went back to the house, helped Carolyn remove the baked goods from the porch, and patched the screen.

Our next door neighbors had a Great Dane that roamed the neighborhood and was especially attracted to our lot when serious jobs were to be done. A couple of times I hit his excrement with my power mower and spread fertilizer over a quarter acre. We had mentioned our displeasure to the neighbors concerning their free-ranging dog but to no avail.

A week after the cake incident, Carolyn had a conversation with our neighbor during which she said, "Fritz, our dog can climb trees." Carolyn asked how she knew that. "Because on two separate days he's come back to the house with a squirrel in his mouth," she said. Carolyn said nothing to her about our recent adventure and reported this to me when I came home from work. I went out to the rock where I had deposited the demised squirrels. The ground around the rock had been clawed up and when I lifted the rock, the squirrels were gone. We never told our neighbors the truth about their tree climbing Great Dane.

Although we had fine neighbors, we spent a lot more time with our friends from Church every October about 100 men from Black Rock Congregational Church went up to Pilgrim Pines on Lake Swanzey for a retreat. There we shared our faith with each other, played tennis or golf, canoed, hiked and some of the brave younger macho guys even went swimming. One year our guest speaker was Father Fullam, an Episcopal priest from Darien, Ct. Unknown to us, he brought his wife with him, and they had their own cabin. The rest of us shared cabins with three to seven other men. The only camp employees there were the cooks and a day manager. This was in the golden days when none of us had cell phones to interrupt a quiet, idyllic getaway. Late Friday night a call came into the office, and the woman calling asked to speak to her sister Mrs Fullam. The person who answered said there were no women at the camp, that the only ones there were a Black Rock group. Mrs Fullam's sister said, "I guess I got the wrong information, I know my sister wouldn't be with a black rock group." When Father Fullam's wife called her sister the next day, her sister was surprised to find that she was with a Black Rock group.

Those weekends were great. The man who put them together was my great friend, Paul Josephson. On one weekend, he was able to get three prisoners from Danbury Penitentiary paroled to us. These men had become Christians through Chuck Colson's Prison Fellowship Ministry. At our closing session, just before we were to have communion, one of the prisoners asked to speak. He told us that he was in prison because of a bank robbery he'd committed in New Jersey and had one year to go before he would be paroled. He said that on this weekend God had been speaking to his conscience about a bank robbery he had committed in Oregon which had never been tied to him. He said it was his intention to confess this to his parole officer when he got back to prison so he could have peace in his heart. He realized that he might have to do more time by taking this step and asked us to pray for him. A bunch of us put our arms around him and did so. This story has a happy ending as the Oregon authorities dropped the charges against him. A year later he came to our weekend as a free man.

The next year Ray Whittles offered to drive up to Lake Swanzey. Two other men went with us. Ray who was in his 80's, was a great mentor and friend of mine. We played tennis many times on his clay court.(He apologized a lot to me about not being able to get much on his serve.) After the retreat we got lost on the way home as we tried to find Rt. 91. We were in the town of Keene. Ray pulled up to a bench where three old codgers were sitting and asked them for directions to 91. He got them and we drove off. Suddenly he said, "I missed an opportunity." He turned to go back around the square When he got back to the old guys, he asked me to get three New Testaments out of the glove compartment. He took them and walked a few steps and said, "Men, thanks for giving us directions. I'd like to give you a book that's given me direction all my life." Wow!! What a lesson that was on how to be a witness of my faith. This challenged me to prepare a witness card, which I've left on airplanes, in Gideon Bibles in hotel rooms and with my tip at restaurants.

In my lifetime I've owned 19 cars, probably half that number from 1975 to 93 when Carolyn also worked and the boys needed cars to get around driving to school, work, church, and athletic events, etc. My favorites were my first, a 53 hard top Bel Aire Chevy and a '58 2 door Opal that wouldn't wear out. A big chunk of money in those years was spent on cars and insurance.

Dave was driving a girl in our family car to JFK when he spun out on the Van Wyck Expressway. That took out the back end of that car. A new back end was clipped onto it, but Glenn continued its destruction when the engine seized because he forgot that cars need oil to lubricate pistons. We bought a Dodge Dart which became Dave's car to use for track meets and work at the Patterson Club, (where eventually all the boys worked, bussing and waiting, etc.) On a narrow road which was blocked by a fallen tree Dave thought he could get around it and did, but the entire side of the car was also done in. Craig was driving the Dart when he rear ended a VW "that suddenly was in his path."

Another incident happened when Craig was using our Plymouth Scamp to deliver Domino Pizza's. He was in a rather dicey section of town on a late Saturday night. After making a half- hearted stop at an intersection, he was pulled over by a policeman who asked Craig to produce papers. He had all of them except the insurance documents. Craig said the officer almost jumped for joy when he had this charge to add to the ticket that he was writing. He told Craig he could not drive the car until the insurance papers were in the car.

So, as I was sitting by the warm stove in my pajamas Craig called me to come get him and to bring the insurance papers. I found them, put on a jacket and shoes and drove to where Craig waited.

I was more than a little steamed up when I finally found Craig. We drove over to the Scamp and I told him I'd drive it home. I put the insurance papers in the glove compartment and started the car. I had only gone about 50 feet when a siren went off and a police car was soon beside me. It was obvious that the policeman who had ticketed Craig had parked a couple hundred feet away and was waiting to see if someone would drive off with the Scamp. The officer ordered me to get out of the car, spread my legs and put my hands on the car roof. He proceeded to frisk me, which made me rather uncomfortable as I was in my pajamas. He read me the riot act, even after he'd read the insurance papers. He wanted to call the Insurance Company to make sure everything was in order. He was obviously disappointed to find out I wasn't a wanted criminal. I complained to a friend on the Fairfield Police Department the following Monday. He said the arresting cop was new and, in his opinion, drunk with power. I was called a couple of days later and told the ticket he'd written for me could be ripped up.

It wasn't only my boys who had embarrassing accidents with cars. I was at a convention at the Eden Roc Hotel on Miami Beach. The Hotel has a fairly steep driveway up to the entrance. One evening there was a line of about six cars in front of me. The doorman came down the line and told us we could leave our cars and they would park them. He instructed me to leave the key in the ignition with the engine running. I got out of the car and walked toward the entrance when I remembered I'd left my sunglasses on the dashboard. I walked back to the car, opened the door on the passenger side, put my left knee on the seat and reached across the dash for the glasses. My knee slid off the vinyl seat, and as I fell my arm hit the steering wheel gear shift and it dropped into reverse. On my knees, I helplessly watched as my car crashed into the grill of the Cadillac behind me. I settled with a wonderful gentleman for an agreed amount as I didn't want to explain the details of that accident to my insurance company.

A few years later Carolyn and I were on our way to Florida. We were driving on 95, and were about to leave Georgia. It was time to fill the tank as gas prices were about ten cents a gallon higher in Florida than they were in Georgia. I pulled off at the last exit and found that the station I wanted was on the other side of a divided highway. I drove west to find a place where I could turn around. The divided section finally ended, and I backed into a driveway to turn around. I didn't notice that the driveway ran over a culvert and was not very wide. Suddenly my Caddy's right back wheel went off the driveway and my car was resting on its frame with the wheel hanging over the deep ditch.

I walked to the road to flag anyone down to take me to the garage where I could either get a tow truck or call AAA. A car, and a pickup truck passed by me, but then the pick up turned around and came back. An older man dressed in bib overalls walked toward me. I asked if he could give me a lift to the gas station. He circled my car and then lay down on his belly to survey the situation. When he got up he said, "I think I can pull you out of there." He went to the back of his truck and pulled out a heavy 50- foot chain and hooked it to our cars frame. He then hooked the other hook to the tow bar of his truck. He pulled his truck up until the chain was taut and told me to put my car in neutral and steer straight ahead. In a few seconds all four of my wheels were on the road. He came back and crawled under the car where the frame had rested and said he could see no serious damage. He thought the car was safe to drive. I thanked him and pulled two 20's out of my pocket to pay for what he'd done.

He asked. “Do you go to church on Sunday?” I said, “Yes” He said, “Put those in the offering plate.” A horrible experience turned into a beautiful one as we shook hands and parted.

Another of the second hand cars we bought was a camouflage green ‘68 Pontiac, ugly to say the least! The boys called it, “The Tank.” The streets up to our house were fairly steep. When we had more than three inches of snow it was impossible to get up the hill. We would get up as much speed as we could, and when the wheels started spinning, head to the curb, leave the car and walk home. We’d go and retrieve the car after the plows and sanders had cleared the road. One Friday night Craig came home from the Patterson Club in a snow storm, had to abandon the car and walk home.

On Saturday morning he and I went to the car with snow shovels and dug it out of the snow that the plows had heaped on it. When we finally got it freed up, I tried to get it up the hill but could not get traction from a standing start. It was early Saturday morning and as yet there was little traffic on the roads. I backed the car down to the bottom of the hill and backed up a couple hundred feet so I could get up the speed that I needed to get to the top. I told Craig to tell me when the road was clear so I could start my run. He looked down the curve in the road and frantically waved at me with both hands to back up. I soon saw why! A black Dodge hatchback came around the curve and was skidding out of control. I sat paralyzed watching the car careening toward me. By the time it reached me, it was coming at me sideways. The impact of the collision caused the hatchback to rip off and fly over the roof of my car. He bounced off my car, spun and went into a utility pole. I got out of my car and went to see how the occupants were in the Dodge. It was a young man and his girlfriend who both exited where the hatch back had been. He had a big cut on his forehead. Other than that, they appeared to be ok. I went to the nearest house and asked them to call the police. I then went to the Pontiac and examined the front of it. There was no visible damage, not even a headlight was broken. After the police left, I got "THE TANK" up the hill and home. After that I always felt less uneasy when the boys went out driving the Pontiac.

I did not endear myself to my sons when I became the recipient of several car loads of envelopes which were offered to me by the Postal Commemorative Society in nearby Norwalk, Ct. These envelopes were covered by U.S. postage stamps that needed to be soaked off. I gave the boys the task of doing this. They were not happy with the assignment. I suggested they place the 9 X 12 envelopes on the back lawn, stamp side down, then in the morning when the dew had dissolved the glue, they could reap the harvest of stamps. Naturally, I advised them that this should not be done when a windy night was forecast as we didn't want envelopes blowing all over the neighborhood. After a night when this did happen, we abandoned that procedure. That meant that they had to soak off the stamps in buckets of water and dry them on newspaper. I was able to accumulate thousands of used US postage stamps because of the Commemorative Society's beneficence and my sons labor. On the other hand I disregarded the Bible's injunction in Ephesians 6:4 which states, "Fathers, do not exasperate your children." I'm afraid I not only exasperated them but also turned them away from ever taking up my beloved hobby, stamp collecting.

One great experience I had with David and some of his friends was coaching the basketball team that played in the church league. David was a good basketball player and his friend Dave Magee was even better. They recruited several others and three African-American boys, who came to our church so they could play on the church basketball team. I'd pick up the boys on the fringe of the housing project for each game and bring them back to the same place after the game. They advised me that it would not be wise for a white "honky" to drive alone into the project. We won the church league title and were invited to play in the Camp of the Woods tournament in Speculator, NY. We won that tournament also.

In 1967, my friend, Paul Liljestrand was asked to become the Minister of Music at Calvary Baptist Church in NYC. The church was on west 57th street, just across from Carnegie Hall. Julliard was only a few blocks away. This enabled Paul to have many musicians available for his major concert series. He invited me to come down to the city to sing in the choir when they sang Handel's Messiah and Brahm's Requiem.

Paul was given an apartment in the hotel next door to the church. This gave him the opportunity to meet and work with a number of world- class musicians. One of them, Simon Estes, hired Paul to be his accompanist when he sang concerts in the U.S. Three experiences stand out from that time. Carolyn and I asked Paul if we could use his apartment for a party after one of the concerts, He agreed to let us do this. We and several other couples drove down from Connecticut with shopping bags full of food and utensils. We had our party after the concert. We then put all the left over food, dishes and utensils back in the bags and started home. A concert crowd was exiting Carnegie Hall as we came out of the hotel. The sidewalk was full of people. Suddenly, the bottom of one bag ripped open and dishes, pans and utensils spilled out on the sidewalk. All of us were doubled up with laughter as we dodge between puzzled pedestrians picking up the pieces. I'm sure they wondered what we well-dressed bag people were doing there.

On another occasion, I was privileged to be at the church one Sunday and went to Paul's apartment after the service. There I met Simon Estes and several other friends that Paul had invited over. At one point Simon was asked if he would sing a bass aria for us. He chose to sing a dramatic aria from Rachmaninoff's opera, "Aleko." At the end of the aria there's a long rest before the final note. During his singing of it, one of Paul's boys had gone off to the bathroom. Simon was near the end of a deep breath that he needed for this final note when the bathroom door opened and the toilet loudly flushed. Instead of singing the last note the great basso doubled up with laughter and we all joined him. What perfect timing! I wish someone had videoed that scene; it was a classic.

When Paul came to Calvary Baptist, the interior gray stone had been painted sky blue. The church had also spent a large amount of money rebuilding their pipe organ. Shortly thereafter, the church decided that they had made a mistake in painting the stone walls and decided to remove the paint by sand blasting. Everyone knew that it would be catastrophic for the pipe organ if sand got into its works. At a prayer meeting, one of the prayer requests was that the job of sealing up the organ would be successful and prevent sand from getting into it. One of the prayers that were offered that night came from an old lady who prayed, "Dear Lord, please don't let any sand get into Mr. Liljestrand's organ." When I've called Paul, many times I ask him if he has this problem and we laugh again. We've had a lot of wonderful times together. He is my dearest friend. *

* Since the time of this writing my great friend passed away. We look forward to seeing him again when we are together in Heaven in the presence of God.

Chapter 17

Bones of Contention

On January 1, 1976, my position as manager of Detergent Phosphates was broadened to include Bone Charcoal and Bone Meal. Stauffer had a plant in Houston that produced these products. The raw material for them was cattle bones from Argentina. There, cattle roamed the pampas. Many of these cattle died and their bones lay in the fields. People collected these bones and sold them to brokers who then shipped them by shipload to our plant in Houston. These bones were crushed and screened. The bone that went through a one inch screen and stayed on a 10 mesh screen were put in a coke oven and Bone Charcoal was produced. What went through the 10 mesh screen was milled finer and sold as Bone Meal. Bone Char was a good profit maker. It was sold to sugar refiners to remove the brown color from the unrefined, raw, liquid sugar. Amstar-Domino and C&H were my largest customers for this product. Bone Meal was considered a by-Product and was not very profitable. It was sold mainly as fertilizer to companies that packaged it in two to five pound bags that were sold by nurseries and hardware stores.

Every shipment of bones that came into the port of Houston was sampled by the FDA before it was allowed to be unloaded at our Houston plant. The bones were tested for Anthrax bacteria. All bone meal was sampled and sent to the Food Research Labs at the U. of Wisconsin. All the finished production had to be passed by the labs to be free of Anthrax before it left the plant. I routinely got copies of these reports and they were also sent to the plant. We had been in this business since 1938, and had never had a positive Anthrax test.

On Monday February 23rd I got a call from the Food Research Lab that they had a positive Anthrax result on a 40 ton rail car, MP 716459. The caller said that he believed this was a false positive, but by law they had to report it to us so we could stop its shipment until the test was verified. I called the plant and found that the car had been shipped to Faesy & Bestoff Inc. in Edgewater, N.J. on January 29th. I made an immediate call to Silas Bestoff and asked if they had received the car. He reported that they had unloaded the car on the 17th into their silo and had processed and bagged the product in the next few days. I told him that they should not ship any of the products that contained the subject Bone Meal as the product might be contaminated. I told him I would call him back after lunch as to what we should do after I discussed this with my bosses

The sales manager and I went to the VP of our division, and he quickly convened a meeting that included our top environmental attorney. We made a conference call to the lab in Madison and the contact they had at the FDA to get their counsel on how we should proceed.

Early in the afternoon I called Sy and told him the findings of the Food Research Laboratory. They were retesting the samples to verify the results. They believed on the basis of years of samples tested that it could be a false positive. However, since Anthrax is a deadly bacterium that could be passed on merely by handling, we had to warn our customers, our plant, and the railroad. Everyone who had been in contact with the bone meal needed to be warned. I gave him the name of the person at the Center of Disease Control in Atlanta and also told him to contact his local board of health for advice. I told him we would pay to clean up his plant and make the space available to store the quarantined products. If necessary we would also dispose of the material. I told him that we would know in a week the results of the retesting and I would call him then. He told me that they would check to see if any product had been shipped. Products had been packaged with the subject bone meal starting on the 18th and it was now the 23rd. Unfortunately, he reported later in the day that some of this product had been shipped.

This was the worst experience I had in my business career! Much of the next five months was occupied with this problem. On Wednesday we had two representatives of the CDC in Atlanta and a bacteriologist from the Food Research lab in Madison come to discuss what action we should take to help our customer and to make sure that no future shipments were made from Houston before we had received an OK from the lab. We were at fault for shipping the bone meal without that approval. We agreed to send two tech service reps to supervise and work with Faesy & Besthoff in the clean up operation. An environmental clean up firm was there in two days. There plant was right next to a Colgate plant and just across the Hudson was Manhattan.

Fortunately for all of us, the Madison lab called on March 3rd and reported that the re-testing of several samples showed no Anthrax in our product. Unfortunately, I was the Marketing Manager between Silas Bestoff and Stauffer Chemical Co. I can best summarize the details of the next months by excerpts from Sy's letter to Wyman Taylor and I, dated June 14th, 1976:

"Dear Sirs,
This is a factual chronicle of the events directly resulting from your shipment to us on January 29th of car number MP716459. Your first advice to us of the Anthrax finding was by Mr. Paul Peterson by telephone on Monday February 23. All the plant and some of the office personnel, my son and the writer, had been in physical contact with quantities of the suspect material- and Bone Meal, being somewhat dusty, the possibility existed that all F&B personnel; all visitors: and our own as well as customers and commercial truck drivers, etc. could have been infected.

Occuring immediately after the media had reported the death from Anthrax of a New Jerseyite, your telephone advice indicating a positive Anthrax finding in the car of Bone Meal shipped to us, created such total chaos in our office, as to almost defy description. One of our office personnel, married and a mother, immediately left the office and didn't return for approximately two weeks. All other plant and office personnel (30-50) did remain, but each and everyone understandably was more than merely apprehensive, and work was virtually at a standstill. Several of our plant operatives became so agitated that they regurgitated before they could reach sanitary facilities (As tension continued to mount my own blood pressure increased, necessitating medical attention for hypertension. The board of Health and your organization did request that all F&B personnel be informed of their possible exposure, but that in the event of any illness in the relatively near future, the attending doctor should be informed at once of possible Anthrax exposure.

Following the processing of the Bone Meal, 136,000 pounds of commercial products were processed through the same equipment as the Bone Meal—again, all before we were advised of the Anthrax finding. Stauffer's instructions to recall ALL this material added to the concern and fears that had already been generated.

The chilling inertia, the routine "buck passing" and the indifference, as well as the professed lack of knowledge or authority of those concerned in the Health Departments, Pure Food and Drug Departments in Washington, Trenton and New York City was appalling then and is still unbelievable. The loss of material and the shutdown of our plant were financially important to us, but even the remote possibility of being involved in a human fatality was of infinitely greater gravity.

Faesy & Besthoff was shut down—and for all intents and purposes, no authority appeared to care whether it was for a day, a week, a month, or forever. Finally on Thursday, Stauffer personnel, Robert Bryant and Charles Helt, engaged the services of the

Industrial and Environmental Pollution Controls Company of Mt. Vernon. They were all present during the sterilizing operation of our plant. It was a F&B crew led by Anthony Besthoff who disassembled our equipment on Thursday and Friday. It was the same crew who supplied the "muscle" from 6AM to 9PM Saturday and then without sleep or rest, worked 23 hours from 7AM Sunday to 6AM Monday sterilizing the plant and equipment with a 5% Caustic Soda solution; then a hot water rinse, and finally with steam.

It was F&B personnel who reassembled the machinery, of course, it was F&B trucks and drivers who had to pick up the suspect merchandise from F&B customers throughout Eastern, Southern, and Midwestern USA. Then it was those same F&B trucks that had to be taken out of service, driven to the truck cleaning station, and then sterilized and washed down with a Caustic Soda Solution, hot water rinse and steam before they could be placed back in service. As the suspect merchandise was returned by our trucks, it had to be re-handled by a F&B crew, palletized and then placed in a segregated area of our warehouse for eventual reloading into three railroad cars which were turned over to the RR for final disposition of your orders.

How much the life of our plant equipment and our trucks may have been shortened by this sterilizing treatment we can't even "guess-estimate". For example, several weeks ago, after the truck sterilization, I received a telephone call from one of our drivers then in DuBois, Pa. that the side of his truck had peeled off from the seams and the contents of the truck were imperiled and the condition of the laden vehicle too hazardous to continue the trip We had to transfer the merchandize to a local trucker for ultimate delivery to the customer. We cannot positively state that the Caustic Soda sterilization caused this incident. Neither can we positively state that it hadn't. In the more than 20 years in which we have operated trucks, we have never had and incident even remotely resembling this occurrence. We have 11 other trailers and I'm certain you will agree there is some justifiable concern as to whether the Caustic Soda sterilization may not have caused undetectable damage to our other equipment which may be evident in the future."

I have a vivid recollection of Sy's call to me on the day after the truck incident occurred. Sy said, "Guess what Peterson, the side of one of my semi trailers just peeled off on the Penn Turnpike. I hope Stauffer can afford to buy me 11 new semi trailers." He had simmered down quite a bit when he wrote this letter that led up to his threat of a law suit if we didn't pay handsomely for our blunder. I continue with excerpts from his letter:

"We lost a combined total of a minimum three weeks production and shipping during the height of the season in one of the best years the Home and Garden Industry ever experienced. Additional plant personnel (of coarse inexperienced) were added and we increased our normal 40 hour work week by 20 to 22 hours overtime. As of May 24, we have reduced our overtime to 10 to 12 hours overtime.

It is three months since the calamitous news. Working at maximum capacity, we are now just up to date, considering the MANY cancellations of placed orders that we were unable to ship on time. Much repeat business that we would normally received, has thus, for patently obvious reasons, been placed with competitive producers. How much this cost us this year and how much it will cost us in the future, is as much a guess as is the loss of confidence and ill will that may have generated with many of our customers because of this years performance. Even our friendliest and most understanding customers have not been happy with the prorated deliveries we had to make and I truthfully can say, that I believe everyone of our F&B customers has had reason to complain, and most of them did!

Because of the seasonal nature of Bone Meal usage, it became imperative that we procure, and procure very quickly, a satisfactory replacement supplier for the contracted Bone Meal which you were now unable to supply. Fortunately we were able to obtain supplies from a domestic producer that we could use, but we had to accept material in bags. Our equipment is designed to handle bulk rail cars or bulk trucks. Bagged Bone Meal costs more than bulk and bags have to be handled from the trucks, placed on pallets then on to a fork lift, then via elevator to the third floor. Then to an area where the bags can be opened and dumped into our system. The empty bags then have to be bailed, taken down to our loading and placed in a refuse truck. All this labor is unproductive, costly, and time consuming. The additional cost to us for bagged material and otherwise not required labor, can be conservatively estimated at 16 to 20 dollars a ton or a minimum of 6 to 8 thousand dollars. The enclosed invoice does not specifically itemize this, nor a number of other more or less similar related and substantial charges, one of which would be the cost for additional thousands of miles and the time required in prorated deliveries over and over to the same customers.

Approximately six weeks ago, pressures and tensions built up to such a point between on of our customers and our then head of the shipping department, That words ensued which made it necessary to accept his resignation immediately. The void created has had to be shared since that time, by already overburdened personnel. During all this time, we endeavored to act with the utmost discretion. Had the media, our customers, Stauffer's customers been informed that Stauffer shipped us a car containing 40 tons of Bone Meal in which the possibility existed of Anthrax contamination, there is no telling how much hysteria and panic could have resulted. We readily concede that Stauffer Chemical may have had some unpleasant moments- but Faesy & Besthoff was, and still is, on the "firing line," through absolutely no fault of ours. A corporation such as Stauffer Chemical is so adequately staffed that it can readily accommodate itself, even to the most extended periods of disruptive confusion and chaos. Modest sized corporations such as ours do not have these resources.

In preparing the attached invoice, we have endeavored to be factual, completely fair and reasonable in our charges. Many can be specifically documented. We believe that Stauffer Chemical Company has a real moral obligation to F&B that transcends the actual dollars and cents expense which we have sustained. We have protected the name, the reputation and the business activities of Stauffer Chemical Company and through absolutely no fault of ours, no carelessness, neglect, indifference or omission on our part, we have been subjected to a series of harrowing business experiences. Some of our employees have been with us for 30 years-my son Anthony has devoted his entire business life to F&B- I was on of the founders of this company 54 years ago. Our careers, our families and our future, everything that we had worked and sacrificed for, was Jeopardized

We have attempted as accurately as possible to indicate a very minimum of our costs, past and future. It is our sincere conviction that we are entitled to much more, and we leave it to you to determine – adequately-fairly- and generously.

Very Sincerely Yours,
SILAS BESTHOFF)"

Silas asked for half a million dollars. After much study of his accountings, our company offered him $300,000. He requested a meeting at his office on July 15th to discuss the issue. He requested that neither side bring in lawyers at this meeting. We welcomed that suggestion. As Wyman Taylor had never been to the plant, I suggested he wear a gray suit because of the dust that covered everything in it. I had not been to the plant since a visit that I made when the plant was being washed down with Caustic Soda. I was shocked to enter Sys' office and find it almost dust free and rid of the piles of newspapers and dust covered books. His desk top was clean!

After a few minutes, we got into a discussion on the settlement he was requesting, and Wyman challenged several of the figures. After about a half hour, Sy opened his top desk drawer, took out a Wall Street Journal and read us an article about Dow Chemical settling a multi-million claim after being found guilty in a contamination suit.

Wyman asked Sy if we could be alone for a few minutes, and he suggested we use the Men's room for our meeting. Wyman had been authorized to go up to $400,000 if we felt this would settle the matter. We did not want to go to court. We agreed to offer him $375,000. He accepted our offer, and Wyman told him he would receive Stauffer's check within five days.

I called Sy five days later and Sy confirmed that he had received Stauffer's check. He also told me that his bad luck was continuing. His Cadillac had been stolen the previous night. Two years later we were again supplying him bone meal, I had lunch with him and he told me his Caddy had been found in Lebanon. I asked, "Lebanon, Pa?" "No," he said, "The country of Lebanon." He was not interested in getting the car back as the insurance company had paid his claim on it.

The Houston Plant fired the control chemist and the traffic control manager because they had not observed Stauffer policy regarding shipments of Bone Meal. I continued to be the Marketing Manager of this product until I was promoted to the Food Ingredients Division in 1984. I was thankful I still had my job and Stauffer had insurance to cover all the expenses that resulted from this debacle.

(Editorial observation)

I'm glad none of this got out to the media. In the next few years the chemical industry was rightly chastised with the Love Canal and Bhopal, India disasters, which caused the deaths and illness of many. I'm sure we all remember the anthrax problem we had after

9/11. I can't imagine how this would have affected me and Stauffer Chemical Company if this incident had happened in today's climate with the media feeding frenzies. I'd probably have been on TV a few times having mikes pushed in my face.

Chapter 18

Travel, Track, Traumas

In late February and April of 1977, we took two trips to celebrate Craig's 12th birthday. Over the Winter break we went to Florida. There we visited historic St Augustine, Cape Kennedy, Disney World and Cypress Gardens, and then spent a few days at Uncle Albin's home in Ft Lauderdale. On Spring Break we took a tour of the Mid-Atlantic States and mid- South. We started at Valley Forge and Gettysburg, then to Washington, Monticello, The Great Smokey Mountains, and ended in Kentucky. We saw the horse country, Lincoln's birthplace, and Mammoth Cave. I was glad we made these long driving trips that year, because in the next two years gasoline went from $1.05 to $3.10 a gallon because of the Iran –Iraq war and the forming of OPEC. There was such a shortage of gasoline that many stations ran out, which in turn caused long waiting lines at the stations that had it. What I remember most about that trip was hearing Kenny Rogers singing on our car radio the sad ballad "Lucille." I can hear it now: "In a bar in Toledo across from the depot, on a bar stool she took off her ring— You picked the fine time to leave me, Lucille, four hungry children and a crop in the field." Our family all learned that song.

At work I lost my long time secretary/ assistant, Marie Schwark, when she became pregnant. We worked well together. She called me POP, which was my sign off on the documents that crossed my desk. She kidded me a lot about my initials. On the day she left I gave her one last piece of advice. I told her not to give her child a name or initials that the child would later be kidded about. Imagine my surprise when the birth announcement arrived telling of the birth of Gregory Alan Schwark! I couldn't wait to write her and report my surprise that the bulge she had in her abdomen was just a little gas.

One of my new responsibilities at Stauffer was to interview college graduates who applied for sales jobs. I recall two of the candidates vividly. One was an African- American who had recently graduated from Rutgers. In the middle of the interview I was called away from my office for about 15 minutes. When I returned, she was asleep. In fact, I had to make quite a bit of racket to wake her up. I apologized for being gone longer than I'd expected, and the interview ended favorably as she was very well spoken. The other two interviewers agreed with the Human Relations department assessment of her, and we hired her to be a rep in the northern half of Ohio.

Our Cleveland sales manager reported that during some of the training sessions she nodded off during the meetings. One day the purchasing agent at Parker Rustproofing called me and asked if I'd approve of his secretary shaking her to wake her as she fallen asleep in that company's reception room. After this event, the company sent her for medical testing. It was found that she had narcolepsy, and medication was prescribed. That seemed to work for a while, but a few months later she was terminated when one afternoon she fell asleep at the wheel of her car and ended up sitting on the roof of it in the middle of a farmer's pond. A news photographer got a good picture of her with bemused cattle looking on as the farmer waded in to rescue her. Stauffer got some notoriety because of this, and a number of my customers sent me clippings of the picture.

Grace Ting was born and raised in Manhattan's Chinatown. She had a B.S in chemistry from NYU. She was hired as our first Chinese-American sales representative. After her two- month training program she was assigned to our Houston office. The day she got there I got a call from our sales manager, Wayne Dake. He said, "Paul, don't you like me?" I said, "Why do you say that Wayne? His answered floored me. "Paul, you sent me a lady who has never driven a car!!! Do you know that the average sales rep in her territory drives 25,000 miles a year?" Five people had interviewed her at Stauffer, and we all assumed that every 22 year- old American knew how to drive a car. Grace had two more weeks of training as we sent her to driving school. She became one of our best representatives.

Speaking of training, my oldest son, David, went out for the high school cross-country team in the fall of 1975 in order to get in shape to try out for the basketball team. He made both teams but found out his real gift was running. As our corporate offices were only a couple of miles from the high school, I'd duck out around three o'clock to be at his meets and come back when his event(s) were over. In his junior year he set a new school record for the mile in 4:3I, and the two mile in 9:42. He also was the high jumper and triple jumper on the track team. In his junior year he was All-State in cross- country and ran the two mile race in the State Championships.

Early in January of '78 he gave me his plans for training for the spring track season. Week of 1-2, run a total of 35 miles. That would build up to the week of 3-4, when he'd run 70 miles. He then would taper off to 35 miles a week with an emphasis on building speed. On several occasions I went down to the track with him and he'd run ten four forties in an hour completing each one under a minute. His goal for the year was to get his mile time to 4:20 and the two- mile to 9:20. (I ran the half mile in high school but never trained like he did.) That year I went to most of his track meets at home and away. What a thrill it was for this frustrated athlete to see a son who was a champion. In his junior year the cross- country team took first in Fairfield County and was third in the state meet. I had the opportunity many times to hug him at the finish line.

On a sunny afternoon I was stretched out on a lawn chair reading the *New York Times.* While I read the boys were racing each other around the house. Dave was giving his younger brothers one long side of the house as a head start and still beating them. I finally had enough of his winning and ranking on them and laid out a challenge. I said, "You still can't beat your father in a 40 yard dash." We decided that a clothes line would be the finish line. We got down in a dash stance and asked Glenn to yell, "go". He did and I got the jump on Dave. With about five yards to go, I had the lead by a step. Then I heard and felt my hamstring muscle pop, and I fell in agony on the ground. No one should run a sprint race without warming up, especially when you're in your mid- forties. Older men still think they can do physically what they did in their twenties. Not true! That why it's rare for a professional athlete to compete beyond the age of 40. This rank amateur was on crutches for over a month paying for his macho stupidity!

Dave applied to several universities that had good engineering schools and track programs. He was accepted by Bucknell. In the fall of his senior year, he was projected to be the top high school distance runner in Fairfield County and one of the top three in the state. Unfortunately, he suffered a stress fracture in August. He tried to run a race at Trumbull H.S. but had to drop out when the pain was too great. He and I went under the bleachers of the track and wrapped ourselves in each others arms. We both cried. It was more important that I was with him on that day of terrible and bitter defeat than it was to be at his many victories when we had hugged shedding tears of joy. In order for the fracture to heal properly, Dave did not participate in the spring track season even though he was captain of the team. He was a role model for many of the boys on the track and X-country teams and a number of them got involved in our church youth group because of his exemplary living as a top student and Christian athlete.

In that year Chesebrough- Ponds bought Stauffer Chemical Company. Chesebrough-Ponds was a major player in the food industry, and Stauffer sold many products to that industry so there were good reasons to make the merger. The new management thought we ought to get a bigger share of the bone char business and they wanted me to get to know more of the people in the sugar industry. This resulted in Carolyn and I being invited to the world meeting of the Sugar Producers in London in late June of 1978.This would be my first trip outside of North America so we decided to spend 10 days on vacation in England after the convention concluded.

Our first priority was the sugar convention, which started on a Friday evening with a cocktail party around the swimming pool. We were talking to a number of people who were sugar refiners when a competitor of mine from India came up to me and introduced himself. After a few pleasantries were exchanged he suggested to me that it was time for us to raise the price of bone char and that they would follow our lead. I quickly turned away from him, took Carolyn's arm, and walked away. Carolyn said, "Don't you know that man was talking to you?" I said, "I know that and I also know I don't want to go to jail for engaging in collusion on pricing." In the course of the next few days I met my other competitor, Ian MacDonald, who supplied all the Bone Char to the world's largest sugar refiner, Tate & Lyle, and whose company was a subsidiary of that company. I told Ian of my strange, awkward meeting with our Indian competitor. Ian said he had also been contacted by him with the same proposal. Ian said anti-trust laws in India were usually not observed. For most of the time in the next four days while I attended meetings, Carolyn enjoyed herself as she went on various tours, especially the trip to Harrods and Fortman & Mason.

After the convention ended, we spent six days in London and took a short trip down the Thames to Greenwich. We went to the horse-guards' stable to see the beginning of the changing of the guard and intended to follow them to Buckingham Palace. While filming that spit and polish group, a friendly lady offered to guide us to the best spots to film the pageantry. All along the route she kept asking me if she was pleasing me, which Carolyn found amusing and generous of her. I told Carolyn that this guiding was not being done out of the goodness of her heart and that she would expect a generous tip at the end of her walk with us. We did give her a good tip, and she gratefully accepted it. We then took the double-decker buses all over London and especially enjoyed seeing Westminster Abbey, Wren's masterpiece, St. Paul's Cathedral, Parliament, The British Museum, the Tower of London with the crown jewels, and the National Art and Tate Galleries.

On one of the double-deckers, we were exiting the top deck when I felt the man behind me take my wallet from my pocket. I slowly turned to him and asked him to give my wallet back or I would publicly report his thievery. He denied taking it and said I'd maybe lost it before I got on the bus. I told him I'd taken money from the wallet when I boarded and I felt him take it. I told him I would not let him pass to go down stairs without a struggle. He suggested that I'd possibly dropped it. I looked back up aisle, and sure enough there my wallet was on the floor. I reached around him and picked it up and inspected it. I kept it in my hand until Carolyn and I stepped off the bus. The two pickpockets dashed by us and ran off. I then told Carolyn why they had left in such a hurry.

The last four days of our trip we traveled to Windsor Castle, Oxford, Cambridge, where we heard their magnificent choir practicing, then took some time to learn to drive on the left side of the road. On the way to Stonehenge we got lost. Suddenly a British Bobbie pulled up beside us on his motorcycle and told me I was driving on the Army proving grounds. He very kindly offered to escort me out. We finally did get to Stonehenge. From there we drove to Stratford. In Stratford - on – Avon I stopped a milkmaid who was driving a bicycle and bought a quart of un- homogenized milk. I thoroughly enjoyed reliving my boyhood by drinking the cream off the top of the milk. Then we drove through the Cotswold Hills and down to Bath, then finished the trip touring several famous cathedrals in southern England.

In late August of that year Dave and I loaded the car with his belongings and set out for Bucknell in eastern Pennsylvania, where he would start his university career. He and I talked most of the way about all that we had done together and of our love for each other. I asked him about his goals. He said to get a B.S. degree in structural Civil Engineering, have a 3.0 grade point average, and run on the Track and X-Country teams all four years. At his dorm after unloading and getting him into his room we hugged each other. I shed a few tears and started back on the 200 mile trip back to Connecticut.

Several times on that drive I had to pull off onto the shoulder of Highway 80 as memories of him overcame me and I would start sobbing. I knew my days of strong influence on his life were over. I thanked God for what he had become and the joys and triumphs we had shared. When I got home I was emotionally drained. Since that time I have advised friends to always take someone with them when they drive their first child to the place where they finally have to let them go. It's a tough thing to do!

That fall I was elected to the elder board of our church. I served on the board for 23 years and for six years was board chairman. One of the duties of the elders was to serve communion the first Sunday of the month. On those occasions we would sit on the first row. One Sunday our pastor changed the order of the service in an effort to give a greater emphasis to our communion. He gave a short sermon on the meaning of the bread, and then we distributed that element. Then he gave a short sermon regarding the wine and we distributed it. My son Craig usually sat in the balcony in back of the church with his buddies. In doing that he emulated his father as a teenager and that worried me. At dinner I asked Craig if he had noticed anything different during the worship service. He quickly answered, "Yeah Dad, your bald spot is getting bigger." I was not surprised by that response. Craig was the sarcastic comedian of the family. His teenage friends loved his "coolness." I tolerated it, barely.

We experienced furious storms in 1978 and '79. On February 6,'78, it started snowing. In the next two days we got two feet of it and had drifts of over five feet. Ella Grasso, the governor, closed the state roads to all except emergency vehicles for three days. Then in August of '79 hurricane "Gloria" hit Long Island and our state. We were sent home from work in the morning. I came home to an empty house. Carolyn had gone home to Michigan a few days earlier to care for her mother, who was dying of Pancreatic Cancer. The boys were kept at school instead of being sent home, to avoid possibly coming home to an empty house with no adult present. At the height of the storm, with tree branches coming down, I got our dog, Cindy, a flashlight and a battery- operated radio and crawled under my large roll top desk. The house shook as several large oaks were blown over close to our house.

When it was all over, I went out to survey the damage. Power lines were down, and we were without power for three days. Within ten feet of the house we had a 70 foot high twin- trunk oak so large that I could not encircle either of its trunks with my arms. It was uprooted and fortunately had fallen away from the house. The root ball that came up was as high as the porch deck. If that tree had fallen on our house I don't think the house would have survived. With all the trees that came down on our land and our neighbor's properties, I ended up with a wood pile that was 10 x 40 x 5 feet high. All thanks to "Gloria," that wood warmed our home for several winters.

Chapter 19

Record Times & Rewards

In 1981, I attended the U S Open Tennis tournament for the first time. I was able to get eight tickets for the Friday before Labor Day and six for the Tuesday after Labor Day. I used the Friday tickets to invite local customers to attend, and Tuesdays tickets were bought by friends who were tennis buddies. This was the genesis of an annual three-day tennis party, a major customer relations/entertainment event for Stauffer's customers. I headed up this event for 20 years. We'd fly our customers in on Wednesday, and for those who came early we'd give them a tour of our corporate headquarters. We'd take them to the Trumbull Marriott where we reserved a block of rooms. That evening we'd have a clam and lobster bake. We'd attend the US Open on Thursday. On Friday morning we would play a couple of hours of tennis at the Trumbull Racquet Club after which we'd have lunch. After lunch we'd get those who had flown to N.Y. back to airports.

The company offices were used to get the necessary number of tickets and to arrange flights on either our corporate jets or commercial aircraft to bring our customers to the event. I paid for the rooms and the dinner using my Marriott Visa card. This is the main reason that I had over two million Marriott points when I retired.

We saw all the greats of that era play: Borg, Agassi, McEnroe, Connors, Edberg, Chang, Sampras, Navratilova, Evert, Graf, and the fantasy girlfriend of many male tennis players, Martina Hinges.

I was there when Noah made his famous between the legs shot and witnessed the greatest tennis battle I ever saw between Chang and Edberg. That match went five sets and lasted over four hours. After I retired it became harder to get a ticket for individual days, I'd have to buy a package of tickets, most of which I sold privately to friends. I'd usually go to the Open with several friends on Friday and the Tuesday after Labor Day. Except for those times when there were rain outs, we had great times with our friends watching the top players play the type of tennis we could only dream of playing.

In the eighties I was not only impressed with tennis players but I was also impressed with my sons abilities. Glenn spent most of his years in high school studying and in 1981 graduated from Ludlowe with a grade point average above four due to all the college level classes he took in Math and Science. He was inducted into the National Honor Society and was the recipient of the medals from the following groups: National Merit, Headmasters award, society of Women Engineers, The Parent's Club Mathematics award. With his grades he had no trouble being accepted by the U of North Carolina, where to our great surprise he declared his major to be journalism. In his freshman class was a basketball player named Michael Jordan. Glenn, who loved basketball, was overjoyed when UNC won the NCAA title in March. I was impressed to see on the list of electives that he took were advanced Calculus, Physics, and Classical Greek. Glenn must have inherited most of his brains from his mother. While at North Carolina he became an active member of Campus Crusade for Christ, and this had a large influence on him as he made plans for his career. A few years after he graduated I told Glenn one of his goals should be to live his life so well that at his 25th class reunion, Michael Jordan would say to the alums that he was proud to say that he was a member of Glenn Peterson's class.

After a year at Bucknell, Dave decided to transfer to Virginia Tech. I was able to see him run many races during this time as well as many road races in Connecticut. On the cross country team he was their number 2 or 3 runner. The team won the metro conference twice in the years he ran. He and the team qualified to run in the NCAA division I championship in 1982. The race was run on Indiana University's course in mid November. It was a wet, drizzly day, and part of the course had ankle deep water on it. I quote from the next day's Roanoke newspaper report of the race.

"The Virginia Tech cross country team behind the running of All-American Steve Hetherington capped its best season ever by placing 14th in the NCAA Championship meet in Bloomington, Ind. on Monday. Hetherington placed 21st overall and earned All-America honors for the effort. He covered the 10,000 meter (6.2 miles) in 30:48. Tech's Dave Peterson just missed All- American honors by finishing 57th with a time of 31:33. The Hokies' top five was completed by Steve Pinard (109th), Mark Stickley (111th) and Dave Montgomery (131st)"

Jim Spivey of Indiana U.,who was recognized to be the U.S. top middle distance runner of that era, finished 40th in the race with a total field of 176 runners. Only half of the entrants were US born.

In the spring Dave ran in the Intercollegiate Championship race for the state of Virginia and set a new state record running the 5,000 (3.1 miles) meter race in 14:04. After that race his coach told me that if he'd been able to put Dave's brain and training discipline into Hetherington's body he'd have an Olympian. Dave's best time for the mile was also achieved that year, 4:18. His achievements that year got him an invitation to run in the Penn Relays in the 10,000 meters race. In that race he was lapped twice by a Kenyan and Ethiopian, who ran the race in under 29 minutes. Both were future Olympics champions.

There were two big races in Fairfield County every year. One was on Thanksgiving morning, which Dave ran in every year from 1980 to 1983. Seven to eight hundred runners ran in this five-mile race and Dave won it three of the four times he competed in it. In 1980 he ran it in a record time 24:03. That's a mile pace of about 4:48. The other big race was run on a hilly 10- mile course through Westport and Fairfield. On Labor Day in 1982 he ran in this race with a teammate from Virginia Tech, Steve Pinard, and set a new record of 51:26.

Dave ended his running career when he graduated in 1983 with a double major in civil, structural engineering and political science. He'd run track and field all those years and finished with a grade point average of 3.006. He exceeded his goal by .006. A couple of years after graduation we stopped at an ATM machine. He asked me to guess what his four digit pass was, I guessed his birthday, 0360. "No," he said, "1404." I remembered. Luckily, I'd filmed that race at the U of Virginia and had relived it many times. I hope you'll forgive me for reliving many of the thrills Dave gave me, but I want to thank him for all the joy he's brought me in my life.

In March of 1983, Craig and I drove down to Virginia Tech to see Dave run the 10,000 meter run at the Metro conference indoor championship race. Dave finished third and was disappointed in his performance. It was good enough, however, to be invited to compete in the 10K race at the Penn Relays in Philadelphia. When we got home, Craig went up to his room and Carolyn gave me horrible news. Three of Craig's buddies had been involved in a car accident on Saturday night. One of Craig's best friend, Dave Hoder was killed and another was in a coma. I waited a few minutes to pull myself together before going to him with this heart breaking news. When I told him, Craig said, "Dad if your joking that's not funny." I told him I would not joke about such a thing. Dave Hoder was nearly always with Craig when they went out and he probably would have been in the car if he hadn't gone with me to Virginia Tech. We both knew that. Our trip, one of the few we took by ourselves, may have spared his life.

Craig was asked to give a eulogy at David's funeral. In it he told of several madcap things they had done together. He explained that he had to force himself to tell stories that would make us laugh otherwise he'd scream. He did a great job in doing the eulogy. Craig's friend, Bob Treash, was in a coma for several weeks, after that he had many months of rehab before he left the hospital. Bob never fully recovered, as brain damage affected his speech and motor functions. (Bob was also one of Glenn's best friends.) Years later, Glenn as a pastor, officiated at his wedding.

In June Craig graduated in the last graduation class from Ludlowe H.S. It closed and was consolidated with Warde H. S. on the other side of town. He ran on the track and cross-country team and finished with better than average grades. He was one of the class cutups. Friends at school and church loved him. He was COOL, the life of the party. He also caused his father much concern. It was pretty well known that Craig had led our pastor's son to have his first beer. Not one of his father's proud moments. In the fall I drove Craig to Indiana University where he set out as a business major. By some quirk of fate, in Craig's first year at Indiana, Bobby Knights' Hoosiers won the NCAA basketball tournament. It didn't surprise me when Craig took electives such as the History of Rock Music

In these years we continued to go each January to the Soap & Detergent Association meeting at the Boca Raton Country Club. In 1983, I was elected to be the Chairman for that meeting. What wonderful memories I have of those meetings, especially of the large iced tureens filled with large Shrimp and Stone Crab claws which were set out each afternoon and evening for our snacking.

Each year when the convention concluded we drove down to Ft. Lauderdale to spend a few days with our aunt and uncle. They had a large orange tree that was loaded with fruit. Every day we'd pick 6 to 8 of them, put them in the refrigerator over night and squeeze them in the morning. I've never tasted sweeter orange juice. We remarked that it would be wonderful to bring some juice home to Connecticut. Uncle Albin said we could and gave us two empty 2-liter Pepsi bottles.

On our last day we squeezed enough oranges to give us a gallon of juice and we filled our brownish colored Pepsi bottles. Carolyn put them in her carry on bag. At the airport that afternoon when we got to security the agent asked Carolyn, "What is in the bottles?" Carolyn answered, "Uncle Albin's Orange Juice." The agent's jaw dropped, and his mouth fell open, but he didn't ask any more questions. I'm sure he later told his friends about the orange juice lady.

That next summer my uncle Albin passed away, but my aunt still invited us to come down to spend a week with her and also to visit a cousin of mine who was dying of brain cancer. This was to be our last visit to their beautiful home, When we got to her house, we rang the bell but no one answered. So we walked around to the back of the house and we saw her asleep in a chair. By rapping on the window we roused her. It was good we did because a pan of water on the red hot stove had gone dry. It was sad to see her in such a reduced state. In the family room were 8 to 10 shopping bags of mail that she had received since my uncle had died. With her permission in the next couple days I went through eight months of mail sorting out the personal mail. I sorted Christmas cards in one pile, the checks and financial statements in another. We found 37 checks that totaled over 48 thousand dollars. We had her endorse them and deposited them in her bank account.

My cousin, Larry, was the executor of my aunt's estate but had not been able to help my aunt because of his brain cancer. We went over to his house to see him and give an account of what we had done for her. His brain was badly affected in the motor area so he could not stand without assistance, My cousin Debbie asked if I'd assist him in taking a shower. I did that but it took over an hour to get the job done and I was totally exhausted.

While we were staying with our aunt, Carolyn asked if she could make her some Swedish coffee bread using my aunts' big Kitchen Aid mixer. Auntie said that would be wonderful. Carolyn got up early in the morning to make the bread. In a few minutes she came back to the room in tears saying she had broken the mixer. I went to the kitchen to take a look. The two inch thick metal shaft from the base to the motor had broken off cleanly. Carolyn said it had broken off as soon as she turned it on. It appeared to me that it had been broken off earlier and been glued together by whomever, the cleaning lady, etc. and not reported to my aunt. My aunt had gone out that morning so I took it to a welder to be fixed. He said that the mixer dated from 1936, and was constructed of white metal, a tin based alloy, which could not be welded.

When my aunt came home, a crying Carolyn met my aunt at the door. She asked, "Has something happened to Paul?" "No", Carolyn said, "It's worse than that; I broke your Kitchen Aid!" She led her to see it. My aunt said, "Don't worry, we'll go to Kitchen Aid and get a new one. I still have the lifetime guarantee." She had received it as a wedding present in 1939.

I can't adequately describe the scene that took place at the appliance dealer's store. I carried the two pieces of the mixer in a box (It must have weighed 35- 40 pounds) into the store and laid the two parts on the counter. My aunt, shrunken and stooped by osteoporosis, looked up at the young clerk and handed him the lifetime guarantee. He said that the guarantee did not cover breakage from dropping but only covered breakage from normal usage. To his credit he did not say, Well lady, looking at you I'd say it did last a lifetime. He said that it was the oldest Kitchen Aid he'd ever seen, a G3, which was the third model Kitchen Aid made. He offered her 25% off on a comparable new model. My aunt agreed, and we took it home. When she passed away in June, as she had no children Carolyn got that new Kitchen Aid which has been used many times to make Swedish Limpa Rye bread, Swedish Coffee Bread, and pepparkakor cookies for me, family, and friends.

The day before we were to leave, my aunt had a doctor appointment at ten o'clock which she insisted on driving to. She had two big Cadillac's in the garage, so got in one and sped out of the driveway with tires squealing. At this point in her life her only view of the road was what she could see between the dash board and the top of the steering wheel. At ten o'clock we got a disturbing call from the doctor's office asking if she'd remembered her appointment. We told them she had and was on her way. Ten minutes later I got a call from aunt Elvira saying she'd been in an accident. She was okay but asked me to come get her. This I did as quickly as possible.

The accident happened when my aunt was making a left turn off Hwy.1 where two lanes turned left. She apparently did not see the car on her right that was also turning left. When she got across the intersection, she headed toward the curb and rear ended him. He was an ex-Navy Seabee. His Dodge, with an Ohio license plate, had its back left fender and trunk pushed in quite a bit. Hardly any damage was done to my aunt's Caddy. Astonishingly, she said to all that she didn't know if she'd hit him and thought that she had maybe just gone over the curb. The officer and the ex-Seabee just shook their heads when she said that. Out of my aunts hearing the Seabee used some language that is unprintable about women and especially old women drivers. She was given a ticket. When we got her back home and laid her down, I called my cousin Larry and suggested we might want to talk to our dear aunt about selling her three Cadillac's and taking cabs the rest of her life. He agreed. We went to his house for dessert that night, hoping and praying that she would be willing to discuss the matter.

After a small amount of chit-chat Larry said to our aunt, "I understand you had an auto mishap today." She looked at me directly and said, "Have you been telling tales out of school?" I answered, "Yes, but only because Larry and I are concerned about your welfare. We swore to Uncle Albin we'd take care of you." In the next minutes we told her that we thought it would be wise to leave the driving to someone else for the rest of her life and that she could sell her cars to finance her travels. She said no a dozen times before Larry played his last card. He said, "As your executor I swore to your husband that I would protect you. I'm going to die of cancer within a year and won't be able to protect you then. For my sake, will you give up driving? Tomorrow you may hit a pedestrian you don't see and you could be sued for millions. Do you want to risk that?" Her final answer was, "I will not stop driving."

After that experience, I thought I might be written out of her will. The next day Larry and I decided to call two retired cousins of my aunt to advise them of Aunt Elvira's health and her need of assistance. Fortunately for all of us, Lillian and Virginia Lynch came down and stayed with her the few remaining months of her life. I don't believe she ever drove again. Two months after her 79th birthday she died in her home following a fall in her bathroom. I was honored by my cousins by being asked to give a eulogy for this great lady who was a second mother to me. She and Uncle Albin gave to me and my family of their love and substance, more than I could ever have dreamed of receiving.

When we got home, I had to repack and fly out to Las Vegas for a sales meeting. While I was gone, Carolyn decided to sweep the garage floor of all the wood chips and bark that comes from having a wood stack in the garage. She got a couple of paper shopping bags full and decided to burn them in the wood stove. Just before going to bed she put them in the stove and closed down the damper. After midnight she was awakened when the smoke alarm went off, and she found the house full of smoke. She went downstairs and saw smoke coming out every part of the stove. She opened the draft and then opened the stove door. Both bags that were smoldering burst into flame, and she closed the door and damper.

In a couple of minutes our neighbor, Frank DaSilva, called and asked if we were ok. Carolyn said she was alright, but that she was alone and didn't know how to turn off the smoke alarm. Frank came over in his bath robe and slippers. Carolyn in her long flannel night gown went down in the basement with him to show him where the alarm box was located. After about five minutes Frank found the right wires to disconnect and deactivated the alarm which by this time had awakened most of our neighbors. Frank and Carolyn opened several windows and doors to let the smoke out. After Frank went home, Carolyn heard sirens as police and fire engines came up our street. She turned out all the lights in the house and prayed they would not come up our driveway. Carolyn was very glad they didn't. We talked about that experience many times with the best neighbors we ever had, Frank and Rosalie.

Now with all my sons gone off, I was shy three men- power in handling snow and leaves. We hired a local snow remover to take care of one problem, but the leaves were another matter. I convinced our neighbor across the street to jointly purchase a commercial size leaf blower to ease our removing hundreds of pounds of leaves that covered our lawn and driveway every fall. It was one of the wisest purchases I ever made. It held up for the 17 more falls that we spent in Connecticut.

In my second term as an elder at Black Rock C. C, I was asked by the Chairman of the board, Dave Topazian, to work with another elder, Len Vidmark, to explore starting a branch church in the Danbury area. There were 10-12 families in that area who attended our church every week, even though that meant a round trip of 40 to 50 miles. Most of them were young families, and because of the distance their children could not come down to Fairfield for the many youth activities. The complete details of our work over the next three years could be a book in itself. I'll try to summarize the steps that were taken in starting the new church:

1. We together drew up a mission statement and by-laws that were in agreement with the families concerned and BRCC.
2. A minimum of ten member families would be required to start the church.

3. These families, would agree to give 10% of their income to the new church.
4. BRCC would give them up to 75% of the mutually worked out budget in their first year of operation, 50% the second year, and 25% the third year, by the fourth year they were to be self supporting. By that time, they were to find a pastor of their choice that would also be approved by Black Rock's board of Elders.
5. We agreed to assign our assistant pastor to be their preacher on Sunday and serve them one other day of the week until they found their own pastor.

The search committee entered into an agreement in 1982 to hold their Sunday morning worship service in a ballroom at The Ramada Inn on Rt.84. Half a dozen other rooms were rented for Sunday school and nursery. The first service was held there in the fall of 1982 with approximately 50 in attendance. Within two years they had outgrown that facility and rented a middle school on Sunday. The name of the church, chosen by the members was Grace Fellowship Church. In a few years the church bought property and built a church. They changed its name to Walnut Hills Community Church. For the first two years, Len or I would go up to attend their services on Sunday and met with them on business matters.

The church now meets in a 37,000sq. ft. building which includes a nursery center, youth center and a library. Its membership is near 2,000 and it is the largest protestant church in New England. We were never asked to give them any financial aid. Those dedicated founding members and their families all worked and gave of themselves with God's help to build up and support the church. One of the great ministries the church started in the nineties was an after school program, day care, and activities for busy working families that attracted people to join their fellowship. I was privileged and honored to be chosen by our church to have a part in the start of a great new sister church.

In the summer of 1983, I was promoted to the Food Ingredients Division as Manager of Food Phosphates. When I called Carolyn with the news her first question was, "Does that mean we won't go to the Soap and Detergent convention in Boca next year? I answered, "Yes." I don't think she was very happy that I was promoted!

On my birthday, December 20th 1983, my sons gave me the greatest gift I've ever received. It was a new Thompson Reference Bible in the New International Version. What made it so precious was what they wrote on the fly leaf:

"December 20, 1983,

To our father, who has made the image of God as our heavenly father, legitimate and meaningful, may the words of Proverbs 23:24 prove true three times over."

Love, David, Glenn & Craig

Proverbs 23;24 reads; The father of a righteous man has great joy. He who has a wise son delights in him. Are you surprised that this Bible is my most valuable possession?
David was 23, Glenn 20 and Craig 19.

Chapter 20

Food, Glorious Food

My promotion to manager of food phosphates coincided with that of the retirement of a director of research of Colgate, whom I had worked with in formulating their fluoride toothpaste. Our director of research, Dr. Toy, invited a number of our associates to celebrate at Peng's Restaurant in Manhattan. Art was a personal friend of the owner and chef who was the "inventor" of General Tsao's Chicken. We got to the restaurant at 6:45pm and parked our car in a garage across the street. The garage attendant asked where we were going. When we said Peng's, he said, "Remember we close at 11:30." Twenty were in attendance, 10 each from Colgate and Stauffer. We were directed to a large private dining room. The restaurant described itself as having, "the most unique and exotic Chinese cuisine for the gourmet." After some opening toasts we were seated and given a menu which Art had selected for us. It consisted of ten courses. (1) A plate with four hot appetizers. (2) Minced squab soup (3) Peking duck (4) honeyed Hunan ham (5) half lobster with spicy sauce (6) General Tsao's Chicken (7) crispy whole sea bass (8) abalone with Chinese vegetables (9) jade noodles (10) desserts, crispy pastries. Items 3 through 8 were brought into the room and prepared for serving so we could experience the aroma of each course. With each entrée a special beer or wine was presented with the entrée. By the time we left the restaurant at 11 o'clock, we had sat four hours experiencing what we all agreed was the most memorable meal we'd ever partaken of.

You who know me know that my favorite cooking style is French. My favorite places that serve that type of cooking were "The Blue Fox" in San Francisco and "La Francaise" in Wheeling, Ill. When I went there I usually ordered veal kidney or sweetbreads. I also liked "Ernie's" in San Francisco for their classy red dining room. In New Orleans we'd go to breakfast at Brennan's and end it with Bananas Foster.

In the town of Westport there were two restaurants that hosted many company functions, La Chambord and Manero's. La Chambord's chef could not be surpassed with his Sole Meuniere and for dessert a Grand Marnier soufflé. Manero's was more of a steakhouse, favored by many who liked a liquid lunch. If you ordered a Martini they gave you a shaker containing two or three drinks. Several Stauffer managers went there nearly every day when they were in town, and some were dumb enough to come back to the office under the influence.

In my history of working in Sales and Marketing from the late fifties to the early nineties, I noticed a couple of interesting and significant social changes. In the fifties and sixties there were few women in our management meetings, and the top jobs were held by WWII vets. Most of them were heavy smokers and were proud of their ability to prove how much they could drink. At our meetings, business and social, nearly everyone smoked. In the eighties and nineties at least a quarter of our number were women. Very few of the men or women smoked, and if they had a drink it was a glass of wine. In fact by the time I retired, smoking was banned in our meetings or conference rooms.

One of my strangest dining experiences came in Foxboro, Mass. at the Yankee Peddler Restaurant. A salesman and I had a late lunch on a Friday with a customer. When we left it was after 2pm. When

I went to the coat room to get my hat and coat, my hat was the last one on the rack. The salesman drove to the next appointment. As we sat waiting to meet with the purchasing agent, I noticed that the feather was missing from my hat band. Upon further examination I found that it was not my hat. It was my size, seven and a quarter and it was of grey felt, but it was not a Stetson and had the initials FHG in gold on the hat band, not POP. Inside the inner hat band was a business card. It was the hat of Frank H Gordon of the Diamond Match Corporation whose office was on Lexington Ave in NYC. On Monday morning I called Mr. Gordon and said that our paths had crossed in Foxboro last Friday and that we had swapped hats. I also said I was going to be in the city on Thursday, and I could come by his office and exchange hats.

There was a long period of silence from his end of the line. He finally said, "I lost that hat in Binghamton, NY two years ago and took the only hat that resembled mine which was also seven and a quarter." At the end of our conversation, he asked if I was happy with his hat. I said, "yes." He said, "Well I'm happy with the one I got so I guess it would be best to leave it at that." I agreed, and so ended one of the weirdest experiences of my life. It's a story I've told many times.

One May my boss and I went to the Chemical Specialties Manufacture's Convention in Chicago, which was always held at the Drake Hotel in the middle of May. For you who may not know Chicago, the Drake is on Lake Michigan. If the wind was from the south or west it could be 60 to 70 degrees. If it was blowing from the north or east, off the lake, it could be 35 to 45 degrees at that time of year. We went out one noon for lunch when the wind was from the west, the temperature was 76. When we came out of the restaurant at 3pm, the wind had shifted to the northeast and the temperature was 38.

One year we could not get a hospitality suite at the Drake so we stayed at the Continental a couple of blocks north on Michigan

Avenue. On the last night of the meeting we invited about 20 to dinner at their rooftop restaurant. Before the dinner, we served them drinks and hors d'oeuvres in our hospitality suite. One of the guests was an ex-WAC captain, who was now head of purchasing for a large manufacturer of cleaning compounds. She prided herself in how much she could drink. She had a number of martinis before we went up to eat and was pretty wobbly when we sat down.

We had our soup course and the salad was served. All of a sudden there was a loud crash when she passed out with her face in the salad. The Maitre d' came over with some smelling salts and she revived, she then quickly slurred that she better go to her room. She was too drunk to stand up. Three restaurant workers carried her laid back in her chair to her room. I accompanied them to the room where we opened the covers of her bed and slid her onto it. It had to be one of my most disgusting experiences as a host in what should have been a great evening. I'm glad to say that I never had to do business with her again as she was fired from her job because of her drinking problem. It was my second worst dining experience.

We had several wonderful dinner parties over the years at the Ivanhoe Restaurant. This was a notorious speakeasy during prohibition days and was famous for being one of Babe Ruth's favorite hangouts when the Yankees were in Chicago. They had a room downstairs called the "Catacombs." Over the years I hosted several dinner parties there. It was known for its good German food. When I hosted a dinner I'd let the maitre d' know who we wanted to roast that night. All of the attendees other than the victim would be informed of what would happen, and we asked them all to keep a straight face as long as possible during the proceedings.

After we'd all finished the main course, a waiter would come and take our order for dessert and beverage. As soon as he left, a large red headed, Wagnerian- sized woman wearing a German outfit would come and start clearing our table. She wore a badly food stained apron on which she continually wiped her hands. She'd first take a flat blade and scrape all the crumbs to the vicinity of the victim. When she got to his area, she'd lean over him mussing his hair, and then scrape all the crumbs into his lap. In doing this work she'd knock one or two of his pieces of silverware on the floor. She'd pick them up, swish them around in his water glass, dry them with her dirty apron and place them back carefully in front of him. The coup de grace came when she went around the table picking up all our dinner plates. She'd get six or so and then when she was on the other side of the table, ask him to give her his plate. He'd pick up the plate and stretch it out to her. She'd then put all the plates on his and naturally, they'd all crash down to the table. That usually was enough to break everyone up and nearly always the roastee had as big a laugh as the rest of us. The waitress would always then come over and give him a big kiss on the cheek.

My favorite restaurant for steak in Chicago was George Diamond's, and the rib-eye was my favorite cut. It was a favorite place for athletes. One night Joe Torre and Bob Gibson of the Cardinals had the table next to us, and they were nice enough to give me their autograph. Unfortunately both The Ivanhoe and George Diamond's closed over ten years ago.

Carolyn and I went to Skippers restaurant at the yacht basin in Norwalk one night and were having a nice dinner. In the middle of our main course a busboy came to refill our water glasses. In filling Carolyn's he over filled it and poured some of the water from her overflowing glass back into the pitcher. I shouted loudly because of his action, and he asked why I was upset. The owner came over and asked what was wrong. I told him what the busboy had done and told him we would be leaving and would not be paying the bill. He did not challenge our decision.

One morning at O'Hare Airport, I went in for a bite to eat before getting my flight to New York. The eatery was full of beautiful black people, and only one seat was open at the counter, which I took. I glanced over to my right and there sat Muhammad Ali. After I introduced myself I gave him my ticket envelope which he kindly autographed.

I got a surprise of a different kind at my favorite eating place in Milwaukee, Karl Ratzsch's. I was eating with friends when a man and woman walked in. I immediately recognized him as a friend from high school and college days. I hadn't seen him for over 30 years. We'd both majored in chemistry and he'd gone on for his doctor degree in Geochemistry. I had followed his career and knew he was a professor at the U. of Wisconsin in Milwaukee. I asked my friends to excuse me and walked over to see Bruce. At first he did not recognize me. I'd grown a mustache, lost most of my hair, and put on a lot of weight since we had graduated from college. Finally, he rose and gave me a hug and introduced me to his wife. After a couple of minutes we exchanged addresses, promised to write, and said we hoped to see each other again sometime.

A few days later I got one of the most depressing letters I've ever received. The letter stated that the woman Bruce introduced to me was not his wife, but a woman he hoped to marry when the divorce from his wife of thirty years was finalized. He told me that his father, who was still living, strongly disproved of his lifestyle, but he had decided to go another way from the way he'd been taught when he was growing up. I wrote and told him I was sorry for the embarrassment I'd caused him and would remember him in my prayers. We have had no further communication.

One of the first jobs I had to do when I became marketing manager of the food ingredients division was to renegotiate our contract with Coca Cola for their phosphoric acid requirement. Five% of a cola drink is phosphoric acid, it's what gives it its bite. All cola drinks have it in the formulation, including Pepsi, R.C. Dr. Pepper. Dentists love it for it eats enamel off the teeth and is also loaded with sugar. The night before the meeting I checked into the Omni Hotel, and just then the Chicago Bulls and Michael Jordan also arrived. The lobby became a frenzy of activity, as all, including me, grabbed a piece of paper and lined up to get his autograph.

The following afternoon we had our meeting with Coca Cola's purchasing department and contracts were signed for the next year's business. In the evening we hosted them and their spouses to a dinner at Nicoli's Roof, which sits atop one of Atlanta's hotels. We all enjoyed a wonderful dining experience and had a good time getting to know each other, and then I received a shock when the check arrived! One line of the check charged us for a Swarovski Crystal Ash Tray - $380.00, which about equaled what the charge was for the ten of us for our food and wine. I thought about how I should handle this new experience. I was quite sure my boss would probably not approve of reimbursing me for that amount on my expense account. I finally decided to tell the guests of my problem and asked them to look around and see if we could find the ashtray. To my, and our group's relief, one of the wives found that it was in the side of her chair and put it back on the table. When our waiter came back, I pointed this out to him and he had it taken off the bill, which I then paid.

As we were waiting for the elevator the Maitre d' rushed out and told us that the ash tray had again disappeared. The same women who had found it in her chair, "tee hee'd", took it out of her purse and handed it over. Everyone looked at the ceiling of the elevator as we descended and there were few words spoken as we parted. What a miserable way that was to end a wonderful dinner. I can't imagine the drive home that the thieving wife and her husband had that night. The head of the purchasing department sent me a beautiful letter of thanks for the dinner and apologized for the behavior of one of the wives. I've never had a Coke since then without this event flashing through my mind. That's maybe another reason why I drink Pepsi.

We had a blast of a lunch one noon at a restaurant in New Jersey. Just as we were about to eat our lunch with one of Stauffers' best sales rep, Tim Gugino, and his guest, there was a large pop at the table behind us. Our guest suddenly had blood running down his forehead into his eye- brow. I said, "Ed you're bleeding!" As he wiped it off, he told us to turn around and look at the table behind us. Tim, who was sitting closest to that table had the back of his blue sports jacket covered with red ooze, as were the people at the neighboring table. A spoiled bottle of Catsup had been opened, and the pressure from the gas inside the bottle caused the catsup to spray all over us. The waiters all came over and helped to clean up the mess. They rushed all the suit and sports jackets to a neighborhood cleaner. None of us who were there ever remembered what we had to eat that day, but we've always been careful since that time to open a bottle of restaurant catsup VERY carefully.

In the eighties we became great friends with Gail and Grady Hubbard, who had been moved to Connecticut by GE from North Carolina. We spent a lot of times together as they also had three great children. One Thanksgiving we were invited to their house for turkey dinner. Grady and I decided that the best time to eat would be between the Packers and Cowboys football game. We got to their house at about 3 pm, and we all gathered in the kitchen to watch Grady carve the bird with his new GE electric knife. He took a couple of slices off the breast and blood started to flow from the bird. He stopped as he realized the turkey was not done. He asked Gail how long it had been in the oven. She said three hours, as it should have been for a bird weighing nine pounds. Gail's daughter loudly interjected, "Mama that Turkey is twice as big as our dog and it weighs ten pounds." Gail went to the waste basket and found the ripped green ticket that showed that the turkey weighed nine pounds. However on looking further she found the other half of the ticket with a one on it. The nineteen- pound turkey had some more slices taken off it and they were laid out and put in the new GE microwave. Then with the other dishes which she had prepared very well, we sat down and thanked the Lord for his bountiful provisions for us. Micro-waved turkey is not a winner. But we've never forgotten that wonderful, happy Thanksgiving.

Chapter 21

Change and Threatening Situations

When I took the job as a marketing manager in the food ingredients division, I joined several friends who had worked with me in the industrial division of the company. Dick Kennedy, who headed the division was a good friend, a tennis partner, and as rabid a baseball fan of the Red Sox as I was of the Cubs. We went to quite a few baseball games and also to the US Open Tennis in September. He had the best business mind of any man I ever reported to. (He should have been president of the company. If he had been, I'm sure a number of bad decisions would not have been made in the '80s.) I had a wonderful team to work with, Randy Zigmont, who was my product manager, Bobby Vaughn, who was sales manager, and Debbie Remillard was a wonderful organizer of anything you gave her to do. These people made my job of marketing manager a joy.

I now was marketing manager to many large companies that made foods and beverages: General Mills, Pillsbury, P&G, Duncan Hines, Pepsi Cola, Coca Cola, Kraft Foods, and Borden's to name a few. These firms used phosphates in their products as leavening agents, acidulents, emulsifiers, conditioners, and mineral supplements. It helped me to have worked in the laboratory with these products 25 years earlier.

An enormous mistake was made when our company's president decided we should build a new electric furnace phosphorus plant in

Mexico. He believed that manufacturers would use our phosphorus to make their phosphates. The problem arose when they would not buy our phosphorus. I headed a team that was sent to Mexico to do a market study of phosphate requirements in that country, after our plant was built. We found that the Mexican government had a tie in with the phosphate manufacturers that used a wet process to make phosphoric acid. This acid was used to make phosphates. It did not produce as pure a product as would be made from elemental phosphorus, but it was good enough for the Mexicans, especially when the government had partial ownership of the manufacturer. The government made sure the phosphate manufacturers used their phosphoric acid rather than our phosphorus to make products.

My problem now was how to relate this distressing news to the CEO and the Board of Directors. This was the most frightening business experience I ever had, to tell our CEO and the board that they had made a bad, multi- million dollar decision when they built the electric furnace plant in Mexico because there was little if any market there for elemental phosphorus. A few months later a decision was made to shut down the new plant.

I was asked to be on the plant inspection team in the spring of '84. The day before we were to go to the Houston plant, Wyman Taylor, the head of the industrial division, burst into my office and told me his wife couldn't go on the trip and wondered if Carolyn might want to go. I said "Wyman, I don't even have to call her, I know she would; she loves to travel." I was right, so Carolyn got to be one of the three wives who made that trip. While we worked at the plant the next day, she got a wonderful tour of Houston, including seeing the mansion of Ima and Ura Hogg, Houston's richest ladies who supported much of the fine arts in Houston. She thought the tour was marvelous! That night we had a banquet at the Petroleum Club and the next morning flew home in our largest corporate jet a Grumman G II.

Another perk that I had was to have use of the corporate box seats at Yankee stadium a couple of times a year. This time, instead of taking customers, I invited our pastor, Stan Allaby and his wife to attend the game because his beloved Red Sox were playing that night. Carolyn was not too thrilled about going to a ballgame, but she came along. The most interesting thing she saw that night were car strippers in the south Bronx taking a car apart. It was a close, low score game with the Red Sox behind by a run or two going into the seventh inning. Our pastor, decked out in his Red Sox jersey and cap, stood for the seventh inning stretch. He was called some pretty foul names and certain fans looked liked they might baptize him with beer. I suggested that he sit down, as I didn't want to have someone in the car smelling like a brewery as we rode home. He complied with my request. At the end of the eighth inning, Carolyn asked, "Can we go home?" I said, "If the Red Sox don't tie the score we can leave in a few minutes." They did tie it up and the game went into extra innings. At midnight she again suggested we leave. Marion, our pastor's wife, who also loves the Red Sox informed Carolyn that no one should ever leave a game before it's over. We left Yankee stadium after the 14th inning, 2am, as the game was stopped by curfew. Carolyn did not go to another ballgame with me for 20 years. We went with her brother and his wife in 2007 to see the Grand Rapids White Caps play the Lansing Lug Nuts. She actually seemed to enjoy it.

In the winter of '84, SAS offered a five day trip to Stockholm and Copenhagen at a rock bottom price. Carolyn and I decided to go, it was our first trip to continental Europe. In Stockholm we stayed at the Diplomat hotel. Right across the water was the royal palace. That night we went to the Grand Hotel and met Barbro Stigo for dinner. Barbro is a sister of one of Carolyn's best friends Kristin Trowbridge. The next few days she guided us on a journey that led us all around Stockholm. Since that time we have been to Sweden three more times, in '91, '04 and '06, and Barbro has always been our gracious hostess in Stockholm showing us places that only a Swede would know how to find.

We took the train and ferry to Copenhagen and spent two days there buying our first Royal Copenhagen porcelain figurine. We consumed a terrific fish called Rot Spotta (sp.) and went down to the icy harbor and saw the statue, "Little Mermaid" who was sitting on a cold rock without a stitch of clothes on. Brrrrr!

That fall a company in Japan met with our company to discuss the possibility of buying our technology for the manufacture of dicalcium phosphate. I was asked to be on the negotiating team. Finally, we agreed in principle to sell them the necessary technology. The next step was for them to visit our plant in Chicago Heights and see our plant in operation. We all got our date books out to select a date. One of them suggested December 7th would be the best date for them. One in our group suggested another date might be better because that date brought back memories to another time when we were surprised by an unfriendly visit by Japanese. They got a startled look when that statement was made. Then one of them burst out, "Ah so, December 8th.!" then they all nervously laughed about what that date meant in Japan- US relations.

At our church we developed close friendships with a number of couples and especially with Don and Gloria Treash and Dick and Donna Schneider. Carolyn and Donna had both grown up in farm country and shared many common experiences. Dick, Don, and another friend Keith Tumulty and I played a lot of tennis together. Dick also worked for Stauffer Chemical. In the early '80s he was named General Manager of Stauffer Chemical Australia. He and Donna moved to Sydney. In the spring of 1985 Dick asked that I come to Australia and New Zealand and give a seminar on phosphates, regarding their uses and applications. We set up a date to do this in the month of November. I was given approval to take Carolyn on this trip and tie it to a vacation.

After our seminar in Auckland, we spent a week touring the South and North islands The South Island with Mt. Cook and Milford and Doubtful Sound are three of the most beautiful places on earth. We also came to love the New Zealanders. We did not find the country to be, as the Aussie described, "a country of 10 million sheep, three million of whom believe they're people." From Christchurch we flew to Sydney and stayed with the Schneiders. I gave a seminar to the sales and marketing people and then spent 10 days touring New South Wales and Canberra, where Carolyn had a special friend, Gini, who was a friend from their nursing school days. We got acquainted with koalas, kangaroos and kookaburras.

On our way back to the States we spent the Thanksgiving weekend in Fiji. There I tried to learn to windsurf on a fairly smooth lagoon. After falling many times, into the sail or with the sail on me, I gave that sport the good-bye. My balance and reflexes at 55 were not good enough to learn that sport.

We learned a major lesson on this trip. We saw many tourists in their 60s and 70s who did little but complain about the length of walks or the number of stairs they had to climb. We were 10 to 15 years younger than most of them and had no difficulty getting around, or on or off buses. We decided that in the next ten years we would take as many trips as we could and enjoy seeing the world while we were fit to do it.

Glenn graduated from the University of North Carolina in May of 1985 with a B.A. in journalism, summa cum laude and was inducted into Phi Beta Kappa. While at the university, he was heavily involved with Campus Crusade for Christ, and because of the influence of many, including our youth minister at Black Rock Congregational, he felt God's call to enter seminary and prepare for the ministry. He entered Trinity Seminary in Deerfield, Illinois the following September, to pursue a Master of Divinity degree.

1986 was a good year for Bear fans, as the Bears demolished the New England Patriots in the Super Bowl. I took the train down to NYC to Dave's apartment and with a number of his friends watched THE FRIDGE, Richard Dent, and Ditka win by the lopsided score of 46-10. The next year Carolyn and I took a Caribbean, Super Bowl cruise, and I had the thrill of having my picture taken with Richard Dent giving me a Bear hug.

Several traumatic events occurred in the late eighties, that shocked the world, and one especially affected me. The first was the explosion of the Challenger space shuttle in '86. We were having lunch in the company cafeteria when it was announced that the rocket tanks had blown up shortly after launching and all seven astronauts were dead. The second shock was the melt down of the atomic reactor at the Russians' nuclear power plant in Chernobyl. The radioactive material from that disaster came down all over the Ukraine and Eastern Europe.

In the fall of 1988 an event occurred which made a dramatic change in my life. It was announced in September that Lever Brothers was going to purchase Chesebrough- Ponds and would divest themselves of Stauffer Chemical after the purchase. We in the Stauffer branch of the company did not know what would happen to us.

Several years before, the Stauffer part of the company, had put in an 80- point program for voluntary retirement. The 80 points were your age plus your years of service. I was about to be 57 and had 34 years with the company so I was qualified for this plan with 91 points. Because I did not want to retire, they agreed to sweeten the package. I met with my boss Dick Kennedy and the human resources representatives, and we worked out a retirement package. I was given an immediate raise to $10,270 a month. This would boost my pension as that would be based on my last five year's average salary. Also, I would receive a supplementary package to make up for the fact that I could not get my Social Security until I was 62. I was also to be given my complete medical benefits for my wife and me for up to one million dollars for each of us.

Even with this fairly generous plan I was not ready to retire. We were financing Glenn through seminary, and I had planned to work until I was 62. I loved my job and was in my peak earning years. Carolyn and I both cried when we finally decided there was no choice other than to take the package and retire at the end of 1988. Without knowing what, if anything, would be offered when the merger took place, it left no logical option.

On my last day of work, a Friday, I walked to my office and found the door closed. When I opened it was full of the people I worked with and loved. There were streamers and balloons on the ceiling. They bid me to sit down at my desk. There before me was a Bismarck, a jelly donut. It had been my habit on Friday to go to the cafeteria and get my tea and get an extra treat, usually a Bismarck. They all knew this was my pattern, so on this last day they treated me. They already had their coffee or tea so I did not hesitate to pick up the jelly donut. I turned it to make sure I bit into it where the jelly was injected. When I bit into it, I felt something solid and sour in my mouth. As I extracted it, I found it to be a small dill pickle. My friends exploded into laughter. I looked at Randy Zigmont, my product manager, who was doubled over in laughter. As I was quite sure he was the one behind this prank, I immediately began to think how I could repay him. That opportunity arose when Dick Kennedy told me that there would be a division- wide luncheon for me at Manero's that noon which Dick was hosting.

I asked Debby Remillard to sit at Randy's table, and if he ordered his usual Gin and Tonic she should go to the bartender and make sure they gave him a glass of vinegar on ice with a slice of lemon. Dick proposed the first toast, glasses were raised, and my eyes turned to Randy. As he took his first sip his reflexes caused him to blow the vinegar out of his mouth. I pointed at him and said, as we had said many times before; "the other shoe dropped." What goes around comes around is a true statement. We had a lot of fun at work, and I would miss that camaraderie when I retired.

A few days later the company had a dinner for Marge Tuttie and me; she was also given an 80- point retirement. Many people said nice, flattering things about me. The major present they gave me was a top of the line Minolta SLR camera with an extra wide angle lens and a 70-210 zoom lens. I was especially happy that Carolyn was present.

In January and February I sat home and moped. I did prepare a resume in case someone would contact me and offer a job. In late March, I got the flu and that developed into pneumonia. Amoxicillin was prescribed to treat it, and I was also instructed to eat a lot of yogurt to keep the right balance of bacteria in my digestive tract. I soon came down with the worst diarrhea I've ever had and lost 15 pounds in a week. I went to my G.P. who ran a culture and discovered I had Clostridium Difficile. He prescribed Vancomysin and within a week my digestive tract was functioning normally, but I had lost 20 pounds the hard way. Within another 10 days, I again came down with diarrhea again.

Fortunately for me my great friend Dr. Dave Topazian suggested I get to Dr Brand at Yale who was the top man on the east coast with knowledge on how to treat C. Diff. He set me on a longer course with Vancomysin and that again stopped the diarrhea. During the time I was battling this illness, I lost 30 pounds. I was down to 155 pounds. Toward the end of the prescribed time to be taking the drug, I suddenly developed ringing in my ears. When I called Dr. Brand to report this development, he ordered me to stop taking the Vancomysin. I asked, "Why?" He answered, "Because it's aural toxic and could cause deafness." I stopped taking the drug, and I thank God the diarrhea did not start again, Unfortunately, ever since that time, now twenty four years, I have had ringing in my ears. Dr. Brand said that was a dangerous side effect of the drug, but it was the drug of last resort to stop C Diff. If that hadn't worked, removal of the Colon would have been the only alternative to keep me alive. So the right decision was to risk ringing in the ears versus the alternatives.

For the next couple of months I worked on getting my strength and my lost weight back. Because of this setback I thought it not wise to attend Craig's graduation from Indiana University where he obtained a B S degree in finance. It seems unfair that I did not give Craig more of my time and attention while he was growing up. I have talked to many people who had older siblings and most of them feel that they got the short end of the stick. I ask his forgiveness as he has been especially good to me, and in the last few years we have become closer than we ever were before. After his graduation, he came back to Connecticut and lived with us a couple of years before getting an apartment with a couple of friends. He got a job in a local bank for a few years before joining UPS, Big Brown.

In late May I got a call from Dick Kennedy telling me that a French chemical company, Rhone-Poulanc, had bought the Food Ingredients Division, and he would be head of that division. The French were sending several of their executives over, but none of them knew much about the phosphate part of the business. He then asked if I would consider taking a job as a consultant, who would report directly to him. I would not have to work every day, but when I did they would pay me $400 a day. I accepted the offer immediately!! The first year or two I spent a lot of time working with cheese industry accounts.

In October of 1987 the Tumulty's and we accepted a Mariott offer to come to Hilton Head Island to have a couple of cheap night stays in return for listening to a sales presentation on time shares. We liked the island with its bike riding paths and an abundance of tennis courts. We both had a lot of Marriott points and believed them to be a top grade operation, so we decided to buy a week there starting in 1988. Later that day, after signing the papers, we learned of the largest crash on Wall Street since 1929. We wondered if we'd made a mistake. We had not. Since that time, we have purchased two more weeks at their Grand Ocean Resort and spend three weeks there each fall. 2010 was our twenty- second year to enjoy it. Because two of our sons live within a five hour drive of Hilton Head, it has been a wonderful place for us, them, and our grandchildren to get together. We also have used it as a place to share with our friends while biking, swimming, playing tennis and of course eating. It has been my joy to prepare Swedish pancakes for our guests using Uncle Bunny's recipe. Each year we go at least once to Mrs. Wilkes Boarding House or Paula Deans' in Savannah.

On December 5, 1987, my oldest son David married Linda Peterson in Raleigh, N.C. This worked out well as he worked there for Parson's in the Structural Engineering department. In the next few years he took on the additional responsibility of being president of the North and South Carolina chapter of the Society of Civil Engineers and is now, one of the eight regional governors.

In July of 1988, we took a 10- day trip to Hawaii's Islands of Oahu, Maui and Hawaii. The highlights of our Hawaii trip for me were Pearl Harbor, seeing the gigantic breakers on the north shore of Oahu, on Maui going on a whale- spotting cruise, and on the big island, seeing red hot lava flowing into the Pacific, which created enormous steam clouds and black sand beaches.

We took a three- week trip to the Pacific Northwest and Alaska in 1989, which started and ended in Vancouver. The first two weeks we traveled by car. We drove up the Thompson River canyon to Jasper and then headed south through the Canadian Rockies. My favorite place in the park is Lake Moraine in the valley of the ten peaks. Carolyn enjoyed having high tea in the dining room of the Chateau Lake Louise. From there we spent two nights in Glacier National Park, staying one night at the Hotel on St. Mary's Lake and then driving on the Going to the Sun highway to Lake McDonald. We then headed west to Priest Lake in Idaho and spent a couple of nights with our friends thc Gregg's, who took us on a tour of Spokane and the Grand Coulee Dam. We ended this two-week trip in Vancouver, where we boarded the Westerdam for our cruise to Alaska.

On the first day of our cruise I won a free plane trip for Carolyn and me, over the gigantic Mendenhall Glacier. I won this by making the closest estimate on the miles cruised from Vancouver to Ketchikan. The highlight of that cruise was the day we spent in Glacier Bay watching icebergs crash off into the bay, and in Sitka area seeing hundreds of eagles catching salmon. Upon our return to Vancouver we took a tour of Butchart Gardens in Victoria, which I believe are the most beautiful gardens I have ever seen. Carolyn had to go to the Empress Hotel to have High Tea.

I invited family and friends to a celebration dinner at the Three Bears Restaurant in Westport on 8-16-88. The guests were asked to write their guess as to what was being celebrated. At the close of the main course I opened the envelopes and read their prognostications. Most guessed that I was going to retire from my job, others that we would be moving to a smaller house or another state. Craig was the only one who guessed it, when I saw it I put it aside to read it last. On that date I was married one day longer to Carolyn than I had been to Lee. I gave her a well deserved toast and presented her with a Lady Di ring, a sapphire surrounded by diamonds. She had helped raise our wonderful sons and made me a more outgoing person. I had many more friends because of her unsurpassed, miraculous gift of hospitality, and also many more pounds because of her superb cooking.

On December 20, 1989, Carolyn invited our closest friends to our home to celebrate my sixtieth birthday. That day I had been to the doctor, who found that I again had Prostatitis. As in the past, he prescribed a sulfa drug to treat it. I got home about an hour before the guests were to arrive and took two of the tablets. Within a few minutes I felt tingling in my fingers and toes. I went to the bathroom and saw my face and ears were red and noticed my fingers were swelling. I showed them to Carolyn, and she immediately said she believed I was having an allergic reaction to the sulfa. She called Norwalk Hospital, where she worked, and they said I should get to the emergency room as soon as possible. Fortunately Craig was home, and we got into his car and raced to the hospital which was about 20 minutes away. I felt my trachea was closing up and restricting my breathing. As Craig went through stop signs and red lights with the horn blaring, I gave him an oral last will and testament. I thought I was going to die of asphyxiation. In the last mile of the trip things seemed to stabilize, and when we got to the hospital they laid me on a gurney and gave me a shot of adrenalin. Within ten minutes all the swelling and tingling ceased, and within a half hour they sent me home for my birthday party. The doctor's parting words to me were, "Never take Sulfa again, or you may not survive!" I went home and had a wonderful birthday party with Korv, pickled herring, Limpa rye bread and Swedish cookies, all of which had been made by my precious wife. I started my seventh decade which I look on now, as the best years of my life.

Chapter 22

A Satisfying Career

I worked 34 and a half years and never changed companies, but their names changed from Victor Chemical Works to Stauffer Chemical to Chesebrough-Ponds. From 1952 to 1958 I worked as a chemist in the laboratory. When I moved to technical service and the product development group, I still spent quite a bit of time working on new products and trying new ideas in the laboratory. Finally, when I was hired as a consultant by Rhone-Poulanc from 1989-1991, I again spent a good deal of time with our chemists thinking of and working on new products. Throughout my career, my scientific curiosity and knowledge of phosphates helped me to come up with new products for our company and customers.

I worked with Proctor and Gamble and Colgate in their development of Fluoride toothpastes. You may remember aerosol toothpaste. Quite a bit of research was done by me on that. I think the product failed because too many children found it was fun to spray toothpaste on their siblings and friends. Also, it was fairly difficult to remove from carpets.

In the 70s I spent a major part of my time working with tablet manufactures introducing them to Di-Tab, a granular dicalcium phosphate which is the main ingredient in many vitamin and mineral tablets such as Centrum Silver. I started by taking them five pound samples of the new product and later marketed it to them in rail car quantities.

My main lab work was with detergent manufacturers to develop products that were new or would compete well with their competitor's products. We worked with processed cheese manufacturers in developing different emulsifying salts. I have my name on several patents that Stauffer filed with the US Patent Office. For each of these patents I got one dollar.

What I cherish most from my sales and marketing career were the comments and letters I and my bosses received about me being consistently a man of my word. I took that very seriously, in that it spoke of my and the company's integrity. Early on I took some criticism for not being a guy who enjoyed bar hopping, but not doing that was more than overcome by my being willing to go the second mile with customers to help them be successful. In a number of cases when customers were not able to get on the spot deliveries, I'd go to our plant and throw a few hundred- pound bags of the product they needed in the trunk of my car and deliver it in order to keep them going. I remember one customer who began making cleaning compounds in a cement mixer in his garage from formulations I'd suggested. A couple of times, I put on coveralls and worked with him to make a better product. When he got to the size where he was supplying truckloads of these products, we were his sole supplier of phosphates. I gave the same type of technical assistance to larger customers such as Calgon, Purex, Economics Labs and Kraft's processed cheese plants. I didn't mind getting my hands dirty: in fact, I enjoyed it.

During my career, I had only two bosses whom I did not like. One of them had no skill in human relations and had to have every question answered before I could make a business decision. Sometimes I'd wait until he was out of town and go to the division head with my proposal. Most times he'd say, "It sounds good to me, why don't we try it? Tell him I approve it." He had confidence in my judgment and it made me work even harder to prove my plan was correct.

When my father died in October 1972, no flowers were sent by the company. This was always done if it was requested by the employee's superior. I was humiliated and hurt when none were sent. Flowers had been sent when my mother passed away in '64. After the funeral, my brother and I had a lot to do in going through his things, deciding who would get this and that and meeting with people concerning distribution of the estate. I spent over a week in Chicago. When I returned to my office, in the middle of my desk was a yellow sheet of writing paper. On the paper was scrawled this message; "The Standard Practices Manual allows five days off in the case of the death of an immediate family member. You took seven days," two will be taken from your vacation days." My blood boiled, but my reason prevailed and stopped me from going to his office and letting him have it. He didn't even send a sympathy card! Fortunately for me I soon went to work with Chet Herring as a product manager, he was a good manager, and I enjoyed working for him.

The second boss was in the business of pushing his agenda, not mine. Most times he wanted me to inflate my forecast, even when that forecast was not achievable. A couple of times I gave him the inflated forecast, and gave my product manager my forecast in case I was ever called to account. Once when he ripped me up for our failing to meet the forecast he'd submitted. I showed him my realistic forecast which he had refused. That did not improve our relationship.

I flew over a million miles between 1958 and 2001, and for the most part it was an enjoyable experience. We got full meals on flights of two hours or more, pillows, blankets and current magazines were offered. On longer flights passengers got slipper socks, and eye shades. Now I don't enjoy flying. Because of "Nine-Eleven." Security checks, crowded planes, removal of meals, flight delays, and unhappy airline people have changed that. I'm glad I accumulated a lot of frequent flier miles which enabled us to take dozens of free flights during the last 20 years. I've used all the miles I had on Eastern, TWA, Pan Am US Air, United and Continental. We used nearly all of my American miles when we flew to Buenos Aires and back from Santiago, Chile in January '08. The only miles I have left now are with Delta and American.

Even though I tried to keep in contact with my friends at work, now, after 20 years, most of those friends are gone. My closest friend from those days was Bill Boyd who lived in Connecticut who I'd see every other year. Unfortunately, Bill died on July 2nd of 2008. There are only about half a dozen who I exchange letters with at Christmas. That's sad but true! The friends that I have and stay close to are those I had in my youth, and those I knew in churches I was actively involved with in Chicago, New Jersey, Connecticut and now Florida. Because of this, I'm very glad that I never was married to the company. When I retired, I did not leave the company, rather, it left me. I've never wished I'd spent more time at the office.

The consulting job with Rhone-Poulanc paid very well but was not satisfying as I was out of the action of marketing and sales. In 1989 I earned $80,000 plus for the consulting work I did for them. I had a problem in consulting as I got only the data their sales and marketing people wanted to give me. I was not always getting all the information that was needed to give good counsel. I was out of the loop. I felt some of the information was withheld intentionally by a couple of young MBA's who resented my position. I told Dick Kennedy that if this continued I'd leave rather than give him bad advice.

In 1991 Rhone-Poulanc made a decision to move their headquarters to Cranbury, NJ. They offered to move me if I wanted to work for them. I decided not to take the offer and thus ended my business career. I was 61 years old. Ahead of me were the most fruitful and rewarding days of my life.

All things considered, I'm glad and proud of my business career. Looking back, I'm glad I did not get into a top position which would have demanded being married to the company instead of my wife. I would not have had the time to spend with my wife, sons and the church that I loved. What I did with them will last forever.

Chapter 23

The Golden Years

We have a plaque in our living room that reads:"That only is important which is eternal." Another statement I read that rang true to me was made by the author Steven King at a recent commencement address: "Your legacy is what you pass on to others, the rest is smoke and mirrors."

Lee and I prayed when our boys were young that at least one of them would be called by God into the ministry. Lee did not live to see this happen, but this prayer was answered when Glenn graduated from Trinity Seminary and felt a call to be a missionary in Kenya serving with Africa Inland Mission. It was with a mixture of joy and sadness that we and our church sent him off in the fall of 1990.

With all of our sons now on their own, Carolyn and I had the opportunity to get more involved at Black Rock Congregational Church. I had sung in the choir, served on the mission board, and had been an elder since 1978. Carolyn, with her unsurpassed gift of hospitality, was asked to head up Black Rock's visitor- greeter program. When we joined the church, it had a membership of 700 and a general fund budget of one million dollars. It had a mission fund budget of 100 thousand, and contributed to the support of 12 missionaries or mission organizations.

As the elders interviewed people who desired to become members of the church, many said they were there because Carolyn Peterson had reached out to them when they had come to the church for the first time. This led us to recruit, train, and be part of a team of greeters at the doors of our church. Each Sunday Carolyn would get the cards that visitors turned in and within the next few days gave them a telephone call. She'd tell them we were happy for their visit and invite their questions. At the end of the call, they would be invited to a welcome dinner. We hosted many of these dinners in our home. The dinner consisted of a tossed salad, lasagna and dessert. Our pastor's wife, Jen, would provide the salad, wives of various elders and staff would make the lasagnas, and the host family would provide dessert and beverages. Four to six couples from the church, including Senior Pastor Steve Treash, would be there to get acquainted with the 12 to 18 newcomers. Seventy percent of those who came to the dinners joined the church.

In the fall of 1987, our Christian Education Pastor Doug Christgau, asked me and a young couple, Howard and Sue Hirsch, to start a class for seekers and new Christians. Howard, who came from a Jewish background, had come to faith in Jesus Christ in the days of Woodstock and had been part of that culture. I met him on a men's weekend and I was amazed at his changed life. Doug felt that Howard and I would make a good teaching team for the class. We had many people coming to our church that had no church background or lacked basic knowledge of Christianity. Most of them had many questions that needed answers before they would decide to be followers of Jesus. Many of the women were single, so Susan was needed to counsel and work with them. I had a good knowledge of the Bible and had grown up in a Christian environment, but had not experienced the life many of them had. Some came out of undisciplined lives broken by drugs or alcohol, or had been turned off by religion when they were young.

The class would begin the Sunday after Labor Day and would go through June of the next year. Our first class session was a get acquainted time. We'd ask them to tell as much as they wanted about their background, what had brought them to our church and what they hoped or expected to get out of the class. We said it was important for them not to skip any of the first four classes because each study was based on what had been taught the week before. They should bring a spiral note book, a pen, and a Bible. If they didn't have a Bible, we'd get them one. We recommended that they get a modern translation such as the New International Version. Over the next 14 years, we were surprised that even a couple of atheists and several agnostics began attending. Both atheists dropped out after a couple sessions, but two of the agnostics came to accept Christ's atoning death for them.

Howard Hirsch died of cancer after teaching for a few years. He was a great witness to those in the class on how a Christian triumphs even when he walks in the valley of the shadow of death. After Howard's passing, I was blessed when Steve and Mary Kay Loomis came to join the teaching team. Mary Kay had come to faith in Christ after she and Steve had married, when she attended a Kay Arthur Women's Bible study. At first, Steve did not accept or understand his wife's new "Religious" lifestyle. He was caught up in trying to get to the executive suite of his company. Finally, because of the prayers of many and the persistent witness of several men, he turned his life over to Christ. I co-taught with them for nine years, and along the way they became two of the best friends that Carolyn and I have.

Each September we started our first class teaching who Jesus was and followed that with a lesson on why it was necessary for Jesus to die to atone for the sins of the world. We went back to Genesis to show the origin of sin and the Jewish system of atonement to have their sins forgiven. Using John 3:16 and Ephesians 2:8,9 we taught that God sent his Son to be the perfect sacrifice for our sins, and all we needed to do was accept his atoning death for our own sins in order to be a follower of Jesus Christ, a Christian. Many in the classes had a problem believing they would not have to do good works to achieve salvation. We usually took a couple of weeks to answer many of their questions on this subject. In the lessons following, we went on to discuss the good works we should do as mentioned in Ephesians 2.

Most of the teaching that followed was based on *Navigator's* teaching guides. These lessons were about what we should do to become more like Jesus Christ. These included personal Bible study, prayer, worship, small group Bible study, how to find their spiritual gift(s) that could be used to serve the church and others and which would give them joy and fulfillment.

Many times, especially when we were in our first years of teaching, Pastor Christgau would sit in on the class in case we needed some answers to tough questions. We told the class that no question was a dumb question. We continually encouraged a questioning mind. By answering questions without judgment, the group responded more easily.

A few anecdotes from our years of teaching: In one of the first classes a young lady described her life as a piece of —. I guess she didn't understand that that word was not used in church. She was a single mother who had no clue as to who had fathered her child. Another woman had come to America in the '60s as one of the hundreds of boat people from Cuba. During the first several sessions she cried. She confided to Carolyn several years later that during that time Jesus was washing her with her tears. We started each class with prayer, and we'd ask the class members to give us their prayer requests. One young woman said she was mourning the death of her cat and to pray that God would help her to get through that loss. She also asked if we believed that her cat would be in heaven. Our answer was that we didn't know, but that heaven was a place that God had prepared and was more beautiful than we could ever imagine. A single businesswoman in her mid 30's said she wanted a baby and asked if there was anything in the Bible that forbade artificial insemination. We took a couple of weeks researching that question.

We told her that there was no mention of artificial insemination in the Bible, but that most counselors advised that adoption was a better route to take for a single parent. In the next several years she adopted two Romanian girls.

We had many in the class who were poor or deep in credit card debt. We and some members in our church who were involved in money management, met with them and helped them set up a budget. We had one class where all brought their credit cards and cut up most of them. In another class we had a student who was a Jewish lawyer. Debbie came to the class believing that Jesus hated Jews because they were the instigators of having the Romans crucify him. She was surprised to find out that Jesus was a Jew. She became the best student I ever taught. When I'd read from books of C.S. Lewis or Bonhoeffer, she'd buy that book and read it before the next Sunday.

Some of the class asked that we personally meet with them to help solve specific problems. I had the joy of doing that with several of the men. Steve and Mary Kay did this also. They spent more time than I with many who were going through divorce, separation and child custody matters. We went as protection several times in cases where an abusive spouse had visitation rights only if they were in a public area.

Bill was a young married man who had become a Christian. He was a deputized, licensed bounty hunter and also worked as a repo man. It was a dangerous job, and he was licensed to carry a pistol. He had been involved in several shoot-outs. He and his wife asked us to pray that he would find another occupation or job. In his teen years Bill was beaten by his father, who on one occasion broke a beer bottle on his head. He had only one remembrance of his father telling him he was proud of him. That took place when Bill graduated from his training to be a Marine at Camp Lejeune, N.C. His father had died a few years ago, before Bill had a chance to make peace with him. He had remorse for this and asked me for advice. We made an appointment with our pastor and asked for his counsel. He suggested that Bill write a letter to His father, granting him his forgiveness, telling him he loved him, and asking his father to forgive him. Pastor said we should then go to his father's gravesite and Bill should read the letter aloud. He could then tear the letter to pieces and throw it to the wind. Bill wrote the letter and we went to the cemetery and followed Pastor's instructions. It was amazing to Bill that this action brought him closure in this matter. A few months later Bill started an auto painting business and gave up bounty hunting. He gave me his badge as a token of appreciation for our prayers and guidance.

One Sunday morning Dick Knudsen came to our class and told the class about his rescue from death. He sat in his car in our church parking lot and debated whether he should use the gun under his seat to kill himself or go into the church and meet with Pastor Jim Marshall. He took the latter action, and a couple of hours later came out of the church a changed man as he had accepted Jesus Christ to be his savior. (I later had the joy of discipling him.) When he went home that day his wife saw such a marvelous change in him that she went to church the next day, met with Pastor Jim and she too came into a relationship with Jesus that changed her life.

Over the 14 years that we were privileged to teach in this class, I estimate that 120 to 150 people attended. When I retired the members of the class, past and present, gave me a scrapbook of letters. It is one of my most cherished possessions. When we moved to Florida in 2001, the class was the hardest thing for me to leave. Every Sunday morning when we drove to church, I'd pray for that class and mourn the loss of teaching people who were pressing on to find meaning in life.

In 1989, I went with a group of men to a Tres Dias weekend at a facility for retired nuns. We desired to spend three days in seeking to know God better. It was a wonderful experience. I learned a number of important things about myself as we meditated in silence and received instructions as a group. Over the next few years I was asked to serve on several teams that put on the weekend and served on three teams as a table leader and speaker. Carolyn went on a woman's weekend about six months after mine, and we were happy to be part of a unique, beautiful spiritual experience.

During the 90's, I was the elder representative to the board of missions. I was now able to go on a number of short- term missions projects. In the U.S., I participated on two building projects for Habitat for Humanity on the lower east side of Manhattan. I also went with three teams to the country of Venezuela. In 1990, in the city of Rubio, we put on a roof, poured the floors and put in the electrical system for a six- room school. We went back to Venezuela in '94 and 97, and built two concrete block, 16- bunk cabins for a Christian camp. On a trip to Costa Rica in 1992 our team built a pavilion at a conference center near San Jose. Carolyn went on two of these trips as cook and nurse and made sure we didn't come down with "Montezuma's revenge" by drinking untreated water. Several people who went on these short term trips decided to become involved in missions as a new career. One of them was a VP on the New York Stock Exchange.

My most memorable trip was to Niger, where we spent two weeks building and modernizing a leprosarium with skylights and a new laboratory. At the time Niger, Haiti, and Burkina Faso were vying to be the poorest country in the world. I can only say that I have never been so moved by abject poverty as I was on that trip. We were encouraged by the medical missionaries to take a tour of the hospital and visit the patients and staff. The chief mason, Terry Moore, and I went on the tour one mid afternoon. The ward that we walked through was oppressively hot and what hit both of us was the odor of rotting flesh. In starkly white beds were the black patients missing noses, ears, fingers, and entire hands and feet. A score of nurses, black and white, were ministering to them all in their white uniforms. Most of the nurses had gray or white hair, and we were told by our doctor guide that many of them had spent 25 to 40 years at that hospital. The smells, the heat, and sight of these afflicted patients had its effect on Terry and me, and without being rude we made as quick an exit as we could.

After walking for about a block in silence, we had the courage to look each other in the eye. We turned and bear-hugged as sobs shook our bodies. You'd have to have had a heart of stone not to have reacted as we did. My emotions and thoughts went first to those beautiful nurses. Who gave them the love and compassion to do that job most of their lives? What had I done which in any way compared to their sacrificial love and care? Why was I blessed to have been born in the U.S. and to have had all the good things of life compared to these poor afflicted people? It made me feel unworthy and helpless and at the same time thankful. I didn't sleep much that night.

The most amazing thing that I learned on that trip was from mission staff members, who all expressed that they loved what they did and that this was where they were content to be. My admiration for them is boundless. To be so filled with Jesus' spirit that they had their greatest joy from their ministering goes beyond human understanding. I prayed that some of that Spirit would fall on me. Some of the verses of one of my favorite hymns came to my mind and I prayed them:

> May the mind of Christ my Savior, live in me from day to day,
> By his love and power controlling all I do and say.
> May the peace of God My Father rule my heart in everything,
> that I may be calm to comfort sick and sorrowing.
> May the love of Jesus fill me as the waters fill the sea;
> Him exalting, self abasing, this is victory.

Following the trip to Niger, Doug Christgau and I flew to Brussels and spent about a week visiting missionaries that our church supported who worked in Paris and Vienna. These ministries, though extremely different from Niger, were none the less spiritually enlightening.

The biggest event in the church's calendar was the annual, week-long missions conference. We, as a mission board, worked with Paul Josephson and his group to come up with a theme, build a set and recruit actors to play out the conference theme. One memorable year we had a large whale fabricated that each night disgorged a wet, sea weed-covered Jonah from its yawning mouth. Another year our Sunday worship service was held at the Bridgeport Airport where we gave a Cessna airplane, "The Spirit of Black Rock," to Mission Aviation Fellowship. The money for that plane came from gifts from the congregation. That was a two- year mission project.

Papua New Guinea was emphasized another year. The missionary speaker brought a native with him. During several evening services the native walked on red hot coals. The man had enormous feet with calluses that were about an inch thick. He did not wear shoes. Fortunately for him, the mission conference was held in the Spring. Another year, our Brazilian missionary brought an Indian dart blower with him who planted several darts in the sanctuary's wooden ceiling.

One of our most remembered speakers was Moses Chow, a native Chinese missionary. In his Sunday morning sermon, he recalled an incident on one of his first long steamship trips back to China. He described a Captain's dinner where a pianist had provided the musical background. When the pianist took a short break, a little boy walked to the piano and began playing. Moses described it thus:"a riddle boy went to the priano and started to pray it. He prayed severah short pieces and when he finry got up everybody crapped." I still can't believe that there was no one in the congregation of about 600 who broke out in laughter, but after the service was over that's all people talked of and still remember to this day.

Carolyn had been the best cook and hostess for many years in a cramped kitchen. She was especially handicapped when we hosted visitor dinners of 20-30 people. Our realtor friend, Gail Hubbard, suggested that we modernize and enlarge the kitchen for no other reason than we would get every cent back when we eventually sold the house. We now had a house with three empty bedrooms and dated bath facilities, so we decided to spend money to modernize both the kitchen and bathrooms. We had the kitchen bumped out 4 feet and put in new cabinets and countertops. An oak floor replaced the previous linoleum flooring. In the work area Carolyn had a new bay window, a new sink and a skylight overhead. The total cost for the work was near $48,000.

Two days before we were to pay the builder I received a notice from the post office that they had a registered letter that I had to come to sign for. I went to the post office and got the letter. Once I was in the car I opened it and a check for $43,800 was the first thing I saw. The letter explained that I was the recipient of a court settlement between 42 former employees who were retired in December 1986 from Stauffer/Chesebrough Ponds. I was completely unaware of this case which had been filed by several employees that were retired as I was when Unilever bought Chesebrough. When we were retired we were supposed to get a choice of two options. We were only offered one, and when it was later discovered that we had been cheated the lawsuit was filed and settled in our favor. I couldn't wait to get home to Carolyn and share this wonderful blessing with her. After I showed her the check and the letter, she said that in her view I was blessed because I had agreed to spend a lot of money to give her a new kitchen, and we had been honored by God because we had opened our home to people who were seeking a church home.

Our church continued to grow and that led us to spend a million dollars to provide a larger narthex with a visitor center and more room to meet and greet. We also enlarged and modernized the kitchen and the main ladies' bathroom. Now there were three morning services each Sunday with an average attendance of 1,000.

On one Saturday in January of '96, so much snow fell and drifted that most roads in Fairfield County were closed by up to 7-foot drifts. At ten pm our pastor decided to call the radio stations and ask them to inform the listeners that we were canceling the Sunday worship services. A problem arose when we and about 100 others did not listen to our radios the next morning and showed up for church. The custodians had not gotten the message and had opened up the church. There were about 20 children who had come for Sunday school. I was one of two elders there, and the people asked us to do a worship service. So we did. Carolyn was asked to play the piano for the opening hymn and I offered the opening prayer. We then asked people to share their prayer requests and we prayed for the people mentioned and other items they had requested we pray about. I then read a Psalm, we sang a hymn that someone requested, and then I read Philippians 2: 1-18. I again read verse 3:"Do nothing out of selfish ambition or vain conceit, but in humility consider others better than yourselves." I asked them if they had tried this and how they were doing. After a few minutes, some stood to their feet and gave their thoughts on that subject. We closed with a hymn and went home. During that service, Pastor Steve was called and came to conduct the last two services.

In 1997, we were surprised when a new home was built on the lot in back of us. When the family moved into the house in February of '98, Carolyn, as usual was the first person to go to meet our new neighbor. She met Diane Cooke and offered to prepare a casserole for them for their dinner. When I brought over the dinner that evening Diane was out but I met her husband Paul and their charming eight year old daughter, Barbara. Paul said we'd get together after they returned from a convention in Cancun. He was the new president of Labatt Brewery in the US.

A week later, Carolyn and I were eating breakfast when I saw a person in a pink bathrobe walking around the Cooke's house. I said to Carolyn, "I bet our new neighbor has locked herself out of the house." In a couple of minutes she was walking toward our house. When we greeted her she confirmed that to be the case. We invited her to come into our kitchen. When she looked at the table, it was half covered by visitor cards and there was a Bible on the corner of it.

Carolyn said, "Excuse the mess, but I'm doing work for our church and the Lord." Diane asked, "Are you people believers?" Carolyn said "Yes." Diane said, "I can't believe this, Paul and I prayed that when we moved to the US we'd get Christian neighbors and a good church, and it's happened."

When they came to our church the next Sunday it was elder Sunday and I was one of the elders who gave a testimony about God's goodness that was shown to me when I lost my first wife. Diane used a lot of Kleenex during the service as she sang songs she loved. It was the start of our beautiful friendship with the Cooke's. We were adopted by Barbara to be her US grandparents. She needed that, as her actual Grandparents lived in Canada and New Zealand. They found, as we knew, that Black Rock Congregational Church was the greatest church they'd ever attended. When we moved to Florida in June 2001, the Mission budget of the church was $660,000 and the General Fund budget was $2.1M. The membership of the church was 950, and the church had three morning worship services each Sunday.

Chapter 24

Thrills, Travels & Travails

In the Nineties, Carolyn and I did a lot of traveling. To get started we cashed in Marriott points and took a week trip to Paris and stayed at the Charles De Gaulle Hotel, which was across from the Crazy Horse, less than a block from the Champs Elysees, and two blocks away from the Arc De Triomphe. We visited four churches: Notre Dame first then Sainte Chappelle, which was our favorite. It seems to have no walls, just stained glass windows that made it airy and light. If I could only see only one cathedral, Sainte Chappelle would be it. It's an architectural marvel. Notre Dame is too dark. I went to St Etienne Du Mont, the church in which one of my heroes Blaise Pascal is entombed. It was very light in the church. I sat there for about an hour and read a number of the Pensee's that he had written which had strengthened my belief in God.

On Sunday I took the Metro to Montmarte to visit a cemetery where I saw the gravesites of some of the men whose works have given me great joy; Berlioz, Degas, and Stendhal. I climbed the hill to the Sacre Coeur Cathedral and got a wonderful view of the city. After walking around Montmarte I got on the Metro to return to the hotel where Carolyn and I would meet our friend Peter Cunliffe. He had invited us to go to the Ritz for tea. On that trip I lost my wallet to a master pick-pocket. I was standing, holding on to a bar with one hand and holding my video camera in the other hand. As the train was at a stop with the door open, a tall young man pushed me into a women's lap as he scrambled for the door. As soon as I got off the lady's lap the car door closed and the train started up. I felt for my wallet and it was gone. He had lifted it from a zippered Velcro pocket that was near the knee of my Safari type pants. Several people looking at me realized what had happened and shook their heads and gave me a look of sympathy, but that didn't help me get my wallet back. When I got to the hotel, with the help of the Concierge I reported the theft of my Amex and Visa cards. Fortunately, as a precaution, I had left my Mastercard at the hotel. Just then our friend Pete came up to the desk and he learned of the theft. The concierge advised him that we should go to the police station and report the theft.

On one of the hottest June days on record we walked to the local police station. It was not air conditioned. The policemen behind the counter were all wearing dress blue shirts, ties and billed policeman's hats. They were sweating profusely and mopping their faces with handkerchiefs. The top of their collars were dark blue from absorbing the sweat. Pete asked them in French why they didn't loosen their ties and take off their hats. They answered in Chorus, "Reglement." They told Pete that they could not remove hat and ties in the office until July first.

We were taken by an officer to a private office to make our report. He had an old ribbon type "Royal" typewriter into which he put three forms and carbon papers. He typed with one finger as we answered his questions and advanced the ribbon reel of the typewriter with the index finger of his other hand. Every few minutes he'd take off his hat and mop his face. I wish I could have videotaped this event as it would have rivaled a Keystone Kops movie. We were glad to get out of there after about an hour and a half. The wallet was never recovered, but I was able to replace my American Express card the next morning. We went back to the hotel, picked up Carolyn, and had a late afternoon tea party at the Ritz.

The next morning Pete picked us up and drove us to Monet's home and gardens in Giverney. This was the highlight of the trip for Carolyn. What a beautiful collage of pastel colors everywhere we looked. Late that afternoon Pete drove a few miles south to Chartres, where we toured the great gothic Notre Dame cathedral built in the early thirteenth century. The cathedral is illumined by 25,000 square feet of "Chartres blue" windows. It was called by Rodin the "Acropolis of France." What a glorious day that was!

The next day we took the Metro to Versailles and spent the day walking on the manicured grounds and seeing the Louies' opulent home. We spent another very hot morning touring the Louvre and in the afternoon the smaller museum, l'Orangerie, featuring our favorite artists Monet and Renoir. On another day we went up to the top of the Eiffel tower, toured the Rodin museum, and went to the Invalides to see the tomb of Napoleon. I walked through the Pere-Lachaise Cemetery and saw the grave sites of Rossini, Chopin, Victor Hugo, Faure and Bizet On our last day we took a cruise on the Seine, had dinner with Pete at a west bank sidewalk café, and then Carolyn and I took a romantic night cruise to see the city of lights, a marvelous way to end our trip. In the next few years we went back to Paris several times to again enjoy the city and especially the new Musee d'Orsay.

On trips we made, starting with the 1989 trip to the northwest and Alaska, I took videos, which I then edited and added music and narration about the places we'd seen. I have had great joy doing this and received many compliments from our friends who have relived these trips with us. I have now transferred all these tapes to DVD.

In June of '91 we took our second trip to Scandinavia. We started our trip in Norway, taking a journey called "Norway in a Nutshell." We boarded a train in Oslo and passed through valleys, lake country, and snowy mountains before finally arriving at the town of Flam on Sonjefjord. We then took a several hour cruise on the fjord, and then boarded a bus that wound our way up a hairpin turn road to the Stalheim Hotel. We got one of the most beautiful views on earth. Our room looked out on the Naeroy Valley, which closely resembles the Yosemite Valley. On each side of the hotel, two several hundred foot waterfalls thunder down to the valley below. We slept with the windows open, under a down comforter and were lulled to sleep by the sound of the waterfalls. (Kaiser Wilhelm summered at Stahlheim for 25 consecutive years in the late 1800's, and there is a monument erected at a lookout point, "Kaiser Hoi", where he used to sit for hours.) We spent three nights at the hotel enjoying the Smorgasbord lunch and dinners. There also was a museum on the premises which depicted life in Norway years ago. It also had a sad history as it was a place for R&R for German submarine crew officers in WWII. They were provided with Norwegian girls for their pleasure. Many bore their illegitimate babies. After the war the Norwegian people and government more or less abandoned these unfortunate victims until public outcry forced the government to make recompense.

From there we took the train to Bergen where we saw Stave churches and enjoyed that sea coast town with its open air fish market. We took a tour bus to Greig's home in Trollhagan, then took the train to Oslo where we went to city hall, where the Nobel peace prize is awarded annually. At the Maritime museum we saw Heyerdahl's; Kon Tiki and Amundsen's Fram which he used on his Antarctic expeditions. We then flew to Stockholm just in time to see the raising of the flower bedecked pole on mid-summer day, June 23rd, in Skansen Park. On the longest day of the year we sat watching a parade of Swedes dressed in their various district costumes and then the decorating and erecting of the pole. On that day the high temperature was 48 F with a wind blowing at 20 mph. We had every bit of warm clothing on that we had with us, and still at times we shivered. Our wonderful friend, Barbro, showed us the sights of Stockholm over the next two days. The restored warship, Wasa, which had been taken up from the mud of Stockholm's harbor was the most impressive thing we saw.

One of the main purposes of our trip was to see the areas where my grandparents lived before they emigrated to the U S in the late 1800's. So on Saturday we took a train to Linkoping to get a Hertz car, which we would use to travel in southern Sweden. When we got off the train, we took a cab to the Hertz Agency and found that it was closed for the long Midsummer Day weekend! What could we do? The cab driver suggested we go to the gas station across the street and ask their advice. When we got there the cab driver told the manager of our predicament. Even though he had several customers to attend to, he called the Hertz owner, who fortunately was home. When their conversation ended he told us that the Hertz owner had left our car at another station up the street, and he would take us there in a couple of minutes. He offered us a couple of sodas while he waited on his customers. I offered him a tip, which he refused. We soon were on our way. He had saved us from having our whole schedule upset and a trip possibly ruined. The Swedes are sometimes said to be cold and unfriendly, he was not one of them.

The next day we were in Habo, where we toured the wooden cathedral in which my maternal Grandfather A.F. Anderson was baptized as an infant. In the city of Jonkoping I saw the place where he met and courted my Grandmother Carolyn, "Mussie." We went on to the emigrant institute in Vaxjo, and I got records on my fraternal grandmother Christina, but nothing on my grandfather. The only thing I had was his name, John Eric, and oral history that he had come to Chicago in 1870. We went to Trolle Lunby and saw the count's estate where Christina had worked as a maid before emigrating. We also went to the church where she was baptized in Kristanstad, and then drove to the glass country and saw glass blowers make beautiful crystal objects. We bought a couple of them at Orrefors and Kosta Boda.

To end our two- week tour we took the ferry from Malmo to Denmark, and spent a couple of days in Copenhagen. We were introduced to a wonderful tasting fish, Rot Spota (sp.) and bought several jars and tins of herring to bring home. We also went to Tivoli

Gardens and then to Royal Copenhagen store and bought a figurine to help us remember our trip.

Back home in Connecticut in mid-August, a friend who owned the largest sailboat in Black Rock harbor asked us and two other couples to take a sunset dinner sail on Long Island Sound. His wife had prepared dinner to honor three of our mates who had August birthdays. We got on board and proceeded with a nice breeze filling the sails to head toward NYC. Every thing went well and we proceeded on a tack toward Port Jefferson, Long Island. The food was delicious and enjoyed by all. Nearing sunset we approached a buoy marker and we were told we were halfway to Port Jefferson. Our captain said we'd better turn back to Connecticut, and we did so. Shortly after that the breeze diminished and not long after that the sails were luffing, and it was decided that we should lower the sails and start the diesel engine to get back to Bridgeport. It soon became dark and one of our group suggested we turn on the running lights. An attempt to do so failed. This raised some fears in us as things like ferry's and tugs towing barges would not be able to see us. A couple of the men who knew about boats tried to determine what was wrong with the lights, but to no avail.

We were headed toward Black Rock Harbor with the tall stacks of the Bridgeport Power Station as our guide when all of a sudden the diesel engine started to make a horrible racket. Our host asked George to man the wheel while he dove below deck to investigate our troubled engine. He shouted up to George to turn off the engine. As we slowly drifted where the waves and tide took us we realized we might be out on the sound for some time.

As most of us had dressed lightly, expecting to be home before sunset, the wives especially, started to get chilled. Our captain's wife brought up blankets from below which our wives quickly wrapped around their bodies. She went below to help her husband. Our captain came up finally and announced that it appeared that the cooling water from the sound had been blocked off by sea weeds and the engine had overheated, hence the clattering. We'd have to wait a while until the engine cooled down before he would restart it. We could see by the line up of other lights and the smoke stacks that the tide was moving us further from our safe harbor.

About a half hour passed when he started the engine, but after about 15 minutes it again started banging and he shut it down. At ten o'clock, most of us had expected to be home by this time and tucked in our beds. This was not going to happen. We suggested our host use his boat radio to call the Coast Guard to report our problem. To this he replied that the radio had not worked for some time. As this event happened in the dark ages before everyone carried a cell phone, we were, as they say, up the creek without a paddle. Things got a little tense and our host's wife, I'm sure, was down in the cabin praying for our safety and that there would not be a mutiny among people who had been friends for years. Two of the four men were not retired and had to be at work in a few hours. It got quiet, as no one dared to say anything that would result in ending long time friendships.

Finally, after several times of start ups and shut downs, our host decided to run the engine even though it might mean its ruin, in order for us to get to port. At 3AM, sounding like the African Queen, we finally got to our mooring. Few words were said as we got into our cars and headed home. We got in bed at 4AM. Carolyn and I were never again asked to sail on our friend's boat, and if we had been asked, we'd have turned him down.

In the summer of 1992, we took a three week trip to Austria and Bavaria. We stayed for a week at the Vienna Marriott. It was right across the street from the Stadtpark and the gold statue of Johann Strauss. We went to all the sites associated with my favorite composers: Beethoven, Brahms, Mozart and Schubert. We bought a week pass to use on their wonderful "ring" transportation of streetcars and subway.

On our first Sunday I experienced the most joyful day I've ever had when traveling. In the morning we went to the Hofburgkapelle and heard the Vienna Choirboys sing Schubert's Mass in G. We then went across the palace grounds to the Schatzkammer to tour the palace and see the crown jewels. Then in the afternoon we walked the short distance to the Spanish Riding School and saw the Lipizzaner Horses put on their marvelous show. That evening Carolyn was worn out and stayed home, but I went to the opera and saw a performance of the Merry Widow. What a day! What joy!!

One morning we walked the wonderful pedestrian street, Karntner Strasse, with its street musicians playing music of my favorite composers. At the end of the street is the enormous St. Stevens Cathedral. There I climbed the 344 stairs to the steeple and got a wonderful panorama of the city and looked north to the Vienna Woods. Near the opera house we went into Sacher's and shared a Torte. Carolyn and I went to the "believed" grave site of Mozart and to the main cemetery where Beethoven, Brahms, Schubert and the Strausses are all buried within a few feet of each other. While Carolyn shopped, I visited the home where Schubert was born and homes where he, Brahms, and Beethoven had lived

We took a day and went to see the Hapsburg's answer to Versailles, the Schoenbrunn Park and Palace. We saw around 40 of the 1,400 rooms of the palace. The most beautiful being "the room of a million" which has rosewood paneling framing miniatures which are painted on parchment. At the palace, Mozart played for and astonished the empress Maria Theresa with his talents at the age of six. In a way, she adopted him. In Vienna, in the square in front of the palace, is a statue of Maria with her 16 children. She didn't spend all her time governing! Mozart, as a child, is in the group. Carolyn and I loved the parks and gardens of Vienna, It is my favorite city.

We took the train down to Baden to see our friend Terry Schneider and his family, who minister at a mission for refugees. Most of these refugees, at that time, came from the war going on in the former country of Yugoslavia. There were also refugees from the many civil wars in Africa. We went into Baden and toured the house in which Beethoven wrote most of his Sixth symphony, and enjoyed a concert in the park.

We then headed west toward Salzburg. On the way we stopped at Melk on the Danube and toured the beautiful Baroque Abbey church. The lavish decorations include frescos, gold ornaments and marble. We got to Salzburg anxious and excited to see the birthplace of my favorite composer, Mozart! That evening we went to a concert at the Residence where a string orchestra played several Mozart compositions, one of which he had played there as a young boy. As there were no rooms available in the city we stayed in the suburbs that night and got up early to have a full day to see the city. We parked in a lot a few blocks from the central city and were told we would have to get our car out of the lot by 6:30pm or it would be locked in for the night.

We immediately went to the museum, birthplace, and home, of Mozart. From there we took the funicular up to the Hohensalzburg castle which looms over the city. At eleven o'clock, I told Carolyn that I wanted to take an overview video of the city at noon, when all the churches bells would ring. She decided to go back down on the funicular and do some shopping. I pointed to a small square where people were playing chess on a 60'x60 foot floor. Around the floor people could sit and watch them move the life size figures. I said, "Let's meet there at 1 o'clock," and we parted. I was at that place a few minutes early and sat down to wait for Carolyn. At 2p.m. I was concerned. By 3pm, I was frantic and went to the police station to report a missing wife, gave them her description, and asked them to check the hospitals and other stations concerning her whereabouts. I left my name and told them I would be back by five. In the next hour I walked back to the parking lot to see if she was there. She was not. I left a note on the windshield for her, telling her I was going back to the chess game. I wrote that we had to get the car out of the lot by 6:30, so if she came back and was lost she should wait there.

At 4:30 I went back to the Police station and they had nothing to report on Carolyn Peterson. By this time I was beside myself with fear and dread that something bad had happened to her.

At six I went to the car intending to drive it out by 6:15. In a few minutes I spied her coming toward the lot. I was filled with relief and rage. When we exchanged our first few words I discovered she had the same feelings toward me. We immediately asked the same question: Where have you been? She answered that she had been sitting in the hot sun in the Mozart Plaza for five hours looking at Mozart's statue. She was hot and exhausted. She said I had pointed to the plaza as the place to meet. It did no good to tell her that I'd said to meet at the chess game. We were so spent physically and emotionally that neither of us could eat that night. She said that if she could she'd fly home the next day. I said I didn't understand why she hadn't gone to the police to report a missing husband. Wasn't she concerned about what had happened to me? I never got to see Salzburg well because of "her" mistake. Carolyn then committed a blasphemy by saying that she never wanted to hear Mozart's music again as it would remind her of that horrible day when she sat there in the hot sun looking at his statue. It was the worst day of our marriage! We never again split off from each other without a clear understanding of when and where we were to get back together.

The next day we drove to St. Wolfgang and had a beautiful room at the famous White Horse Inn looking out at the Lake. The sound of silence was broken only by the paddle wheel boats that plied the lake. We needed that. In the next few days we saw the Krimml waterfall which drops 1,250 feet and is the highest in Europe, went to Heiligenblut which has the church that had been seen on thousands of calendars and the village of Hallstatt which sits on a mountainside with houses that look like they're sliding into the lake. Some sit on pilings reaching out into the Lake. We went to Berchtesgaden and took a tour of Hitler's Eagles Nest. After going to Kitzbuhel and Innsbruck, we headed up to Bavaria where we visited many Baroque churches and three of mad Ludwig's castles, and then we went to Munich. The day before we flew home, we went to see the concentration camp at Dachau. It was raining and we added our tears to the rain as we toured the camp where Dietrich Bonhoeffer spent most of his last days before being hung as a martyr for being a patriot. The statement cut into granite as you leave that camp still echoes in me. "Those who forget the past are condemned to repeat it." Santayana

That September my son Glenn married a school teacher he had courted in Kenya. She was Canadian and the wedding was to take place in New Brunswick. As we had never visited the Maritime Provinces we took the opportunity of touring them in the week before the wedding. We drove along the sea cliffs of Nova Scotia, saw the tidal bore come in at the Bay of Fundy and learned much about Bell's inventive genius at his museum. We had a couple of lobster feasts with our friends the Tumulty's, who accompanied us on the trip. Glenn and Wendy were married on a bright crisp day.

In the nineties, as a native Chicagoan, I had the thrill of watching Michael Jordan and the Bulls dominate the NBA. The Bulls would have won eight straight championships if he had not decided to take two years off in the prime of his career to become a mediocre baseball player. I believe he was the greatest athlete of the 20th century. He combined his superb athletic ability with an even greater will to win. In 1994 we also started the "Peterson March Madness Championship", in which we compete every March in picking the winners in the NCAA Basketball tournament. Now the grandchildren are involved in it. A trophy is presented to the winner and their name inscribed on a plaque if they win. You have to be a Peterson to enter the contest.

In September of 1993, we went on a guided trip to Italy. Just minutes before our flight was to leave we learned that we were first time grandparents of Matthew Victor Peterson, who was born to David and Linda in Raleigh N.C.

We started the tour in Milan and took a bus south to the major sites in Venice, Florence, Assisi, Rome, Sorrento, Capri, the Amalfi coast, and ended in Sicily. In Venice, I was walking beside another guy as we walked over the short, narrow, Bridge of Sighs. Just in front of us was a huge woman who spanned the width of the twenty foot long bridge. In the middle of it her beeper went off loudly; beep, beep, beep. My companion turned to me and whispered, "Look out, She's backing up!" We both doubled over in laughter. It's the best-timed joke I've ever experienced.

In Florence we first went to see Michelangelo's *David*. I was moved to tears by the beauty of this masterpiece. In Rome I was also overwhelmed by his fresco's in the Sistine Chapel. I was also maddened because I could not take pictures of it. We were told the Japanese had copyrights on them. (I'm afraid that someone might decide to copyright the Grand Canyon. It's ridiculous!) You could purchase a Fuji VHS of it. We didn't like Rome very much because of the pollution and noise, especially Vespa beep beeps. St Peter's and the coliseum were overwhelming. The other thing we had to look out for was Gypsy children who were excellent pick-pockets. In Italy I got good exercise climbing stairs up to the domes of cathedrals in Milan, Venice, Florence (469 stairs), and at St Peters. For natural beauty you can not beat Sorrento, Capri and the Amalfi Drive that winds down the coast high above the Mediterranean Sea. The town of Positano, where Sofia Loren lives, was especially beautiful. The country side was hilly and covered by neatly kept farms, fruit orchards, Bougainvillea covered walls and vineyards.

We didn't have pizza the entire trip, but had some great meals, especially in Bologna where we had one of the best meals of our life. The other surprise was that we saw very few Mama Mia type women. Most of the women were slim, beautiful and well dressed.

On Sicily we saw the smoking Mt. Etna and many Greek and Roman ruins. Near Palermo we toured a cathedral that had mosaics of over 50 Bible stories. It was overwhelming as was our check- in at the hotel in Palermo where we saw half a dozen men, Mafia, cradling automatic rifles. The monthly meeting was to be held there that night. It's a shame that that was our last glimpse of Italian life.

In February of '94 we went to Puerto Vallarta for a week. I flunked the snorkeling course as I couldn't keep water from filling my mask.

Our major trip that year was to Israel and the Greek islands, and was led by our Pastor Dr. Stan Allaby. It was of value in that it made the Bible stories we'd read over the years live. On Masada we experienced one of the hottest days of our life and later in the afternoon went down and floated in the mineral filled water of the Dead Sea. Our group took communion at the site of "Gordon's Calvary and the tomb. It was a deeply felt spiritual experience. I thought the most beautiful area in Israel was the Sea of Galilee and the towns around it. The thing that was most annoying was the hundreds of children everywhere that pushed us to buy post cards or supposed relics.

On the second part of the trip we flew to Athens and toured Athens and the area of Corinth. From there we took a cruise to the islands of Mykonos, Rhodes and Patmos and then docked in Turkey to visit Ephesus. At the dockside were many kiosks selling LeCoste shirts and Channel #5 at low prices. I cautioned Carolyn not to buy any of it but she had to spend some money. The large size Lacoste shirt shrank so badly that even the Alligator crinkled, and the Channel # 5 was alcohol with a couple of drops of the real stuff in it. (Carolyn donated the perfume and shirt to Goodwill when we got home.) After the ship returned to Athens we toured the Acropolis by day and later viewed it and Mars Hill in the evening.

That fall we went to Raleigh to see Dave's family and our first grandson, Matthew, who now was 13 months old. I was giving him a "horsey back ride" on my shoulders as we walked around the house. I remembered at every door to duck down so that his head would not hit the lintel. I came into the living room where Carolyn and Linda were sitting. When I got close to the center of the room Linda yelled, "Stop! Stop!!" and screamed just as I walked Matthew's forehead into the whirling ceiling fan. Matthew screamed and Linda grabbed him from my shoulders. Fortunately the fan blades were not moving at a high speed and were blunt so the skin was not broken. Grandfathers can have good intentions but can be dangerous!! I'm glad Linda allowed me to touch her boy again.

In March '95 we took a break and flew to Aruba. We stayed on the south side of the Island. The north side of the Island is rocky and windy. Because of the strong trade wind all the trees foliage is on the leeward side of the tree. We took a ride on a submarine that had large windows in the side which enabled us to explore a reef and the sea life.

Our major trip that year was a three- week trip to the Benelux countries, and France and ended in Cologne, Germany. We flew to Amsterdam in late April and rented a car. We got lost several times trying to get to the Marriott hotel where we stayed for a week. We spent a couple of days seeing Amsterdam. The highlights were cruising on the canals, touring Anne Frank's home, and walking through the beautiful Keukenhof Gardens where the tulips and flowering trees were at their peak.

At our first breakfast at our hotel, we each had two demitasse size cups of coffee for which we were charged $16. (No free refills) Carolyn looked around the next morning and discovered they had a coffee urn in the lobby where hotel guests could get coffee free. From then on Carolyn's first action each morning was to go down, and get coffee. One morning she got on the elevator and greeted a couple. Carolyn asked if they were Americans. "Yes," they replied. The ensuing conversation went something like this: "Where?" They answered, "New Jersey." "Where are you from?" Carolyn answered, "Fairfield, Connecticut." The lady said, "I work at a mission with a young man who's from Fairfield." Carolyn asked, "What's the name of the mission?" She answered, "Africa Inland Mission," Carolyn said, "That's our son Glenn." That's Carolyn. If I'd been on the elevator, I'd have looked at the numbers as the elevator descended and never started a new friendship with Tom and Gail Claus. Carolyn invited them to our room to meet Glenn's father. They came to the door just as I was getting out of the shower. I covered myself with a towel and opened the door. I found out in the next few minutes that Tom was a Wheaton graduate and had his doctorate in chemistry. We had more things in common with them than just the mission. We did some touring with them and had dinner with them that night. In the next few years we got to know them better when they moved to Connecticut and joined our church. (How much richer my life has been because of Carolyn's extraordinary friendly nature.)

We saw most of Holland by taking day trips by car out of the city. We went north to the island of Marken and saw the old Holland. At the old Holland, I had the joy of eating a whole fresh herring with onions. We saw most of the people wearing traditional dress and riding bicycles, and salt water surrounded fields and windmills. Going west we visited Corrie Ten Boom's home and clock shop in Haarlem where she and her family ran a way station to help Jews and other refugees escape from Nazi oppression.

On the way to Brugge we stopped at Waterloo to see the field where Napoleon had his final defeat. In Brugge we cruised on the canals and enjoyed the city that is noted for its lace and chocolate. Continuing south we crossed the border into France and visited the famous gothic cathedral at Rouen before arriving at the beaches at Normandy where we spent a couple of days. We walked on the invasion beaches and toured the town of St Mere Eglise, which the 82nd division captured. We toured the museums of D day and the war. I walked on Omaha Beach. It was easy to see the advantage the Germans had in defending the bluffs as the men of the 1st and 29th divisions landed on the beaches below. What a hell that must have been. At the cemetery I sobbed as I read the data on the markers of the men buried there. Most of them were in their late teens or early twenties. While in Normandy we toured Bayeux, where we saw the ancient tapestry which depicts the Battle of Hastings fought in 1066.

One of the main purposes of our trip was to pay tribute to my cousin John Burton Anderson, a B-24 pilot who died when his plane was downed over Germany. His remains are buried in St Avold Cemetery in eastern France. On the way there we visited Reims, and were touring the cathedral when suddenly we heard a men's chorus singing, "Holy, Holy, Holy, Holy is the Lord." It was like being transported to heaven. It turned out that they were a men's chorus from Wales. Outside the church was a monument commemorating Joan of Arc's martyrdom, and then to the technical College where the Germans surrendered on May 8, 1945, VE day. At St. Avold we paid tribute to Burt by placing flowers on his grave. After saying a prayer we went on to Luxembourg.

We found Bastogne and visited the museum containing maps and memorabilia on the Battle of the Bulge, which took place in and around there, then we went to the cemetery where Gen. Patton is buried among his men of the 3rd Army. We drove east to Bonn to visit the Beethoven home, but it was being renovated. Our last stop was Cologne on the mighty Rhine. There we saw the great Cathedral and then flew home.

In '95 and '96 our hearts we gladdened by the arrival of two more grandsons; Joshua born on 6-14-95 to Glenn and Wendy, and Daniel born on 5-9-96 to Dave and Linda. Now we had three, grandsons. What a blessing it was to get these precious gifts from God. We started wondering if we would ever have a granddaughter.

In June of '96 we flew to Switzerland, which to me is the most beautiful country on earth. Its roads are superb and well marked and signed. We also found the people to be friendly and hospitable. We stayed in a couple of hostels and beautifully kept older hotels. In Tolochenaz I saw the beautiful home and grave of my dream girl, Audrey Hepburn, whose body is buried in a nearby church graveyard. We visited several wood carvers, whose houses fly little white flags to denote their occupation. We bought several carvings. There were two highlights on the trip. We stayed at a Bible School in Beatenburg in a large dormitory room. Our balcony faced the Jungfrau massif, with the Jungfrau, Monch, and Eiger mountains directly in front of us. We sat on the balcony many hours watching hang gliders soar up and down the air streams on the mountainsides. The last two days of the trip we went down to Zermatt with its Matterhorn. We stayed on the fourth floor of the Julien Hotel in a room with a balcony that faced the mountain. One of my major regrets is that I didn't come to Switzerland at a younger age and climb the Matterhorn.

We liked Switzerland so much that we decided to go back there again the next year in the company of Don and Gloria Treash and Pete and Jackie Cunliffe. Don was working for Nestle in Vevey, Switzerland and Pete and Jackie lived in a Paris suburb. We flew to Zurich and met Don and Gloria, rented a van, did some touring in the Geneva area, and then were joined by Pete and Jackie. We went back to Beatenburg and did a lot of hiking in the Jungfrau area. On the last part of the trip Pete guided us to several places in the French Alps near Mount Blanc. We had a great meal of cubed steak which we prepared to our liking on a brazier on our table. We had an exciting experience which Pete will never forget. In Paris we went into an underground parking lot and were going down a circular driveway to a lower level when the roof of the van scrapped the roof of the garage, He had to back up the ramp with a stick shift transmission and nearly burned the clutch out. He sweated a lot in getting us out of there.

Our family kept growing, Andrew Peterson was born to Glenn and Wendy on 10-1-97 and Stephanie on 3-12-98 to Dave and Linda. This was a very significant event as there had been 16 males born on my branch of the family tree over the last hundred years and not one female before Stephanie came along. We had been blessed to have Linda and Wendy join our family of men through marriage, and we were very happy when Laura married our youngest son Craig in June of '98 in Youngstown, Ohio.

In the spring of '98 on Mother's Day weekend, a group from our church flew to Bermuda for a few day's which we spent at Willowbnk. We enjoyed motor biking around the island, and swimming at a number of beaches, and watching the sea green waves curl up on the pink sand. One night the guests at the resort were thrilled to hear our group sing "Tuna Casserole."

Carolyn retired from Norwalk Hospital on 1-1-95 and we went south for six weeks. At the generous invitation of my brother Will and his wife Eunice, we spent a week with them and then went to a rented condo in Port Charlotte for the month of March. We repeated this practice for six years. On most years we invited friends and family to join us for a few days. One of those years, while at my brother's, a friend of theirs came up from Naples and invited us all out for dinner at the Green Flash Restaurant. The friend brought a lady friend with him that looked like she'd just been on a shopping spree on Rodeo Drive. We were all dressed casually so she really stood out. I happened to be seated beside her. The waitress came, and as she handed out the menus she announced the "specials." When she came to take the orders the lady placed her order to the waitress in a whisper. She wanted the spinach that came with another dish but the waitress said she could not get that as a side dish. She asked to see the maitre D'. He came and agreed to let her have the spinach. In a few minutes our soup and salads came. Our lady got two desserts. One of them was, a caramel custard. When a number of people commented on that, she said that she had followed the practice of eating desserts first and salads last all her life, as had her two sons. She said desserts curbed the appetite so one would not over eat and also no sweets were in the mouth at the end of the meal to attack one's teeth. As a result no one in her family ever had cavities. When her fillet Mignon came, it was so rare that blood was all over the plate. She ate it quickly and we got to converse. She told me of her membership on the board of the Civic Opera and Chicago Symphony and the Naples Symphony. I told her of my love of classical music and my involvement with choirs. She asked me where we were staying while we were in Florida. When I said Port Charlotte she reacted like I'd said Gary or Newark, and encouraged me, as a man of culture, to find a place in Naples next year.

Several times during the meal she looked me in the face and said I had a striking resemblance to a person she knew but she couldn't pin it down. Near the end of the meal she said, "Eureka! You're a twin of Cardinal Bernardin. (The Cardinal of Chicago who had recently passed away) You have his kind blue eyes, and soft baritone voice. If I put a Cardinal red hat on you, you could pass for him. I have a son who works in Hollywood, and if they ever make a movie of his life I'll suggest you for the role." Wow!! Sad to say friends, the call has never come. When we parted at the end of the evening, Carolyn asked how I'd like to be married to her? I said that I didn't have enough money to even pay for her wardrobe. Besides, I like desserts at the end of the meal.

In July of '99 we traveled to Michigan for Carolyn's family reunion. Her brother Carl allowed us to use his house trailer while we were there. Every morning Carolyn asked me to go immediately to the house to get her first cup of coffee. Carl had an awning over the patio which was attached to the roof of the trailer. It was supported by two aluminum poles opposite each corner of the trailer. One night there was a heavy rain. When I opened the trailer door in the morning, it was blocked by the water-filled awning. I used one of my arms to push up on the pool and finally got enough clearance to squeeze out and jump down. The water I had displaced then flooded back in a wave and in an instant caused the aluminum pole on my side to crack, and come down. The awning full of water hit me and knocked me to the pavement. I fell on my right shoulder and my head hit the pavement. There I lay soaked with water and a bleeding head. Carolyn opened the door and told me that she was very unhappy that I'd broken Carl's awning pole. I restrained myself from saying something nasty back to her.

For weeks I couldn't do anything with my right arm. It was especially painful for me to buckle my seat belt. The doctor reported that I had a slight tear of my rotator cuff and suggested surgery. I declined, but that ended my tennis playing days as I could not serve or hit balls over my head without great pain. I had to settle by watching the greats play that September, when Pete Sampras and Martina Hinges starred at the US Open. It was the nineteenth straight year I'd attended the Open.

Chapter 25

Out with the Old in with the New

As we came to Florida in those years, we debated on where we should spend the remaining years of our life. When Carolyn and I were courting, she told me that she wanted to make that decision, as she'd seen many people who had that decision made for them. Most of those people had ended up in places that were not to their liking. I had wonderful sons, but I knew that it would be far from ideal for me or them if I had to live with them in the last days of my life. We knew that even though we loved Connecticut, taking care of a big house and the upkeep of it would soon be too much for us to handle. We needed to downsize.

We had wonderful friends, the Josephsons and Greggs whose judgment we admired. They had moved to Shell Point Village in Fort Myers, Florida, and were very happy with their decision. In 1996, Paul Josephson asked us to spend a couple of days at Shell Point and see what it offered. We accepted his offer. We liked what we saw, but I was concerned that I would not be happy living with so many OLD people. Carolyn disagreed and said that she felt it would be the right place for her. The next year when we came to Florida we got in contact with Jan Coay, one of Shell Points retirement counselors. We looked at some apartments and got facts and figures from her, and we asked many questions. Over the next few years all our questions were answered. When we attended the ground- breaking ceremony for the Woodlands and saw the plans for the apartments, we decided to buy. The clincher was their offer to guarantee us life care even though we would not move in for a year and a half. Another factor for me was that I was starting to see the residents were not as old as they had looked when we first visited.

Now that we had committed to move in two years we looked through our four bedroom house, full basement, attic, and two car garage, and we realized we'd have to get rid of a lot of stuff. We had boxes in the attic and basement that hadn't been opened since they were put there years before. After we decided what furniture, china, silverware, crystal, appliances, linens, tools we would take, we asked our children and their wives to choose what they wanted of our possessions. We felt that was the wise thing to do as it would prevent possible future squabbles. We decided to take only eight place settings of our fine dinnerware and give the other four settings to the wives who would eventually get the rest. I was deeply disappointed that none of them wanted my 7-foot 4-inch Sailfish that I'd caught in 1973. I blame Carolyn for that because she talked much about it being a wonderful dust collector. (Now, I bet one of my grandsons would love to have it.)

In the attic I had every issue of *National Geographic* since 1944, and in a book case a complete set of the Great Books. These I donated to a school library. In the basement I had 150,000 Baseball and Football cards. I donated 130,000 of them to the Connecticut Children's Hospital. I still have the rest that I need to dispose of before I pass on. From my stamp collection I donated 206,000 used stamps to the Christian and Missionary Alliance. This is only a small part from my lifelong hobby of stamp collecting.

It took us about two years to sort through everything. We threw out a lot, donated much more to charities, and set aside in half the basement what we thought would sell at a tag sale. Carolyn damaged her hips going up and down stairs and in bending and lifting. Even though it was a lot of work, she had a lot of wonderful experiences with her friends in doing it. Monetarily, I think we would have made out just as well if we'd donated all of it and claimed the tax deduction.

One Saturday when I was taking boxes down from the attic and going through them with Carolyn, I opened a large box and found it contained all the paraphernalia of Lee's from our wedding in 1958. There were scrapbooks of the shower, wedding flowers, the cupola from the cake, her gown and the guest registration book. Carolyn said, "I think my parents drove down to Chicago for your wedding. Let me see if they signed the wedding registry." She looked and found the signature Carl & Edith Friske, the next name was Carolyn Friske. She said, "I have no memory of being at your wedding." This saddened me as I thought a single girl would have wished that she was the one marrying me. Fortunately for me, she did get a second chance 15 years later.

In May of 2000 we had two tag sales on Fridays and Saturdays. It rained on both weekends. We had a lot of help, especially from our friends the Munson's. Hal put up many signs giving directions to our house. In April of '01 the house we'd lived in for 29 years sold for $500M more than we had paid for it in 1972.

Pastor Steve Treash insisted that the church give us a reception on the Sunday before we left in honor of the service Carolyn and I had given over 25 years. A book of remembrance was given us which contained letters and pictures. Many kind words were said. Leaving Black Rock Congregational Church and the joyful duties that we had was hard for both of us. As we started looking for a new church in Ft. Myers, our hearts and thoughts were still at Black Rock.

We hired a lady to sell our remaining furnishings and goods and moved to Shell Point Village, 10303 Rosemont Ct. Ft Myers Florida. We moved into a 1,500 square foot apartment on the fifth floor. A few days after we moved in we had a terrific thunder storm one night. At about 3am I awoke and heard the hum of an electric motor and rain beating on the window. I said to myself, "Oh no the sump pump is going and we're getting water in our basement." In a matter of seconds I was fully awake and realized I wasn't in Connecticut any more and no longer had a sump pump or a basement that leaked. I was so glad, that I woke Carolyn up and told her of my experience. We laughed and rejoiced that we would never ever have a leaking basement or home owner worries again.

We tried out a few churches that were recommended. One was too informal and contemporary and the other unfriendly to visitors. The third one was to our liking, Covenant Presbyterian, which had a great choir and organist and the best preacher I have ever heard, Dr. David Swanson. In the days and months ahead we also found him to be a wonderful pastor.

When our good friends, the Cooke's, moved to Belgium, they left us a number of their appliances to sell. They then asked us to use their money to come and visit them in Brussels, and travel with them for a week in Belgium and Prague. Before this invitation came, we had planned to take a river cruise on the Moselle, Rhine, and Saar river and then go to Switzerland and take the Glacier Express trip to St. Moritz. We decided to combine these trips and flew to Brussels in Mid-August.

We were met at the airport by Diane and Barbara. That day the baggage handlers staged a walkout strike so it took us two days to get our luggage delivered to the Cooke's gated home on embassy row. The trip had taken a lot out of Carolyn, and her hips were really bothering her. Paul Cooke rented a wheel chair to enable her to get around on the cobble stone streets of Brussels, Brugge and Maastricht, Holland which we toured in the next few days.

On a weekend we flew to Prague and stayed for several days again using the wheelchair so that Carolyn could see the castles, churches and especially the Swarovski Crystal store where she bought a Garnet ring. I was able to get five tickets for us to attend a performance of Don Giovanni in the opera house where Mozart conducted its first performance in 1780. We all enjoyed it Barbara especially as it was the first opera she'd ever attended. Of great interest to me was the monument in the main square of the city that commemorates the martyrdom of John Hus, who was burned at the stake in 1415. We flew back to Brussels where Paul and Diane gave us royal treatment, taking us to restaurants where I had veal kidney and sweetbreads, dishes not often on the menu in the US. They also took us to the American Club, where Carolyn and I had our first Swedish massage. In the main square, which was brightly lit at night we enjoyed hearing a number of musicians perform in solo and small groups. One afternoon Carolyn taught Barbara how to make a great apple pie. Diane was kind and got me some herring that I had for lunch on a couple of days. In the evening Barbara entertained us by singing the Yentl song from "*Fiddler on the Roof*"

On the last weekend in August we said goodbye to the Cooke's at the railroad station, where we got a train to Trier, Germany, That evening we got on our river cruise boat and began our one week cruise on rivers of Germany. On the boat were 88 Germans, ten Americans and two English ladies. We stopped at least once each day to tour castles, museums or to tour a city. On several evenings when docked, wineries were visited and wines tasted. On the Moselle and Main rivers we went through 6-8 locks. On the Rhine we passed the Lorelei rock on which many ships and their sailors had perished. We sang the Lorelei song in German as we passed it. In the city of Mainz we spent several hours in the Gutenberg Museum and saw his movable type press. It was demonstrated and a printed page was produced. (I believe this invention was the most important invention in the last millennium, in that it mass produced and disseminated, on paper, knowledge to the common man.) I would have liked to have spent a half day at that museum. The largest city we visited was Frankfurt, that was reduced to rubble by bombing in WW11. Most of the historic area was rebuilt brick by brick and around it is a very modern sky-scraped city. There we toured the home of the great German writer, Goethe. The cruise ended in Wurzburg. We disembarked, rented a car and drove south to the walled medieval city of Rothenberg for the weekend.

Our timing could not have been better as they were having a folk heritage festival. On that weekend we walked that beautiful city in which no vehicular traffic is allowed. Cannons were fired down the street and many Bratwursts were consumed by us and the people. There was a great fireworks show at night that we watched from our window. We saw many families with beautiful blue-eyed, blonde children. A blacksmith had set up a forge where he hammered out several swords and pikes. At one point I came upon a clarinetist clad in lederhosen, sandals, and a Boston Red Sox cap, playing one of my favorite pieces of music the adagio movement of Mozart's Clarinet Concerto in A. It was an out of this world experience!

We got in our car and drove to Zermatt, Switzerland where we spent one afternoon, again looking, from the balcony of the Julien Hotel at the Matterhorn. The next morning we boarded the "Glacier Express," which wound its way along river valleys, on the sides of mountains, and through many tunnels to the city of St. Moritz. The scenery was spectacular, and the sky blue the whole trip. The railroad is a masterpiece of engineering. What a beautiful country is Switzerland. The Swiss say that when God created the earth, when he was finished he kissed the area which is now their homeland. It is surely the most beautiful country that I've ever seen!

At St. Moritz we rented a car and drove down to Lugano with its lake and then to Lake Como. We stayed two nights in a hotel on the edge of Lake Lugano. A great place we visited was Swiss-miniatur, a model of Switzerland built on a scale of 1 to 25. It included buildings, trains, boats, airports, and cable cars, all running. It was a joy for a 71 year old boy to see. On September 11th we set out for Zurich. On the way we stopped at the beautiful little town of Appenzell, and finally arrived at the Movenpick hotel at the airport around 3 pm. We were to fly home the next morning.

When I walked into the lobby, it was filled with wide-eyed people looking at the TV showing one of New York's twin towers that was on fire. When I asked a man what had happened, he said a jet passenger plane had flown into it. He didn't know how that could have happened as it is far from the airports. As we watched, another jet came from the right and hit the other tower. We suddenly knew that these were not accidents but deliberate acts. By the time we went to bed we knew that the U.S. had been attacked by terrorists, and that until the situation could be stabilized there would be no flights landing in the US for a while.

I called the front desk and was assured that we could have our room for another night. I took the shuttle to the terminal to talk to American Airlines as their phone lines were all busy. I got my tickets exchanged for a flight the next day, the 13th, but they could give me no assurance that they would be able to fly. Chaos reigned at the airport. I went back to the hotel and waited for good news; none came. The next day I went back to the terminal, got in line, and was told they were not going to change any more tickets until the government ok'd them to fly. They had no idea how long it might take to get that clearance. If the terminal was bad the day before, it was now bedlam.

Late that afternoon when I came back to the hotel, for the first time in my life my hands were shaking, I was a nervous wreck. Fortunately for us, we had left our itinerary with Diane Cooke. That night she called. After a few minutes of talking with me she knew I was a wreck. She told me what she and Paul were hearing from the US embassy. Then said some of the most beautiful words I've ever heard. "Paul, you know where you have a home. Why don't you and Carolyn get on a train and come home to Brussels?" We were overwhelmed by their wonderful offer and took the train the next evening to Brussels. The Cooke family was at the station to welcome us home with hugs and kisses. We were to stay with them for 10 more days, in which time Paul Cooke, with his connections, was able to get us on a flight back to the US. On Sunday we went with them to the American Church and had a blessed time of worship with other Americans. We shared in songs, prayer and communion with others who were going through the same anxiety that we were experiencing. Belgian National TV was there and picked me out to interview. That interview was on the TV that night.

During those days in Belgium, we were told by the embassy to keep a low profile. The Cooke's were advised to take all stickers or I.D's off their cars that might let enemies know we were Americans. We had our tickets changed to fly home on the 23rd. When we landed in the U.S. everyone cheered as we touched down. We arrived home in Ft. Myers at midnight on September 23rd.

Before we had left on our trip, Carolyn had scheduled hip replacement surgery for November. She was now using a cane to get around. When we went shopping, she used a motorized cart to get around. When we went to church Dr. Swanson noticed her on a cane, and I told him of her upcoming hip surgery. He asked me to let him know when the surgery was scheduled. As we were not members of the church, which had over 1,500 members, I did not think it was right to call on his services.

A couple of weeks later, on Thursday, we were called and told of Carolyn's sister in-law's death in Grand Rapids. The funeral was to be on Saturday morning. We got tickets and flew up to Chicago. There we were to get a mid- afternoon flight to Grand Rapids. When we started on our approach to O'Hare, the pilot told us to make sure we were buckled up tight, because due to extremely strong winds we might have a rough landing. The four- engine plane bounced as we were coming in to land. I said to Carolyn, "If it's this rough on a big plane I don't look forward to a small jet flight to Grand Rapids." We got into the terminal and went to the gate for our next flight and found the boarding area jammed with people as the two previous flights scheduled for noon and two had been cancelled because of high winds in Chicago and Grand Rapids. All the people there were hoping to get on the next plane that would be cleared to fly. The agent told us there was only a thirty percent chance the 4 pm flight would leave and that would be the last flight of the day. The high winds were not expected to diminish before 6 pm.

I said to Carolyn that we would not be able to make the viewing that night, which we had hoped to do. If we missed the last flight at 8 pm we would miss the memorial service on Saturday morning. I told her that we ought to rent a car and drive to Grand Rapids that evening. She agreed to that plan, and I left for the rental car area to try to rent a car. While I was gone a middle-aged man and a younger woman, who had heard us talking, asked Carolyn if they might ride with us if I got a car. She said that she thought I would be agreeable to that. When I came back, the 4 pm flight had been cancelled and we decided to drive to Grand Rapids with two strangers.

We got on 294 and headed for Michigan. We agreed to stop at the last oasis before Indiana and get a Big Mac supper. Our passengers insisted on paying for our meal. During the next several hours of our trip we exchanged life stories and learned much about each other. The young wife was going to a basket weaving convention at the Amway Hotel, and the middle- aged man was returning for his mother's funeral. She lived in Dallas; he in Ft Myers Beach, Florida. During our trip they both used their cell phones to call their spouses and told them where they were and what they planned to do. The young woman's husband, from what I gathered, was not too happy that she had chosen to drive with strangers. The man told his wife where he was, and that the two people giving him a ride had not tried to extort money or rob him so he felt he would arrive safely in Grand Rapids. We arrived in Grand Rapids at about 10 pm and dropped the lady at the Amway Hotel; we then took him to the airport where he had his truck. As we dropped them off, they offered us money to pay their share of the trip, but we refused them. The next day when I turned the car in I found $80 in the rental agreement. The bill was only $62 so they were more than generous to us when we had assisted them in getting to their destination. Do unto others as you would have them do unto you, works.

After Colleen's memorial service, Carolyn suggested to her brother that he might take her great friend Nellie Barr out for dinner some night. They were married in February 2003. I got a new sister-in-law who had been on the beach at Pentwater with Carolyn when we first got acquainted in 1973.

When we got home, Carolyn scheduled her hip surgery for the day before Thanksgiving. We checked into the hospital at 5 am. As we walked into the pre-op waiting room, there was Dr. Swanson, to give her words of assurance and offer a prayer to God for a successful surgery. That action of David's made it easy for us to decide which church we would join. On the day after Thanksgiving when I came into her room, there he was at her bedside visiting with her. What an extra-ordinary servant of God!

After several days at the hospital, Carolyn came back to Shell Point for her recovery and physical therapy. I had to fend for myself for a couple of weeks. I did not enjoy my cooking, doing shopping or the laundry. Fortunately, a few friends dropped off casseroles to sustain me. Carolyn had bought six pairs of extra-large panties that would fit over her surgical dressing. After a few days she gave me four of them to launder. She had fears that I would put them in a dryer that was too hot and for too long as that would shrink them. I was instructed to dry them at low heat and to take them out before they were completely dry. I was then to let them air dry by hanging them up on the dresser or door knobs. When I came the next day with her clean laundry she took them out of the plastic bag and inspected each item. There was another lady patient in the room and her husband was visiting her. Carolyn suddenly exclaimed, "I gave you four panties, there are only two here!! Where are the other ones?" I said, "I don't know." She told me I'd better find them. Her room mate's husband sided with me when he said; "If you had given him four and he came back with five then you'd have something to be upset about." When I went home I found the other two hanging on a door knob.

Carolyn had her other hip replaced in April of 2002. For that second surgery we had to report at pre-op at 7am. Once again Pastor Swanson was there to meet and pray with us before she went into surgery. Two years later when we were members of the church he asked me to be a candidate to serve on the Elder Board. How could I say no to his request? A couple of years later I agreed to lead a men's Bible study group, and also joined the choir. I admired Carolyn's determination to do all the exercises so that her recovery went fast, and she was soon taking her morning walks at a good pace.

When I came to Shell Point I got a computer and hired a tutor to teach me to use it. The first task I took on was going through 3,000 slides of family and trips. I got rid of about a third of them and edited many of them by cropping and then putting them on disc and making prints of many of them. I went through all my photographs and updated my photo albums. The other project I pursued was getting all the information I could on my forbearers and have now traced my ancestry back to 1800. All my Swedish ancestors who came from Sweden in the late 1800's were former soldiers, farmers or maids.

In 2004 we took a trip to Norway, Sweden, Finland and the St. Petersburg area of Russia. In Norway we again went to Stalheim with our friends, Don and Gloria Treash. Then we took a ship up the Norwegian coast all the way to Kirkenes, which is right across from Mermansk, Russia, 72 degrees north of the equator. For three days we never saw a sunset. Because of the warming effect of the gulf stream, we saw strawberries growing in Tromso, Norway. We flew back down to Oslo, stayed there a day and then flew to Stockholm. We spent a couple of days there before parting. Carolyn and I took an overnight ferry to Helsinki and then a train to St Petersburg. After seeing the Hermitage and Catherine the Great's enormous "summer cottage," it was easy to understand why the Russian people finally had enough and threw out the Tsars. It's too bad they didn't have a better option than Communism under Lenin and Stalin.

Since my rotator cuff was injured in the late nineties I have not participated in sports so have found it helpful to work out at Shell Points fitness center in order to try to maintain muscle tone and a healthy heart. This has also helped me burn off calories in order to keep my weight in check.

I have found this especially good in keeping my waistline from getting more than 40 inches and keeping my weight under 200 pounds on my 5'10 frame. I dimly remember back in the sixties when I had a 30 inch waist, was a quarter inch short of 6 feet tall, and weighed 155lbs

I was quite proud to get my weight up on the abs and back machine to 125 pounds. One day as I pushed back I over did it and got a severe pain in my lower back. When I went to Dr Hicks the next day she asked how much weight I was using. She said very loudly, "Paul, you're an old man. You'll never be a Charles Atlas, don't go over 75 pounds." I was properly rebuked, but I think half the floor heard her rebuke and gave me smirky smiles as I exited the examining room.

During the last few years two beautiful grandsons were born to Craig and Laura, Anders in May of '02 and Mathias in June of '04. We are rich to have three wonderful sons, their wives, and seven grandchildren. I pray that in the days I have left I will be a good grandfather and example for them.

Chapter 26

The Homestretch

I am now in the eighth inning of my life, but that does not mean I'm not ready to start new projects or plan for, or have dreams for, the future. In the 90s I started a new hobby before we moved from Connecticut, the collecting of un-circulated 50- state quarters. Starting in 1999 the US Mint issued five state quarters each year. In Connecticut I had accounts at two banks. At each bank I had a friendly teller who would put aside two rolls of quarters as each new quarter was issued. Fortunately when we moved to Ft. Myers, I found two banks where a teller did the same for me. This program ended in 2008, but the mint knows how to get more income and issued six more in 2009 for six territories. I've been able to supply my grandchildren with the ones they've missed. This has given them and me joy.

At Shell Point I served three years on the Fine Arts committee, which advises regarding artists we should try to bring to our community to perform. In the first years I showed videos and DVDs of the trips Carolyn and I have taken., and I present Movies or DVD's of concerts on one Sunday of each month from October through June. These were presented in our surround sound Grand Cypress Room. We invited our audience to give suggestions regarding what they wanted to hear. I now show classic movies, made in the 1940's to 2000, that our older audiences like.

At our church, I was asked to serve as an elder. I also started a early morning study group at a local Perkins restaurant. We met at 7am for prayer and study of the Bible or Christian classics of C.S. Lewis, and then had breakfast at 8am. I resumed singing in the choir when my term as a serving elder ended in 2006. I enjoy singing under director, Phil Chandler, and organist Claire Fasse.

In 2002, we decided to go north for two months during the summer months. We have alternated traveling to New England on the even numbered years and staying in Wisconsin and Michigan in the odd numbered years. We spent most of our time with friends in Connecticut and then two weeks at a cottage on Lake Annabessacook, which is east of Augusta, Me. This enabled us to spend time with Glenn's family, whom we see less than Dave's and Craig's family who live in North Carolina and Georgia. When we go to the Midwest, we spend a few days in the Chicago area seeing old friends and visiting my hometown. Then we go up to Door County and stay in Ephraim with a beautiful view of Lake Michigan. This area is Scandinavian heaven for Swedish descendents like Carolyn and me. It also helps that we have lifelong friends there, Bill and Betty Peterson. While in Ephriam we eat a lot of Whitefish and go to a couple of fish boils. I also consume a lot of pickled herring. I do a lot of reading and work on Sudoku, crossword and jigsaw puzzles. After two weeks there we take the Badger ferry from Manitowoc to Ludington and spend most of our time with Carolyn's family in the Grand Rapids area.

We had two very memorable experiences in 2005 on our trip north. We stayed a couple of nights with our great friends Paul and Rae Liljestrand in Thomasville, Ga. On our first night we retired to our guest bedroom and in a few minutes fell asleep in their antique double bed. Several times during the night I awoke to the sound of, CRICK, CRICK, CRICK, but then went back to sleep. At about 3am I awakened as my side of the bed crashed to the floor pinning me between the side board of the bed and my wife was on top of me. Carolyn finally got off me and turned on the light. We found that the 2X2 rail that was glued to the side board had failed, causing the box spring, the mattress and us to end up on the floor. We remade the bed and spent the rest of the night sleeping inside the bed frame.

I don't think anyone should be surprised that an elderly overweight couple might cause this to happen. I'm just glad that we could tell them the next morning that we were not engaging in marital activity when this happened. Paul and Rae, being our age, believed our report. Our hosts were glad to find that neither of us was hurt by the collapse. Now if I ever again sleep in an antique bed and hear a strange Crick, Crick, I'll turn on the light and investigate before I climb back under the covers.

In July of 2005, our three sons rented two large beach houses on Emerald Isle, N.C, to have all the family celebrate my 75th year. Dave and Glenn's families stayed in one and Craig and Laura and their boys stayed with us. Our daughters in law, planned all the meals and other eating arrangements, and our get-togethers on the beach, and evening fun time on the larger house's back porch. They were nice enough to play one game of Trivial Pursuit with me and let me win. We have wonderful memories of that weekend, which ended with having a great family picture taken on the beach. After that we went to Wilmington, N.C. to visit friends from our Connecticut days. From there we set out for Door County for two weeks and then went to Michigan for Carolyn's family reunion.

In November, we took a Caribbean Cruise with several other Shell Point couples. The cruise took us to the Panama Canal, which we saw for the first time, and the island of Jamaica. In Panama we went through the lock to Lake Gatun, and then took a train across the isthmus to the Pacific side and Panama City. We learned much about the building of the canal, and that led me to read David McCullough's great book on the subject: <u>The Path Between The Seas.</u>

Carolyn had always wanted to take a trip to Sweden with her brother to show him the country where their grandparents were born. She signed up for a 12 day back- country roads trip for July of '06 that took our group of 15 people to see nearly all the major sites in the southern third of Sweden. The tour was run by Anderson Tours in Lindsborg, Ks.(We would highly recommend this trip to anyone of Swedish descent.)

Before taking the tour we spent several days in Norway, Flew to Bergen, and then by bus went to Stalheim once again before taking the boat on Sognefjord to Flam. We then took the train to Oslo for a night before taking an overnight sleeper train to Stockholm. We met our Sweden tour director at the airport and started the tour, which began with a castle palace. Upsala was next, where the Provost of the University gave us the best guided tour I have ever had. We then went up to the lake country and down the west coast to southern Sweden, where my grandparents came from. Following this we visited the Crystal centers and the emigrant institute in Vaxjo. At the end of the trip we spent a couple of days in Stockholm, where, once again, Barbro Stigo extended herself in guiding us around Stockholm. A highlight was seeing the changing of the guard at the Royal Palace. While on the trip, I noticed that I had a balance problem and was fearful of standing unsupported at high places.

In August, we went up to Maine and on the way stopped to spend a couple of nights at our friends' time share at Jiminy Peak in the Berkshires. They had a split duplex apartment on the second floor, facing the mountains. When we went to our room that evening, the sun had just set and the sky was a beautiful shade of violet. Carolyn went out on the open deck to enjoy the view and invited me to come out join her. After a couple of minutes Carolyn said we'd better close the door or our bedroom would soon be invaded by bugs. I closed the door. The colors went from violet to purple and soon to a gray and then very quickly it was dark and it was time to go inside. What a shock it was to find that the door had locked when I closed it.

After a few minutes, we started knocking on the building's metal siding, and Carolyn called out for help. We got no response! We then began shouting and soon were feeling our voices strain. The temperature was dropping rapidly as our calls bounced off Jiminy peak. It was now dark and I could not see the ground below, so I wisely decided not to jump from the balcony. Finally a man in the unit below us called up and asked us what was wrong. We told him we were locked out and asked him to call the front desk and send someone that could let us back into our unit. A few minutes later a woman went to our hosts' door and told them of the distress of their guests. They came into our bedroom with their mouths agape and opened the door and let us back inside. When we got in we looked at the door. Near the door knob was a small sticker that read: "Make sure the reenter button is out before going out on the deck." We learned the truth of that message the hard way.

In late September we settled in for our three weeks stay at Hilton Head, I went, as I had for years, to the Bike Shop to rent a bike. I got set to pedal away and put my left foot on the lower pedal while holding the handle bars straight. I felt unsteady and thought, "How do I get my right leg to the other side of the bike?" This was one of the most frightening experiences of my life. I had ridden bikes all of my life and automatically put my left foot on the lower pedal and then pushed off with my right foot and swung the leg over the back of the bike to the right pedal. I immediately knew something was radically wrong with my balance or brain in that I could no longer make the right moves automatically. During the next three weeks I fell three times when dismounting, fortunately injuring only my pride.

When we got back to Shell Point I made an appointment with Dr. Yallof. He asked me to do a number of things like walking a straight line and standing on one foot. He asked me to walk toe to heel. I could not do it without falling to one side or the other. At the end of the exam he recommended I see a neurologist, Dr. Davis. After his examination he called the hospital and set up appointments for me to have an MRI of the brain and a spinal radioactive dye tap into my spinal column, a Cysternogram.

When the test results came back, Dr. Davis asked me to come back and see him. Carolyn came with me. When we came into his examining room his first words were, "Would you be willing to have brain surgery if it would save your life?" How's that for bedside manners!! He said it was clear from the tests run that I had hydrocephalus, an abnormal amount of fluid on the brain, causing the brain to be pushed down and this would eventually cause DEATH. That did not give me much of a choice. Fortunately, when I was having these tests run at the hospital, I asked the persons who were running the tests who they would choose if they needed brain surgery. Two names were on most lists and Dr. Correnti was on all of them. So I told Dr. Davis that I would appreciate it if he would set up an appointment for me with Dr. Correnti. I met with him, and he described a surgery in which a shunt would be put in my brain's right ventricle that would drain excess spinal fluid into my abdominal cavity. The surgery was set for January 4th, 2007. The last time that I had spent a night in a hospital was New Year's Eve 1929. Seventy- seven years had passed since then, and as I considered that, I thanked God that I had been so fortunate!

As I went into surgery I had a perfect peace. When I came back to consciousness the only person there was Pastor Stu Austin sitting across from me. What a wonderful sight that was! He prayed with me for a swift recovery, and in a short time I was put in an intensive care area with other patients who had neurological problems. We were in a semi-circle around a nurses' station that had a direct sight line to each patient and our monitor screens. I had a lot of sensors and IV's in my arms and was limited in my movements.

Early on my third night, the nurse came over to my bed and asked me if I was ok. I said, "Yes." She advised me to calm down, lay back and close my eyes. In short order, she was back again with another nurse who checked me over and then told me that my heart beat was up to 140 beats a minute, and she believed I was having atrial fibrillation. They called for the heart doctor to come and examine me. They asked me if I'd ever had atrial fibrillation before, and I said no. After the Doctor examined me, he prescribed a drug which would be IV'd. They asked me to sit up. When I did, I got a strong urge to urinate and asked the nurse to get me the urinal bottle. She brought me the bottle, but with all the tubes and wires I had in my arms I could not get it down to my crotch. I said to the nurse, "You'll have to help get me into the opening." She did that job, and in a minute I was relieved and glad that I had not wet the bed. The nurse came over and asked what I was smiling about. I said, "You're a member of a very small group. In all my life only a few people have touched that part of my body, a doctor or two, my mother and father, probably my youngest aunt, my wives and now you're in the club, a very exclusive group." She and I had a good laugh over that experience, and she told me that was not her first time to provide that service. There are times in your life when modesty takes a back seat.

When I was discharged from the hospital, they gave me a narcotic that gave me wild delusions, and in addition made me car sick on the way home. They quickly took me off that drug and I found that extra strength Tylenol was sufficient to dull my pain.

In the next months I had strange, sharp shooting pains and abnormal spasms that my surgeon said were normal for a person who'd had brain surgery. Each time I'd report these abnormalities to him he'd say, "Paul, you've had brain surgery and the brain is readjusting to the results of that invasion." He said it might be six months to a year before things got back to normal. He was right. My balance situation improved immediately. In September when we again went to Hilton Head, I rented a bike and rode nearly every day with no problems. As I'd start rolling I'd say a prayer of thanks to God, for his mercy to me and for the doctors, surgeons and modern medicine. I have since learned that this surgery was first performed in 1972. I have met three others at Shell Point who have had this operation. I've thought often about my blessing and the fact that there are probably old people all over the world who stumble and fall and believe this to be normal for their age and don't have the wherewithal to have it diagnosed and corrected.

In October '07 we took a Caribbean cruise to Bermuda with several other couples. This time we took buses around the island to various beaches and scenic lookouts. It reinforced our opinion that it is our favorite island. When we arrived at Columbia, Carolyn went shopping for an emerald, as she reminded me we would have our 35th anniversary in May 2009. I bought the ring she chose after she promised to stay with me at least until then.

In February 2008, the leadership of our church made a courageous decision to leave the Presbyterian USA denomination. Our reasons for leaving were well founded. The denomination by its actions, had violated the teaching of the Bible and its own Book of Order on such critical things as the standards of Ordination and, most importantly, had denied the necessity of trust in Jesus Christ for our salvation. The core verse for this belief is John 14:6 where Jesus said; "I am the way the truth and the life. No one comes to the Father except through me." Some in the denomination said there may be other ways to God. We said if you say that, you deny the central tenant of our faith and it's no longer Christianity!

In order to leave the denomination, the local Presbytery laid out very severe guidelines and punishments. We had to have a two-thirds turn out of our membership on the Sunday of the vote, and three-quarter vote of those members voting yes in order to leave the denomination. If we did win the vote, it was understood that we could take nothing from the church property and we would lose the property. Even though we had a generally elderly congregation, many of whom were homebound and students who were away or in the service and could not vote by absentee ballot, we got the necessary quorum and 76% of the vote to leave. We were told to be out of the church building by Easter Sunday.

Three miles from us the church found a Brazilian Assembly's of God Church that used the building only a couple of days a week and had their worship on Saturday night. We were able to rent the church for the rest of the week. On Palm Sunday we had our first worship service in the sanctuary. The two Brazilian pastors welcomed us. It was one of the most wonderful services I've ever been part of. We were without our choir robes or music, pew Bibles and hymn books, but were there as a united group of believers. In the next few weeks donations poured in for office furniture, computers, hymn books, pew Bibles, Communion Service equipment, etc. This has turned into one of the most exciting and challenging spiritual experiences of my life. Our choir attire is now white tops and black skirts or slacks. The congregation seems to like it. When the church divided, half the choir, along with the director and organist left and are a valuable part of our new church. All but two of the elders came with us as well as the entire Pastoral staff. The church business manager, whom we love and miss, stayed with our former church. Now in a time of serious recession we are raising capital to buy land and build a new church building. The church is looking to God for guidance and direction in this matter.

In July, we went to the Northeast, along the way spending time visiting friends and family in Georgia, North Carolina, Virginia and Connecticut before arriving at our cabin on Lake Annabessacook. We had delightful times with Glenn and his family and in the last couple of weeks of August had the pleasure of having Gail Hubbard and her husband stay with us two nights. They brought eight lobsters for us to feast on. Don and Gloria Treash then came for a few nights' stay in our guest cabin. One evening we decided to go to a historic theatre and see the play, "Arsenic and Old Lace." We were told that our view of the stage would be somewhat obstructed. When we took our seats we found that meant we could see only half the stage at most and Don only a third of it. The actors were great and we had a lot of laughs. When we were leaving I asked Don if he had enjoyed it. He came up with a classic line saying, "That was the best play I never saw."

The church that Glenn pastors, Hope Baptist, has now built a larger sanctuary, where we enjoyed worshipping. The highlight of our trip was witnessing our son baptizing our grandson Joshua at a lakeside service. We were also joined by our son Dave and his family for a couple of days. It was great to see five of our grandchildren together.

On our way back to Florida we stopped in Washington, D.C to see the National Cathedral and the Korean and WWII memorial. The Cathedral is magnificent, and I felt the Korean War memorial accurately portrayed that war. The WWII memorial could have been made more meaningful. Over 400,000 thousand Americans lost their lives in that terrible war with Germany, Italy and Japan. To emphasize that, they could have put the number of how many had died from each state on the 50 individual state columns.

When we got back to Shell Point Carolyn found out that there was going to be a trivia contest called Shelleopardy! It was a take off on Jeopardy, and she entered my name as a contestant. My competitors were two Shell Point employees. I was able to win and got a $30 gift certificate for Publix which we used to buy two T-bone steaks and a box of Dove bars. I also got a Shelleopardy T-shirt to wear. It was nice to get a payoff for all the trivia knowledge I carry in my head.

Because 2009, was my eightieth year Carolyn decided to honor me by taking a cruise to Antarctica. We flew to Buenos Aires and boarded the ship on January 17th. It was a nice warm summer day. The next morning we docked in Montevideo where I was able to see some of the remains of the German Battleship Graf Spee, which was trapped by the British and damaged so badly that the Germans scuttled it in the Platte river estuary in December of 1939. Sailing from there to the south, we docked two days later in Stanley and enjoyed a marvelous tour of the main Falkland Island. We boarded 4- wheel- drive vehicles and drove for more than two hours over paved roads then gravel and finally peat moss bogs. Driving on these bogs was like a thrill ride at Disneyland, and it really shook up our old bones. Finally we arrived at volunteer point where we saw thousands of penguins of several species, including Magellanic, Gentoo, and the majestic King variety. This experience in itself was worth the trip. We took over 100 pictures on this part of the trip.

The next couple of days were spent heading south for the Antarctic Peninsula. On the second night we were crossing the "Roaring 50's" latitudes south of Cape Horn, where the Atlantic meets the Pacific, and got into one of its powerful displays. Early in the evening we went out on deck seven and saw waves of 15 to 20 feet and felt near gale force winds. Fortunately we were on a ship that is 990 ft long and has all the modern stabilizers. Even then we staggered along while having one hand on a rail or bulkhead as we walked. At 2:15 am we were awakened by a loud bang. Carolyn's bed fell off its risers, items on the dresser and shelves fell to the floor. The next morning the captain in his morning message reported that we had experienced gale force winds that reached up to 75 mph and at 2:15 we had been hit by a rogue wave that he estimated was 50 feet high. Several glass doors on the ship had been broken, and he warned us to be careful as we moved around the ship.

During our two week cruise I read several books and went to the ships lounges at least once a day to play Trivial Pursuit. I won several "Princess" ship store prizes. As we approached Antartica, we began to see icebergs of all shapes sizes and colors, glacier covered mountains, sea birds, Minke and Humpback whales. It was spectacular to see Chinstrap penguins swimming alongside our ship, leaping out of the water as they darted along.

In the morning we came to Elephant Island where Shackleton left most of the crew of the shipwrecked *Endurance* while he and several others made their incredible journey in a converted lifeboat over 500 miles of roaring ocean to the tiny island of South Georgia. Now, after seeing that part of the world, I am even more in awe of that miraculous achievement.

After a week of sailing around the peninsula, we crossed back over a much calmer sea to the strait Magellan and cruised on the Drake Passage, where we saw more penguins and several seals and sea lions. We went ashore at Ushuia, Argentina, and toured the most southern city on earth. Our next day took us to Punta Arenas, Chile a very pretty town that was clean and featured a town square with a large statue of Magellan. The following day we cruised on fjords of Chile, which are more rugged than the Norwegian Fjord's. Our cruise ended as we headed for the port of Valparaiso, where we disembarked the ship in the morning and spent the rest of the day touring in and around the capital city of Santiago. We would have liked to have spent more time in this large, modern, beautiful city. On a tour of the city we learned that the first president of Chile, elected, in 1810 was Fernando O'Higgens (put that in the trivia part of your brain). On that day we toured a modern winery, saw a Chilian rodeo, had a great meal and went up a funicular to an overlook of the city of almost five million people. This was the most enjoyable and educational cruise I have ever taken. We were amazed by Antarctica's imposing mountains, glaciers, caves, icebergs and wild life. We were not surprised to talk to people who were on their second or third trip to that continent.

Back in Florida during Easter week, much time was spent in rehearsing with the choir Faure's Requiem, which we presented on Maundy Thursday and then in rehearsal of Easter Anthems which we sang in all three services on Sunday morning.

In April I watched the Tar Heels win the NCAA Basketball Championship. I was glad for Glenn's alma mater to win in that it enabled me to win my fifth Peterson March Madness trophy with 160 points. This year there were nine Petersons who made picks on who would win each game. This was the sixteenth year for this competition.

We spent July and August in the upper Midwest: in Wisconsin in Kenosha, Spooner and Door County, then in Michigan where

Carolyn fulfilled a life time wish to stay one night at the Grand Hotel on Mackinac Island. It cost half a grand to do that. It was her early birthday present. During most of the month of August we stayed with her brother and spent a lot of time with Carolyn's friends and relatives. We drove to Sawyer, Michigan and took the train to Chicago to see wonderful friends, Roy and Rose Sandstrom, Mary and Ken Bell and Barb and Ralph Swanstrom. We had a great time with them and enjoyed seeing my home town particularly Marshall Field's and the new Millennium Park.

On December 21, 2009, Carolyn orchestrated my eightieth birthday celebration in the Grand Cypress Room at Shell Point. All of my family was present and a family picture was taken (see page 310). Over 100 other relatives and friends were here from as far away as Chicago and Connecticut. A catered dinner was served and a program followed which included a quiz about events that occurred in 1929. Carolyn wonderfully led the program that followed the dinner. My grandson Joshua played one of my favorite pieces of music on the Clarinet, (The Adagio movement from Mozart's Clarinet Concerto) and my oldest Grandson spoke of our playing baseball together and his EPIC victory in a game of Monopoly. Carolyn and Mary Kay Loomis spoke and then my three sons. In their roasting they did it lightly as they recalled things that I had done that deserved to be critiqued or wondered about. Their words of remembrance and praise were beyond what I deserved. In my reply I thanked God and my family, for the joy, strength and love they have given me throughout my life. Except for my wedding days with Lee and Carolyn it was the most joyous day of my life! The evening ended with a showing of pictures of my life journey, and praise to God with the singing of *Great is Thy Faithfulness.*

That night when I went to bed I was so emotionally pumped up that I laid awake for most of the night as I relived the event. I thanked God for the wonderful family and friends with which he has blessed me the past eighty years. I thought again of a verse the boys referenced in the Bible they gave me 28 years ago, The father of a righteous man has great joy; he who has a wise son delights in him (Proverbs 23: 24). I Do!

Eighty two years ago I was starting my life as a fetus in my mothers' womb. I would see the light of day on December 20th 1929, and be named Paul Oscar Peterson. In June, Carolyn and I started our eleventh year as residents of Shell Point Retirement Community.

GOD HAS BEEN GOOD TO ME!!

Boy's in pool with Dad, Florida 1974

Paul with his seven foot "Championship" Sailfish, 1974

Paul and Carolyn's wedding 1974

Dreaming of the future

Carolyn and Paul at Boca Raton C.C. 1975

Our family at home in Fairfield, Ct. 1983

Paul at Glacier Bay, Alaska

Paul and Carolyn at Mt Blanc, France 1998

Paul "climbing" Matterhorn 1998

Paul Peterson Family

Chapter 27

What's Ahead?

In my memoir I have reported the events, things and people that have influenced my life. God has allowed me to live a wonderful, satisfying life. What lies ahead for me? He knows and my times are in his hands.

There are many verses that David wrote that have and will continue to guide me. Psalm 31:14, 15, "But I Trust in you my Lord. I say my times are in your hands." And then in chapter 32:8 God says, "I will instruct you and teach you the way you should go; I will counsel you and watch over you."

I've seen people who are old at fifty because they have given up on their dreams and ideals. Years and the sun wrinkles the skin, so does smiling, but giving up hopes and dreams wrinkle the soul. Worry, doubt and fear are what bow the head and stoop the body. Whether a person is 18 or 80 they should have in their heart the love of discovery, the challenge of events, the joy of wondering what's next in life. I am no longer able physically to climb the Matterhorn, but I can still picture myself on the final ridge. When I was visiting a cemetery in Paris I came to a statute of a mountain climber. The inscription read, "He died climbing." I'd like that to be said of me.

"Never let success hide its emptiness from you. And so keep alive the incentive to push on further, that pain in the soul which drives us beyond ourselves. Whither? That I don't know. That I don't ask to know."

Dag Hammarskjold

After my first wife Lee's death, I claimed several verses that have guided my life since that time. Isaiah 41:10 "So do not fear, for I am with you; do not be dismayed, for I am your God. I will strengthen you and help you; I will uphold you with my righteous right hand." Jeremiah 29:11-13 "For I know the plans I have for you, declares the Lord, plans to prosper you and not to harm you, plans to give you hope and a future. Then you will call upon me and come and pray to me, and I will listen to you. You will seek me and find me when you seek me with all your heart."

In the last 10 years my body has told me that I'm an old man. The first shocking experience came when I grabbed a bat and wiffle ball and went out on the front lawn with Joshua and Andy to hit a few balls to them. I threw the ball in the air and when it descended into the strike zone I swung and missed. I repeated this routine and missed again, again and again. I remembered the many times I'd gone out with my sons and done this for an hour never missing the ball. In fact, I could hit them grounders, line drives, long fly balls or pop-ups when they requested them. Now, 40 years later, my hand / eye coordination is all but gone. I can't even tick a twelve inch wiffle ball. Five years ago my balance left me when I was discovered to have hydrocephalus, which caused me to lose my balance. I'm thankful that through the hands of a great surgeon and God's healing touch, that I can now again walk a straight line and ride a bicycle. But as many friends my age know it's a major task to get up and down from the floor without the pull of a helping hand or some chair or stand to push up on. While going to the bathroom for the second time the other night, I wondered how long it might be before bladder control is a memory and diapers are required. I had a dream a while back that my face from the nose up was covered by a tangle of long hairs emanating from my nose, ears and eyebrows. Why does all the hair that used to grow on the top of my head now grow profusely from these other places?

A poem of Edna St Vincent Millay – *Grown Up* - rings true to me. "Was it for this I uttered prayers, and sobbed and cursed and kicked the stairs, That now domestic as a plate, I should retire at half past eight." I don't Twitter, Tweet or do Face Book, but I do toot oftener than a few years ago. When a check out man asked me at Publix; "Paper or Plastic?" I told him," It doesn't matter to me, I'm bi-sackual." He gave me a strange look.

So how should I cope with this slightly impaired body? I have been privileged to see the great violinist Itzhak Perlman several times in New York and once at Interlocken in Michigan and many more times on television. He had polio as a child and has braces on both legs and can walk only with the aid of crutches. He makes his way toward center stage with a smile on his face, gets to a chair, puts his crutches on the floor, unclamps the braces, tucks one leg back and pushes the other leg forward. Then he bends down picks up his violin, puts it under his chin, does a little final tuning and nods to the conductor that he's ready to play.

In November of 1995, Perlmann was only five minutes into a concerto when one of the strings of the violin broke with a loud pop. The conductor brought the orchestra to a stop and everyone wondered, what's next? The great violinist sat motionless for a few minutes with his eyes closed, and then he signaled to the conductor to begin again. He played with passion and power such as most had never heard before. They could see him modulating and recomposing the music in his head and fingers as he proceeded. He got the three strings to make sounds that they had never made before. When the concerto ended there was an audible gasp and silence in the hall. Then everyone stood and cheered, doing everything they could to show how much they were in awe of what he had done. After a few minutes he smiled and raised his bow in the air as a signal that he wanted to say something. He smiled, wiped the sweat from his face, and then as the crowd quieted he said, "You know, sometimes it is the artist's task to find out how much music you can still make with what you have left." Shouldn't that apply to all of us?

It is my task in this fast changing, morally declining world to live my life as the apostle Paul admonished me to do in Philippians 2, "Do nothing out of selfish ambition or vain conceit, but in humility consider others better than yourselves. Each of you should look not only to your own interests but also to the interests of others. Your attitude should be the same as Christ Jesus: who being in very nature God, did not consider equality with God something to be grasped, but made himself nothing, taking the very nature of a servant, being made in human likeness. And being found in appearance as a man, he humbled himself and became obedient to death- even death on a cross!"

This I purpose to do, with what strength and gifts I have, until I'm called from this earth. I know, "That in all things God works together for the good of those that love him, who have been called according to his purpose. Who shall separate us from the love of Christ? Shall trouble or hardship or persecution or famine or nakedness or danger or sword? No, in all these things we are more than conquerors through him who loved us. For I am convinced that neither death nor life, neither angels nor demons, neither the present nor the future, nor any powers, neither height nor depth, nor anything else in all creation, will be able to separate us from the love of God that is in Christ Jesus our Lord." Romans 8:28, 35, 37-39.

Addendum

My Beliefs and How I Came to Have Them

I believe that God created the heavens, earth, and human beings. He created me to have fellowship with Him and enjoy Him forever.

Why do I believe he is the creator of all things? Because the Bible says so, also, Copernicus, Galileo, Newton and Pascal were Christians who believed that God manifested Himself in the creation. He put our planet earth in part of our galaxy, the Milky Way, and gave it properties that would enable living plants and animals to live on it. No other planet in the known solar systems matches our planet earth in being able to support life. There is a fraction of a billion chance that with all the criterion needed to support life, that this could have just happened. That was the main purpose for the work the above mentioned scientists did, and further discoveries have confirmed their work. The chance that life was started by a spark in a swamp is a leap of faith greater for me to take, than a belief that a creator God did it all. Scientists, have been sending electric shots into mixes of amino acids for decades and not produced life or viable cells.

I do believe God's creation happened over eons of years and that there were prehistoric forms of life, dinosaurs, etc., that walked the earth and disappeared before the creation of man took place. I do not dispute the fossil records. I believe that the creation of Adam and Eve was a specific act of God, and he breathed into them the breath of life as the Bible states. Even though the most advanced of the apes have 99 plus percent of our DNA, they do not have the ability to reason that God put into his creation of human beings. He also made us to have fellowship with Him. All human beings have in them the desire to worship. Pascal said; "There is a God shaped vacuum in every heart, and man is restless until it is filled by Him."

He also said; "If you believe and God exists, you gain everything. If you disbelieve and God exists, you lose everything." If I believe that I am here by blind chance, or evolution, life has no eternal purpose and I am not accountabe to anyone.

I believe that all mankind, starting with Adam and Eve, has sinned. Romans 3:23, "For all have sinned and fall short of the glory of God." God gave us the Ten Commandments as listed in Exodus Chapter 20 to obey. His Son expanded upon them when he gave his Sermon on the Mount, as recorded in Matthew chapters 5, 6, and 7. These were not suggestions! I confess that I have broken many of them at some point in my life. God gave us these commands for our good and to regulate our society. If we disregard them, it leads to anarchy and our destruction.

I believe that God's son, Jesus, came willingly to earth to die on a cross to pay the penalty for the sin of all of mankind. In living his sinless life on earth by word and deed he taught us how we should live our lives. I believe that I can do nothing in my own strength to obtain forgiveness and obtain salvation. Ephesians 2:8, "For it is by grace you have been saved-through faith and this not from yourselves, it is the gift of God, not of works, so no one can boast." I accepted His free gift and am saved. I also believe that there is only one way to obtain our salvation. Jesus said in John14:6, "I am the way the truth and the life. No one comes to the Father (God) except through me." People who believe there are many ways to God are trusting in a rope of sand.

I believe that all who have accepted Jesus Christ are given the presence of the Holy Spirit in their lives when they make that decision. Jesus promised this to all believers, as recorded in John 14:26:" The Holy Spirit—will teach you all things and will remind you of everything I have said to you."

I accepted Jesus' free offer of salvation when I was nine years old because I wanted to obey him and go to heaven when I died. I admitted to Him that I had sinned, lied, cheated, disobeyed my parents and asked His forgiveness and help to live a life pleasing to Him. My mother quoted these verses to me to assure me of my salvation. John 3:16,17. "For God so loved the world that he gave his one and only Son, that whoever believes in him shall not perish but have everlasting life. For God did not send his Son into the world to condemn the world but to save the world through him."

I am ashamed to say, that in my younger years I did not practice what I believed in my heart. I acted as a Christian on Sunday, and when I was with my church peers, but when I was with my neighborhood and school buddies I acted and talked as they did. I was a hypocrite. Many times I did things that I knew displeased God, and I lied to my parents many times when they asked where I had been or where I was going. As I knew that Jesus had taught many times that he was coming again, I actually prayed he would not come when I was doing things that were wrong or was in places I shouldn't have been. I was not living a joyful, fruitful Christian life.

When I got to Wheaton College I started to study much that grabbed my attention and rang true to me. From Shakespeare: "Look thou be true, do not give dalliance too much rein, the strongest oaths are straw to the fire in the blood. Be more abstemious or else good-bye your vow." and C.K. Chesterton, who wrote; "Christianity has not been tried and found wanting. It has been found difficult and left untried." Dietrich Bonhoeffer who wrote, "When Christ calls, he calls us to come and die." This called me to make a serious commitment to his Lordship on my life. Then in a class in apologetics, I came across the Great writings of C.S. Lewis. When I read *Mere Christianity,* the final paragraph of the chapter "The Shocking Alternative," put it straight to me to get serious about my faith in Christ. "People often say about Him, I'm ready to accept Jesus as a great moral teacher, but I don't accept his claim to be God. A man who was merely a man and said the sort of things Jesus said would not be a great moral teacher. He would either be a lunatic-on the level of a man who says he is a poached egg- or else he would be the Devil of Hell. You must make your choice. Either this man was, and is, the Son of God: or else a madman or something worse. You can shut him up for a fool, you can spit on him and kill him as a demon; or you can fall at his feet and call him Lord and God. But let us not come with any patronizing nonsense about His being a great human teacher. He has not left that open to us, he did not intend to."

I was in my junior year at Wheaton when I experienced my first extraordinary spiritual touch of God. I was standing in the balcony of Pierce Chapel and the faculty and student body were singing the hymn, "*Have Thine Own Way. Lord."* I started singing the second verse:. "Have thine own way Lord, have thine own way, search me and try me, Master today." Those were the last words I sang as I was choked up by the Holy Spirit as he said, "Do you mean that?" I sat down and with tears asked Jesus to take my life and run it. That decision has made all the difference. I'd accepted him as Savior; now I accepted Him as Lord.

I felt the abiding presence of the God after the sudden death of my beloved wife Lee in April 1973. I could have been angry at God. Instead I was led to remember such Bible verses as Isaiah 41:10, "So do not fear, for I am with you, do not be dismayed for I am your God. I will strengthen you and help you, I will uphold you with my righteous right hand." Hebrews 13:5," Never will I leave you; never will I forsake you," and Verse 8 reads, "Jesus Christ is the same yesterday, today and forever", and Jeremiah 29:11-13: "For I know the plans I have for you declares the Lord, plans to prosper you and not to harm you, plans to give you hope and a future. Then you will call on me and come and pray to me, and I will listen to you. You will seek me and find me when you seek me with all your heart." Many times when I reached out for Lee in my half sleep to touch her, when the reality of her loss hit me, these verses flooded into my mind.

Another reason for my belief in God is that I have seen how he has worked in others' lives and turned their lives from darkness to life. In the New Testament we have the account of the changed life of the apostle Paul. In the early centuries of Christianity, the conversion of Augustine, and in the era of the slave trade the ship owner, John Newton, who wrote the words of the hymn, "Amazing Grace how sweet the sound that saved a wretch like me." I saw personally how Jesus changed the lives of many that I taught in the Seekers' class at Black Rock Church in Connecticut from 1986 to 2001. One young single mother comes to my mind. She said that when she became pregnant she had no idea who the father might be because she had sex with so many different men. In a few weeks she decided to accept Christ and to give up her immoral lifestyle. She got into a woman's Bible study that met on another day of the week and was excited about her new life. A few weeks later she came to the class and started crying. She said she'd had a bad week and she had doubts that she was a Christian. She said that in her job as a loading dock supervisor at the Post Office she had to get the workers to do a better, faster job in getting the trucks out. On one particular day she had used her former profane language to get them moving and felt that to be a sign that she was not a Christian. I asked her if she had ever felt remorse after using that language before she had come to Christ. She thought for a moment and said no. I told her that was a sign that she was a follower of Jesus because the Holy Spirit had prompted her to have remorse at this step back. I asked her to read Romans 10: 9,10. I asked her if she believed that was true for her? She said yes. We as a class prayed for Leslie and several months later she reported that her filthy talk had disappeared from her vocabulary. We were a witness to God's power in her life. In that class we had many other proofs of God's life- changing power. What greater proof can there be of God's existence and power!

I believe that the Bible is the verbally inspired word of God and is without error in its original writing. Jesus said that He is coming again and that He will take those who have put their faith in Him to heaven. I believe there will be a last Judgment for all mankind, and that those who committed the unpardonable sin of rejecting his salvation will be condemned to hell. I also believe there will be a judgment of believers where we will be rewarded for what we did in the name of Jesus Christ. In light of that I will continue to do what I can for Christ and his kingdom.

Statistics

On my 81st birthday I was 29,574 days old (12-20-10)

When I was 22, I was 5 feet 11 and three quarters inches tall and weighed 130 pounds.
At 81 I am 5 feet 10 inches tall and weigh 200 pounds. All that weight has pulled me down.

My blood pressure is 130/70. I have borderline high cholesterol but do not take any medication for it. I've had several spells of atrial fibleration.

I have ringing in my ears (tinnitus) that was caused by the drug Vancomicin, which was taken to cure an intestinal ailment that I had in 1989.

I take half an aspirin tablet and centrum every day along with Prilosec for a mild acid reflux problem. Several nights a week I have a small glass of red wine, which I believe is beneficial for the heart. I eat Herring every day to get fish oils. This is my favorite "medicine."

I have lived most of my days in five states: Illinois 10,527; Connecticut 8,266; Florida 2,887;
New Jersey 1,926; and Indiana 1,757. I have been in all 50 states, and have spent 445 days outside the USA.

I've owned 19 cars and estimate I've driven about 900,000 miles. My favorites were a 53 2dr Bel Aire Chevy a 60's Opal and my present '98 Toyota Avalon. I have bought only 4 new cars.

My first airplane flight was in 1959 when I was 30, since then I have been on 1,312 flights and flown 1,054,000 miles.

Obsevations and Counsel

My observations of events in our country give me great concerns for the future. The USA is now 233 years old, so I have been alive for over a third of its history. Over the last 50 years I have read a lot of history and have been impressed by the character of the men who were the founding fathers. Especially impressive were our first two presidents. Washington prayed to God many times for guidance during the Revolutionary War. Those prayers were answered by miraculous victories against overwhelming odds. I believe God's providential blessing on our victory is obvious. (Read David McCollough's "1776" and his biography "John Adams") John Adams was one of a few members of the Continental Congress who did not own slaves as it clashed with his beliefs. He was the main drafter of the Massachusetts Constitution as well as the US Constitution, which flowed from it. In 1756 while at Harvard at age 20 he wrote this in his diary. "I am resolved to rise with the sun and study scripture on Thursday, Friday and Sunday morning, and to study some Latin authors the other three mornings. noon and nights I intend to read English authors… I will rouse up my mind and fix my attention. I will stand collected within myself and think upon what I read and what I see. I will strive with all my soul to be something more than persons who have less advantages than myself." Are there any students at Harvard who do that today? He wrote, "Our Constitution was made only for a moral and religious people. It is wholly inadequate to the government of any other." He asked for, against some opposition, a delay in signing the Declaration of Independence, in order to have a day of prayer observed before it was signed on July 4, 1776.

Not all the founders of our country were Christians, but the great majority were men who believed in a God that guided the purposes of men. Read the Declaration of Independence, The Bill of Rights and the Constitution and notice how many times God is referred to and called on. Adam's also gave this ominous warning: "Democracy while it lasts is more bloody than either aristocracy or monarchy. Remember democracy never lasts long. It soon wastes, exhausts and murders itself. There is never a democracy that did not commit suicide." Adams also gave this warning. "Ambition is one of the more ungovernable passions in the human heart. The love of power is insatiable and uncontrollable." How apt that is in this year.

Throughout our history our presidents and leaders have beseeched the blessing of God on our country's decisions. We acknowledge on our currency that we trust in God, and until the last few years public prayers were offered to God in our schools along with a posting of the 10 Commandments in our schools and public buildings.

The Frenchman Alexis De Tocqueville reported on what he observed on his investigating of what made the US a great country in the mid 1830's. "I sought for the greatness and genius of America in her commodious harbors and ample rivers- and it was not there.... In her fertile fields and boundless forests-and it was not there, in her democratic congress and her matchless constitution- and it was not there.... Not until I went into the churches of America and heard her pulpits flame with righteousness did I understand the secret of her genius and power. America is great because she is good, and if America ever ceases to be good, America will cease to be great."

The US since WWII has been the most powerful, prosperous and proud nation on earth. It seems to me that we relaxed and let down the bars and enjoyed our success. In the late 50's we were given the Playboy philosophy of Hugh Hefner who said, "If it feels good do it." Dr Timothy Leary who worked at Harvard introduced us to LSD and preached turn on, tune in, drop out, which ushered in the flower children of Woodstock. We've pooh-poohed the need of a relationship with God and preached that greed is good. Now some say that the only absolute that is in effect is that there are no absolutes. We've lost our moral compass. It has put our country on a slippery down slope. Our modern day prophet and preacher Billy Graham who spoke of the need for righteousness has been silenced by old age and no one of his stature has risen to stop a runaway train. On the political front we need statesmen. Instead we have politicians who do what's needed to get reelected and get rich along with it.

In the last few months I've collected a number of clippings from newspapers and magazines that illustrate where we're at:

"28% of Americans say they would lie, cheat or backstab to keep their job.

In 2008 Americans used 350 tons of cocaine – half the worlds' consumption.

In 2008, 1 American in 31 was in jail or prison; in '82 it was 1in 77; in '72 1 in 683; in '52 1in 6,739.

In the year 2006, 17,600 deaths resulted from accidents caused by drunk drivers. That's more than 4 times the number of our troops that have been killed in the Iraq war!!

Why aren't people marching on Washington over this issue!! Sweden, which takes drivers' licenses away for life and give long jail terms for this offense, annually has more people die by hitting moose than because of drunk driving.

In 1982 the average household saved 11% of their income, in 2007 the savings rate was 1%.

In 2008 the US birthrate for girls 15 to 19 was 42.5 per 1,000; England was second with 29.7 per thousand.

Here is the percentage of Americans that don't think the following activities are sin. Adultery 19%, using hard drugs 35%, having an abortion 44%, having sex before marriage 55%, getting drunk 59%, gambling 70%. (It would have been interesting if they had asked if they believed that there was such a thing as sin.)

In the 80's only Nevada and New Jersey had casinos; now 12 states do and 48 allow some form of gambling or lotteries.

In 1990, eight percent stated they had no religion. In 2008 that figure rose to fifteen percent."

Now we are in the worst economic disaster since the great depression. This disaster which was caused in large part by bank and financial institution personnel who believed greed was good and by consumers who borrowed beyond their means and ran up credit card debt to buy what they didn't need in order to make others envious of them. In the early 40's my hero C.S Lewis wrote this in 1942 in his preface to The Screwtape Letters: "The greatest evil is not done in those sordid dens of evil Dickens loved to paint but… in clear, carpeted, warmed, well lighted offices, by quiet men with white collars and cut fingernails and smooth shaven cheeks who do not need to raise their voices." I think this well describes Bernie Maddof and some of his cronies on Wall Street that brought our country to near financial collapse in 2008.

My mother and father and most of my aunts and uncles passed away in the 60's and 70's. Many times when the local news (crime report) is reporting another routine mass killing, child murder or a ED commercial is shown, I visualize how shocked they would be if they suddenly came back and were watching with me. It would be hard for them to believe how bad things have become in our beloved land.

In light of this bleak scenario how should Christians live?

Jesus great commission (Acts 1:8) is still as applicable to us as it was to his disciples. "You will be my witnesses to the ends of the earth." He sent the 12 out with these words; "Be as shrewd as snakes and as innocent as doves." The entire Sermon on the Mount in Matthew 5,6,7 taught us how to live as Christians. Jesus also said in Matthew 10:39 "Whoever finds his life will lose it and whoever loses his life for my sake will find it." The apostle Paul writes in Romans 12:20, "If your enemy is hungry feed him, if he is thirsty, give him something to drink. In doing this you will heap burning coals on his head."

Financial advice: I have found none better than is found in my favorite Shakespeare play, Hamlet where Polonius gives this advice: "Neither a borrower nor lender be, for loan oft loses both itself and friend, and borrowing dulls the edge of husbandry."

There will be times when you have to borrow money to buy your first home or for student loans. These are loans which will in the long run enable you to grow your wealth as property values generally appreciate and what you spend to learn more will help you advance in your career. AVOID ALL OTHER DEBT.

Use a credit card as a convenience instead of carrying a lot of cash. Pay your credit card bill completely every month. Do not get into credit card debt. It has brought financial ruin to many people. I have in my life have had to counsel several people on how to get out of their credit card debt. You don't need more than four credit cards. I have only once had to pay interest on my credit card debt when I mislaid a statement I received from Mastercard. Delay the temptation to go into debt to gratify your greed not your need. Phillippians 4:19 says; "And my God will meet all your needs according to his glorious riches in Christ Jesus." The important word is needs not greeds. Get into the wonderful habit of tithing 10% of your earnings to your church. God has given you all you have, the least you can do is give back to him from what he has given you.

I have owned 19 cars, only 4 of them were new. I've saved a lot of money doing this as a new car's value depreciates greatly in the first several years. In Connecticut, where I bought most of the used cars, I had two friends who ran auto repair shops. Many times they would tell me of a car that would be for sale that might be a good buy. I also have a good friend who kept his cars in top condition. I have bought several cars from him.

Learn to appreciate good music. It will bring you great joy all your life. My definitions of peace are the Adagio movements of Beethoven's fifth piano concerto, Mozart's 23rd piano concerto and his final Clarinet concerto. When I've had a hectic day I have come home, sat down, closed my eyes and listened to music such as this. I hope some of you will be the recipients of my large collection of CD's and DVD's.

Develop a quiet time with God and His word. Have a time of journaling in your Bible study. Answer these questions as you read a passage of Scripture: What did it say to the people who lived in the time it was written? What does it say to me today? How should these words affect the way I live my life?

Make close friendships with people who build you up, help make you a better person. Separate yourself from those who would influence you to do what is wrong or cause you to disobey Gods commandments.

I love and agree with this statement of President Theodore Roosevelt: "It is not the critic who counts, not the man who points out how the strong man stumbles or where the doer of deeds could have done better. The credit belongs to the man in the arena, whose face is marred by dust and sweat and blood, who stands valiantly, who errs and comes short again and again….who spends himself in a worthy cause who, at the best, knows, in the end, the triumph of high achievement, and who at the worst, if he fails, at least he fails while daring greatly." The other speech that has given me great courage when I have been challenged is found in Shakespeare's play, "Henry V", play Act IV, scene three, which begins, "My cousin Westmoreland?" (I leave you to look it up and be inspired,. maybe even memorize it)

This quote of Santayana is so true: "Those who cannot remember the past are condemned to repeat it." How true this was as WWII was brewing.

These are words of wisdom from lessons learned in my experiences of living:

> Don't drive alone when you take your child to college as you won't be able to see the road when you drive home.
>
> Be a person of your word, keep your promises no matter what it costs.
>
> You can't love your children too much, you get it back in unconditional love.
> Spend time at home with your family. I've never met a man who wished that he'd spent more time at the office.
>
> Give your children the opportunity at age 13 to choose where the family will go in the U.S. on a family vacation and work along side them in planning it. It was one of wisest things

I ever did. They will be gone from the nest in a few short years.

Be real; you can get by with charm for a few minutes, after that you better know something.

Go to church as a family on Sunday. If you don't go, they may not go when they leave the nest.

To love and be loved is the greatest thing in all the world.

Make minor decisions with your mind, make the big decisions with your heart.

Fill your life with experiences, not excesses.

Go on at least a couple short-term mission trips, for example Habitat for Humanity, World Vision, Builders w/o borders. I assure you, you'll want to go on more.

Adopt a third world orphan and contribute to their support.

Accept the fact that you are responsible for what you do.

If you want to get the best out of life, give it your best.

Treasure your children for who they are, not for who you want them to be.
If love isn't shown and taught in the home, it's difficult to learn it outside it.

Trust is the most important factor in life's relationships.

You should not do things that wouldn't make your mother proud.

> Love will sometimes break your heart, but it's worth it!
>
> It's as important to forget a wrong as it is to remember a kindness.

Live your life so in the end you can rest in scriptures such as Romans 8:28, 35-39 and 2Timothy 4:7,8 and as you pass into his presence in heaven may you hear the doxology of Jude vs. 24, 25.

I've had a wonderful life of growing in knowledge and experiences involving loving relationships, but I sure wish that I'd climbed the Matterhorn. I've spent my life climbing. I'd recommend you do the same.

Favorites

Bible Readings

Psalms 8, 19, 23,
37,42,46,51,84,91,100,103, 150
Proverbs 31:10-31
Isaiah: 40, 41:10,11, 43, 53, 55
Jeremiah 29:11-13
Lamentations 3: 22,23
Matthew 5,6,7,
John 3, 11,14,15,16
Romans 8, 10,12
Philippians 2, 3
1 Thes.4
2 Tim.3
1 Peter 1
Heb. 4, 12
1 John 1
Jude 24,25

Hymns

When I Survey the Wonderous Cross
Beneath the Cross of Jesus
To God be the Glory
My Faith Has Found a Resting Place
Jesus the Very Thought of Thee
And Can It Be?
Immortal, Invisible God only Wise
Love Divine all Love Excelling
May the Mind of Christ My Savior
Jesus Thou Joy of Loving Hearts
Rejoice the Lord is King
Glorious Things of Thee are Spoken
Jesus Thy Blood and Righteousness
Jesus Lives and so Shall I
Gracious Spirit Dwell With Me

Favorite Christian Books

Confession's of St Augustine
A Serious Call to a Devout and Holy Life- Law,
Fox's *Book OF Martyrs'*
Mere Christianity -C.S. Lewis
Screwtape Letters- CS Lewis
The Great Divorce- CS Lewis
Surprized by Joy CS Lewis
The Cost of Discipleship- Bonhoeffer
Prisoner for God- Bonhoeffer
The Return of the Prodical-Son- Nouwen
Pensees – Pascal -*Morning and Evenings*
Spurgeon

Favorite Books

I have been a voracious reader of U.S. History especially of the Revolutionary, Civil War and WWII eras. I have read Catton's books on the Civil War and Churchill's six volumes on WWII. I have also read biographies of the men involved in these conflicts; Lincoln, Lee and Stonewall Jackson in the Civil War and Manchester's great biography on Churchill, two volumes titled: *The Last Lion.* My favorite authors for these eras are Shirer, Manchester, Doris Kearns Goodwin, McCullough and Ambrose. I would recommend them highly. Must reads are McCullough's *1776* and biography of *John Adams.*

For my Grandchildren I recommend these books I enjoyed as a child; *Black Beauty, Hans Brinker And the Silver Skates, Tom Sawyer, Hucklebery Finn, The Last of the Mohicans, Robinson Crusoe, The Bounty Trilogy, Two Years Before the Mast, Oliver Twist, Great Expectations, A Tale of Two Cities, The Red Badge of Courage.*

As an adult, these are my favorite novels: Austin: *Pride and Prejudice, Sense and Sensibility*; Dickens: *Bleak House, David Copperfield, Great Expectations, Little Dorrit, Nicolas Nickelby, Oliver Twist, Our Mutual Friend*; Dostoyevsky: *Crime and Punishment,* (MY FAVORITE)*The Brothers Karamazov*; Pasternak: *Dr. Zhivago*; Stendahl: *The Red and the Black*; Tolstoy: *War and Peace.* For a fun read: John Grisham's novels.

My favorite comics; #1 Calvin & Hobbes (I have a number of his Collection books which contain much wisdom.) #2 Peanuts

Favorite Painters; Rembrandt, Renoir, Homer, Wyeth

Favorite Places

Cities: US Chicago. San Francisco, Palo Alto, and San Diego
Foreign: Vienna, Paris, and Florence

U. S. A.: Yosemite Valley, Grand Tetons, Glacier National Park, Grand Canyon. Canada: The Valley of the Ten Peaks and nearby Lake Louise, in Rocky Mountain National Park, Butchart Gardens Victoria, B.C.

Most beautiful countries: Switzerland, New Zealand, Norway. Cities: Vienna, Paris, Florence Areas, Europe: Netherlands: Keukenhof Gardens, (in the Spring); Switzerland; Interlocken-Beatenberg with the Jungfrau, Monch and Eiger Mts., Zermatt, Matterhorn (Stay at the Julien Hotel with a room on the south side top floors with the Matterhorn in your face, Lake Lucerne and the city, Lake Lugano,. Italy: Tuscany and the city of Florence. Sorrento, Capri, the Amalfi Drive, Positano. Norway: Stalheim Hotel, near Bergen (Stay on fourth floor with view of the valley.) and cruise on Sojne and Gehringer fjords.

New Zealand: North Island: Auckland, On the South Island Mt. Cook, Christchurch, Milford and Doubtful Sounds, Lake Te Ana. (Friendly people)

Favorite Island: Bermuda ; Close by, friendly people and pink sand beaches.

Favorite Music

What a debt of gratitude I owe to my mother who by listening to great music on our radio became the one most responsible for a life I have lived enjoying it. There have been few days in my life when I have not either listened to it or sung it in numerous choirs, or quartets. I started collecting recordings of such works as March Slav and the Piano Concerto #1 of Tchaikovsky and Beethoven's 5th Symphony. They were recorded on 78 rpm records. Today I have a collection of over 300 CD's and 150 Tapes of great music from Baroque to Broadway and Swing era classics. Mozart, Schubert and Brahms are my favorite composers. Here is a listing of my favorite Classical works.

Adam: O Holy Night sung by Bjorling, Albinoni: Adagio in G, Alven: Midsummer Vigil Bach: Toccatta & Fugue in D for Organ, Brandenburg Concerto's # 2 & 4, Mass in B minor, St. Matthew Passion, Concerto for 2 Violins, Air on a G String, Jesu, Joy of Man's Desiring. Barber's Adagio for Strings Beethoven's: Symphony's # 3, 5, 6, 7, 9 Piano Concerto's # 1, 3,4,5. Violin concerto, Triple Concerto, Missa Solemnis, Romance# 2 for violin, piano Sonatas # 8, 14, 17, 21, 23, 26, 32 Leonore overture # 3, Egmont, Fidelio Overtures. Boellman: Suite Gothique for organ Brahms: Symphony's # 1,2,4 Piano concerto's 1&2 Violin Concerto, Double concerto, Alto Rhapsody, Requiem, Liebeslieder waltzes, Academic Festival Over.

Berlioz: Symphonie Fantastique, Nuits de Ete, Roman Carnival Over. Bizet's: L'Arlesienne Suite# 1, Duet from The Pearl Fishers- Au Font du Temple Sani, Bjorling/Merrill Casals: Song of the Birds: Chopin: Piano Concerto's I & 2, Grande Valse Brillante, Fantasie Impromtu, Polonaise in A, Military Polonaise, Nocturnes in D, E Ballads 1,2 Sonata I&2 Waltz in A flat, Scherzo.# 2 Andante, Spianeto& grand Polonaise, Fantasie Impromtu. Debussy: La Mer; Clair de Lune

Dvorak: Cello Concerto# 2, Symphony "New World" # 9 Symphony # 8 Aria "Oh Silver Moon" Faure: Requiem, Pavane, Franck: Panis Angelelecus Gluck: Dance of the Blessed Spirits Greig: Piano Concerto, Peer Gynt Suites, Holberg Suite Handel: Water Music Suites, Royal Fire Works Music, Messiah Largo from Xerses Haydn: Creation Oratorio, Cello Concerto, Trumpet Concerto ViolinConcerto; Symphony's, 22,49,53,59,60,71,82,83,88,92,93,97,98,99,100,101,103,104. Hummel: Trumpet Concerto Liszt: Piano Concerto's 1&2, Funeralles, Les Preludes, Liebestraum #3. Marcello: Oboe Concerto. Mendelssohn: Violin Concerto, Symphony's 3, 4 Piano trio, Elijah Oratorio, Piano Con. #1.2 Midsummer Nights Dream Music, Songs w/o Words, Octet for Strings, Mussorgsky's: Pictures at an Exhibition for Piano – Ravel: Symphonic orchestral transcription of it.

MOZART: Ave Verum Corpus, Concertos for Horn #1-4; Con. For Flute and Harp, Piano Con. #s 9,15,20,21,23, 25,26,27; 2 Pianos K365, Clarinet in A K602.Adagio in C for Oboe, Exsultate Jubilate, Operas: Marriage of Figaro, Magic Flute, Don Giovanni, Symphony's# 25, 29, 35,38,39, 40, 41 Eine Kline Nachtmusik Divertimento K136, Requiem, Sinfonia Concertante K 297B; Piano Sonatas K280,332,333,545,570,576; Sinfonia Concertantes K297B, K364. Puccini: La Boheme

Purcell: Trumpet voluntaries: Rachmanioff: Piano Concertos1&2, Rhapsody/ theme Paganini, Vocalize; Respighi: The Pines of Rome. Rimsky-Kosakov: Scheherazade. Rodrigo: Fantasia para un Gentil Hombre. Rossini: Overtures; La Gazzz Ladra,. Semeramide, William Tell. Saint-Saens: The Swan, Piano Concertos 2,4:; Cello Concerto, Violin Concerto#3: Symphony #3

SCHUBERT: lieder, Impromtu's op. 90,142 My signature piece #3 in G flat, Mass in G, Songs for Male chorus, Piano Sonatas in B flat, & A major Symphony's 1,3,5,9; String quintet,(Trout) moment musicaux op.94 Incidental music, Rosamunde. Schumann: Tramerei, Symphony's 1, 4 Piano Concerto, Kinderszenen, Sibelius:

Finlandia, Swan of Tuenela, Valse Triste. Smetana: The Modau. Sousa: Stars & Stripes Forever, Washington Post, El Capitan, Semper Fidelis J. Strauss: Tales from the Vianna Woods, Artists Life, Blue Danube, Voices of Spring, Radetsky March, Liebeslieder waltzes Opera, Die Flatermaus R. Strauss: Waltzes from Der Rosenkavilier Stravinsky: The Firebird. Suppe: Poet and Peasant and Light Cavalry Overtures. Terrega: Recordes De Le Alhambra (favorite guitar piece) Tchiakovsky: Piano Concerto# 1, Violin Concerto, Romeo& Juliet Fantasy, Mozatiana, Nutcracker, Sleeping Beauty, Swan Lake suites; Serenade for Strings, 1812 Overture, Symphony's 4,5 Verdi: Requiem Opera La Traviata Vivaldi: The Four Seasons. Gloria, Concerto for 2 Guitars. Wagner: Overtures: Rienzi, Tannhauser, Preludes: Die Meistersinger, Lohengrin prelude and prelude to Act III. Prelude and Love Death, Tristan & Isolde. Weber: Overture, Der Freischutz, invitation to the Dance, Clarinet Concerto in E. Widor: Tocatta from Sym. #5, organ, Wienawski: violin con.#2. Williams: Fantasia on a theme of Tallis.

I have many recordings of the Robert Shaw Chorale. I love the choral music of John Rutter.

Popular

Autumn Leaves, September Song, It's Magic, Stardust, Edelweiss, Climb Every Mountain, You'll Never Walk Alone, Tenderly, Some Enchanted Evening, Maria. Both Sides Now, Send in the Clowns, This Nearly Was Mine, Bridge Over Troubled Water, Many of the great hits of Glenn Miller and Tommy Dorsey including; Moonlight Serenade, In the Mood, Tuxedo Junction, String of Pearls, Opus #1, Chattanooga Choo Choo. I like almost all of what the Carpenters did but since then most Pop, Rock has been noise, too assaulting and unintelligible for my hearing!! I love the clear soprano voice on Judy Collins.

110 Favorite Movies

Adam's Rib
African Queen, The
The Age of Innocence
Amistad
Arabesque
Arsenic and old Lace
Babette's Feast
Blob, The
Born Yesterday
Breaker Morant
Breaking Away
Bridges at Toko-Ri, The
Bridge On The River Kwai, the
Bridge Too Far, A
Bullittt
Butch Cassidy--Sundance Kid
Captain's Paradise, the
Casablanca
Chariots of Fire
Christmas Story, A
Citizen Kane
The Cross of Iron
Day of the Jackal
Diabolique
Dial M for Murder
Diary of Anne Frank
Doctor Strangelove
Doctor Zhivago
Dollars
84 Charing Cross Rd
Elvira Madigan
Field Of Dreams
Flight of the Phoenix
The French Connection
Fried Green Tomatoes
Gallipoli
Gandhi
Gaslight
Gettysburg
Gone With the Wind
Great Escape, The
Great Expectations
Great Train Robbery, the
Hamlet
Henry V
High Noon
Hustler
How to Steal a Million
In- Laws, The
In the Heat of the Night
It Happened One Night
It's a Mad, Mad World
It's a Wonderful Life
Jaws

Kramer vs Kramer
Lady Killers, The
Lavender Hill Mob, The
Lawrence of Arabia
A Man For All Seasons
Man in the White Suit, The
Mash
Miracle Worker, The
Mr Holland's Opus
Mutiny On the Bounty '35
My Big Fat Greek Wedding
My Fair Lady
North By Northwest
Notorious
Nun's Story, The
Odd Couple, The
Oliver Twist
On Golden Pond
On the Waterfront
Out of Africa
Patton
Pianist, The
A Place in the Sun
Places in the Heart
Pride and Prejudice
Rear Window
Remains of the Day
Roman Holiday
Russians are Coming, The
Sabrina
Saving Private Ryan
Schindler's list
Sense and Sensibility
Shane
Sleepless in Seattle
Some Like It Hot
The Sound of Music
Stalag 17
Stalingrad
Steel Magnolias
Sting, The
3 Days of the Condor
Take the Money and Run
To Catch a Thief
To Kill a Mockingbird
Topkopi
Tootsie
The Train
Treasure of Sierra Madre
A Trip to Bountiful
Twelve Angry Men
Von Ryan's Express
Wait until Dark
What about Bob?
Witness
Witness for the Prosecution

Favorite Actresses: Audrey Hepburn*, Ingrid Bergman, Grace Kelly, Meryl Streep
Favorite Actors: Alec Guinness*. Gregory Peck, Cary Grant, Anthony Hopkins, Laurence Olivier
* Favorite

Family Tree

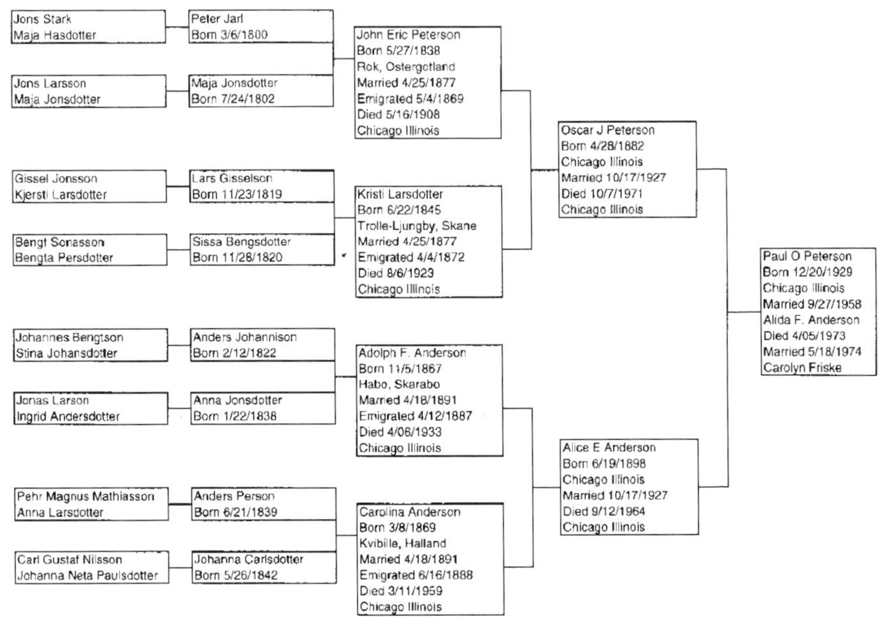

Paul Peterson
Ancestor Chart
Jons Stark
Maja Hasdotter
Peter Jarl
Born 3/6/1800
Jons Larsson
Maja Jonsdotter
Maja Jonsdotter
Born 7/24/1802
John Eric Peterson
Born 5/27/1838
Rok, Ostergotland
Married 4/25/1877
Emigrated 5/4/1869
Died 5/16/1908
Chicago Illinois
Gissel Jonsson
Kjersti Larsdotter
Lars Gisselson
Born 11/23/1819
Bengt Sonasson
Bengta Persdotter
Sissa Bengsdotter
Born 11/28/1820
Kristi Larsdotter
Born 6/22/1845
Trolle-Ljungby, Skane
Married 4/25/1877
Emigrated 4/4/1872
Died 8/6/1923
Chicago Illinois
Oscar J Peterson
Born 4/28/1882
Chicago Illinois
Married 10/17/1927
Died 10/7/1971
Chicago Illinois
Johannes Bengtson
Stina Johansdotter
Anders Johannison
Born 2/12/1822
Jonas Larson
Ingrid Andersdotter
Anna Jonsdotter
Born 1/22/1838
Adolph F. Anderson
Born 11/5/1867
Habo, Skarabo
Married 4/18/1891
Emigrated 4/12/1887
Died 4/06/1933
Chicago Illinois
Pehr Magnus Mathiasson
Anna Larsdotter
Anders Person
Born 6/21/1839
Carl Gustaf Nilsson
Johanna Neta Paulsdotter
Johanna Carlsdotter
Born 5/26/1842
Carolina Anderson
Born 3/8/1869
Kvibille, Halland
Married 4/18/1891
Emigrated 6/16/1888
Died 3/11/1959
Chicago Illinois
Alice E Anderson
Born 6/19/1898
Chicago Illinois
Married 10/17/1927
Died 9/12/1964
Chicago Illinois
Paul O Peterson
Born 12/20/1929
Chicago Illinois
Married 9/27/1958
Alida F. Anderson
Died 4/05/1973
Married 5/18/1974
Carolyn Friske

Siblings of Paul Petersons Grandparents

Anders Person & Johanna Carlsdotter
Married: August 22, 1868

MM Carolina Josefina, born: 3/8/1869

Johan August	**2/1/1871**
Carl Gottfried	**9/26/1872**
Per Alfred	**7/1 /1874**
Mathelda	**11/1/1876**
Johan Albin	**12/6/1878**
Nils Adolph	**7/30/1881**
Alfred Severin	**2/13/1885**

Anders Jonanisson & Stena Svensdotter, married: 4/9/1849

Gustaf Julius	**4/12/1850**
Emma Charlotte	**1/30/1852**
Frans Levin	**10/3/1854**
Johan Emil	**10/8/1858**
Mathilda Gustafra	**10/8/1858**
Half Brothers & Sisters	

Anders Johanisson & Anna Jonsdotter married: 4/12/61

Elias	**11/2/1861**
Carl Victor	**5/18/1863**
David Alfred	**6/24/1865**
MF Adolph Fritz	**11/5/1867**
Gustaf Robert	**12/11/1870**
Anders Albin	**3/30/1873**
Anna Elizabeth	**11/3/1881**

Siblings of Paul Petersons Grandparents

Lars Gisselsson & Sissa Bengsdotter

Married: March 22, 1845

FM Kjersti Larsdotter	**6/22/1845**
Bengta	**9/29/1847**
Else	**05/26/1850**
Ola	**11/5/1850**
Bonde	**10/23/1855**
Anders	**01/14/1861**
Else	**03/14/1863**

Peter Jarl & Maja Greta Jondotter
Married: 1822

Fredica Sophia	**06/7/1823**
Carl August	**06/21/1827**
Charlotta	**02/3/1830**
Per Leonard	**01/9/1834**
Anna Marie	**12/6/1835**
FF Johan Eric	**05/27/1838**
Frans Oscar	**05/27/1838**
Frederick	**12/22/1840**

Anderson Grandparents

Wedding picture of maternal Grandmother Caroline Anderson, 1891

Wedding picture of maternal Grandfather A. F. Anderson 1891

Adolf Fritz Anderson was born in Habo, Vastergotland, Sweden to Anders and Anna Jonson on 11/5/1867. He moved to Gustaf Adolph parish in1874. In 1869 one of his older brothers emigrated to the U.S., and in 1882 another followed. He moved to Jonkoping in 1886 and settled at Tyska Maden #7. While living there he met his bride to be, Carolina Josefina. In Jonkoping he was a carpenter apprentice. "America Fever" was pretty strong at that time. In 1886, 169 persons emigrated from that parish, which had a population of 8,300.

A.F caught that fever and emigrated from Gothenberg on March 25,1887. He left for two reasons. At the age of 13 he became a Christian and became a diligent student of the Bible. He was convinced by his study that believers in Jesus Christ should be baptized by immersion. He was baptized and became a member of a small Baptist house church in Jonkoping in 1882. As the Lutheran Church was the state church, the Baptists were a persecuted minority. That was one of the reason why he decided to emigrate, the other was that there was little economic opportunity for a person of common stock. In America a couple of his brothers were becoming relatively wealthy.

He sailed on the packet ship, "Romeo" for Hull, England. In England he transferred to the ship S.S. Arabic, a 2,787 ton ship which arrived in New York on April 12, 87 with 988 passengers made up of English, Irish, Norwegian, and the majority, 535 Swedes. He was passenger # 669, 20 years of age, a male laborer. He was located in: # 2 steerage with one piece of luggage. He settled in Chicago, started working as a wood worker and attended night school. (One of the things he made was a platform, oak, rocker for his wife to be. This rocker is still working and is a possession I'm proud to have.)When AF had earned enough money for her passage to America he sent for her.

Carolina Josephina Andersdotter was born in Kvibille, Halland, Sweden on March 8, 1869 six and one half months after the wedding of her parents, Anders and Johanna Persson on 8/22/68. At the age of 17 she moved to Jonkoping and began to work as a maid. She moved again in Jonkoping to Kyrkokvarteret # 17. While there she was converted to Christianity in 1885 while attending a Baptist church in Halmstad. There she also met and became engaged to AF. Anderson. A little over a year after he had taken the ship, "Romeo," to Hull, England, she took it, on 6/1/88, and then transferred to the S.S. City of Chester, a 4,440 ton ship. It arrived in New York on 6/16/88 carrying 824 passengers made up of Russians, Romanians, English, Scotch, Irish, Danes, Norwegians, and 180 Swedes. She was in #2 steerage, passenger 277, 18 years old, a house servant with all her possessions in one piece of luggage.

In Chicago, Caroline and Adolf continued their courtship They attended the Addison St. Baptist Church where she was baptized in the winter of 1890. They were married 4/18/1891.Shortly after this he turned his wood turning skills into fashioning ornamental iron, and joined the Ornamental Iron Workers Union. He became a naturalized citizen on 10/29/1892. In1894 he founded the AF Anderson Iron Works.

Caroline and A.F. were the parents of five children: Bernard, born on 11/25/ 93; Judith, 10/ 9/96; my mother, Alice, 6/19/98; Roy, 6/17/01; Elvira, 4/21/07.

A.F. also was an officer and director of the Chicago City Band & Trust Co. In the 1920's, he ran on the Republican ticket for state senator in Illinois, but was defeated.

The family's first home was at 1216 W. 59th St. Many neighbors were also Swedish emigrants. By the 20's he'd moved up the financial ladder and built a three story brick home in Hyde Park, at 6841 Bennett Ave, a mansion.

He and his wife were founding members of the Englewood Swedish Baptist Church, the church I attended as a boy. He was a teacher of a Bible class, and served twice as Sunday School Superintendent. He also served as a Deacon and trustee at various times, and as church Vice Chairman from 1921 until his death from pneumonia on April6,1933.

He and Caroline were presented with 11 grandchildren and 23 great-grand children.

His word was bond. His verbal commitments were always carried out. By chance, when I was a teenager I met a man, who had done business with him. He looked me in the eye and said; "Young man you have a lot to live up to, having AF as a grandfather." Those words many times were brought to my mind when I was tempted to do things that might bring shame to my family.

My grandmother, "Mussie," spent her life successfully being a wife, mother, and grandmother. She spent many of her latter days teaching an older women's Bible study at our church. She was a devoted follower of Jesus and loved people. I never heard her say an unkind word about anyone. She was like a second mother to me. After AF died, our family spent every summer with her at their cottage at Bass Lake. Many nights, when I passed her bedroom I saw her kneeling in prayer at the bedside.

When the family was rushing around, many times she would say "There's no cow on the ice," or in Swedish, "Det ar ingen ko pa isen" This referred to her being brought up on a small farm in Sweden when they had only one cow for their family. In the Fall or Spring the ice on the lake was too thin to support a person or animal. If the cow got on that ice and fell through it was goodbye to their milk supply. The cry, "There's a cow on the ice," got everybody moving. In her mind, any happening less significant than that did not require quick action.

She had a stroke that left her completely helpless when she was 85, She lived on five more years and died three days after her ninetieth birthday, March 11,1959.

She and AF's bodies are buried in Oak Hill Cemetery.

Peterson Grandparents

Wedding picture of paternal Grandmother Kristine Peterson 1877

Wedding picture of paternal Grandfather John Peterson 1877

My paternal grandfather, Johan Eric Peterson, was born on 5/27/1838. He had a twin brother, Frans Oscar. They were born in Rok, Ostergotland, Sweden, to Peter Jarl and Maja Jonsdotter, and were their sixth and seventh children. Their father was a Lifeguardsman (a soldier). Soldiers were like today's National Guard. As part of their pay they were usually given a small farm, or croft to work. In the late 1860s he lived in Elfsby/ Alvsby and worked as a farmhand. He used the name Jarl as well as Petersson. He later moved to Mortanas, Varmdo, Stockholm lan and from there emigrated, to Anerica on 5-4-1869 at the age of 30.

He arrived sometime in June and went to work as a driver of horse-drawn street cars. The next year on October 8-9, The Great Chicago Fire destroyed most of the city. The fire moved NE from Jefferson & Dekoven Street, wiping out three and a half square miles of the city, including the business center. Over 17,000 buildings were destroyed and 100,000 people, one-third of the population, were made homeless. The exact number who lost their lives, while never known, was estimated at 300. There is no record of his witnessing the fire.

His signing of written records, Citizenship paper, land grant documents etc., with an x may indicate that he was illiterate.

The parents of my grandmother, Lars Gisselsson and Sissi Bengtsdotter, met in Trolle-Ljungby, Skane. They were married there on March 22, 1845. My grandmother, Kristi, was born to them on June 22, 1845. Doing the math it's obvious that Sissi was pregnant when they were married. Parish records read, "The parents did not keep their seven children in school very much." Lars was a farmer who knew how to make love. (The fact of the matter is that both of my grandmothers were conceived out of wedlock.) This is the only skeleton in my ancestral closet that I know of. At the age 17, Kjersti moved to the parish of Nosaby in November of 1862 to work as a maid. She returned home in October 1871 and prepared to emigrate to America. On April 4, 1872 she left Kristianstad. We don't know what port she left from except we know it was not Gothenburg, as there it would have been recorded. She arrived in New York in May of 1872 and came immediately to Chicago. At the Second Baptist Church on 18th and Dearborn, she came to faith in Jesus Christ and was baptized in early 1874. We have no record of where she lived in Chicago, or where or when she met John.

John and Christina were married on April 25, 1877, in the Second Church by Dr. Frank Peterson. They lived at 3248 State Street where their first two sons, Frank and Albert were born. Both of these sons died before they were three. My father, Oscar, was born to them, at home on April 28, 1882. John was almost 44, Christina nearly 37. John became a naturalized citizen of the U.S. in February 1883 and decided to homestead in Clark, South Dakota. (Their life stories continue in Oscar's life story.)

Oscar J. Peterson

My father, Oscar Peterson, was born to John and Christine Peterson on April 28, 1882, in their home at 3228 So. State St. Chicago. Attending Christine during the delivery was Midwife Maria Fridenschmid. Christine had given birth earlier to other sons, Albert, born in 1878 and Frank in 1879. Both of them died in infancy.

John, became a naturalized citizen of the U.S. in February of 1883 and took advantage of an offer to homestead in Clark County, South Dakota. He left his job as a driver of horse drawn streetcars and moved the family there in May. He was given two horses and a cow and 160 acres to farm. His first job was to build a 16 x 24 ft. clap board, one room house before winter arrived. My uncle David was born in that house on October 9, 1884. After five years of farming, John was deeded the property by an act of President Benjamin Harrison in 1889.

Dad spoke many times of the hardships in trying to farm on the wind swept plain and of the cruel winters. Tragedy came in February of 1890 when the four horses and the cow contracted "Hoof and Mouth" disease. Three marshals came and rounded up the animals. The family gathered in the house and rifle fire punctuated their sobs as the dream of successfully homesteading in South Dakota died. Seventy years later my dad could still remember the five shots. This disaster caused the family to move back to Chicago in spring of 1890.

Within the next eight years they moved twice, first to 36th and Wallace for three years, and then to 29th and Poplar for five. In that period Oscar contracted TB, "Consumption", and did not attend school for three years. In a two year period he had it so bad he coughed up blood several times. The low point came one late afternoon when he heard the visiting doctor tell his parents, that he probably wouldn't live through the night. Fortunately for my father the doctor was wrong. He survived the crisis, which he credited to his mothers fervent prayers. At the age of thirteen he went back to school and entered fourth grade. He graduated at age 17 from the Holden Grammar School. That was the end of his formal education. They again moved to 856 33rd Place, near Halsted Street, and lived there six years. When the family had returned from S.D. his father resumed his job with the street car company and was given the job of caring for16 horses, but when the street cars went to electric power that job ended. John went to work for the Al Wolf Mfg. Co., a company that sold plumbing supplies. He worked there until his death from pneumonia in 1908. He had a tough life for 70 years. He was buried in Oakwood Cemetery at 67th and Hyde Park Blvd., Chicago.

Dad's first job was with a meat packer, Morris & Co. At night he studied in preparation to take the exam to be a US Postal mail clerk (a mail sorter) in the main P.O. in Chicago. He learned where every street in the city of Chicago was located. This was before the system of Zip Code was used. I remember as a boy the many times Dad was called by friends, and asked "Oscar where's so and so street?" He prided himself in being able to give them the location. He also told the story over and over about the physical he passed to get the job. The doctor weighed and measured him at 5'10 and 125 lbs. and said "Well kid, you just made it" The minimum weight for the job was 125 lbs.

He got a superior rating on the exam in knowing the city street locations and was assigned "to throw," (sort), incoming mail for the entire city at the main Post Office at Randolph & Michigan. He started on the night shift in November of 1900 at an hourly wage of 37 cents an hour, working 48 hours a week, Monday thru Saturday. This gave him a yearly income of $923. By 1904 the PO needed more room and moved to Clark & Jackson.

In the first decade of the century my fathers' first love was the Chicago Cubs. If you wanted to get him excited you would ask him about his favorite team. He'd tell you of the team they had from 1906 to 1910. This team was managed by the "Peerless Leader", Frank Chance the first baseman. They played on the "West Side" grounds. Dad attended many games as he worked nights. Tinker to Evers to Chance had a poem written about them. He told me many times about the "Bonehead" play by Merkle of the Giants that got the Cubs into the last World Series that they won against Ty Cobb and his Tigers. The '06 team that had a 116-36 record, a .731 winning percentage that is still a record; how in 1907 and '08 they won back to back World Series four games to none and four games to one. He'd go on about the Cub pitchers, Pfiester, Reulbach, Overall, and "Three Finger'" Brown who pitched four complete games allowing the Tigers 0,1,1,1,runs in these games for an ERA of 0.75. The great Ty Cobb hit .200 in two series. Catcher Johnny Kling threw out Cobb and picked off other base runners with his snap throws. Dad lived off the memories of these teams for the rest of his life because they never won another World Series, even though they played in seven others, and they haven't won any in my 81years. Unfortunately, he passed on "Cubitis" to me and to two of my three sons.

After his father's death, my dad, Uncle Dave and their mother moved to a flat building at 6034 Peoria. He lived there until 1928. When his brother married in 1914, Dad was left with the care of his mother. The last year of her life she was bedridden and he got his cousin Ethel to come and help until she passed away in 1923. He was a man who believed strongly that children's main responsibility was to take care of their parents. You didn't get married unless you had enough money to support your parent and wife. Later in his old age he decried children who put their parents in "Old Peoples' Homes." My brother Will and I were told many times that he never expected us to treat him that way. If we decided to do that he said he'd rather be taken out behind the barn and shot.

In 1926 he met my mother Alice Anderson, at the Englewood Swedish Baptist Church. She was the 28 year old daughter of AF Anderson. They were married on October 17, 1928 and had a gala wedding reception at the Windemere East Hotel. Oscar was 46, Alice 30. They moved into a new apartment building at 7120 Peoria. I have an unsubstantiated belief that AF gave them a financial assist in getting this apartment for one of his favorite daughters.

I'll say more about my dad when I tell the story of my life, but I want to let you know what I received from him besides his love for the Cubs.

My father was 47 when I was born. He never acted like an old man when he rolled on the floor with me and my brother. We'd go out and play catch many times. In 1940 our family took a trip to Sister Bay, Wisconsin. While playing with other kids they asked me where my father was, I pointed him out and they said, that's your grandfather. I'd never noticed until then that my dad was older than the fathers of most of my peers.

He showed me how to build with blocks and boards and how to use tools. He gave me an appreciation of the joy of hard work and perseverance. One of my favorite bed time stories that he read me was "Perseverance, Cork and Glue." A fun thing to do with me was to dig out a stump or a big rock from the lawn or garden area using a pick and shovel and a long 4x4 as a lever. We had fun accomplishing things by hard physical work. He had a great love for roses and dahlias. He showed me how to prune roses, spray and fertilize them and protect them from the killing winter cold. We shared the joy of cutting wood and splitting it. Every fall we'd dig up the Dahlia bulbs, separate the clump of new bulbs, and store them in peat moss in the cool basement, then plant them in the spring when the "eyes" sprouted from the bulb. His Dahlias in front of our home were the envy of the block.

One very different thing about him was that he never drove a car. As he always used public transportation as he was growing up there was no need to have a car. My mother was the driver of our family car. I've often thought about what our friends and neighbors thought of that. It never bothered him as far as I could tell.

He had loyalty in his commitment to Jesus Christ, his wife, and sons and, job. He worked for the USPS and the Civil Service from 9-4-00 until 4 -30-52, fifty one years and 8 months. When he was 65 his boss called him in to inform him that in 45 years he had been out sick only 28 days and he had accumulated a record 362 days of sick leave. (This came from a person who, at age 11, was not expected to live until morning.) The boss ordered him to be" sick" an average of one day a week until he retired, not wanting Washington to know about this as they might decide to cut back on sick leave benefits.

In1934 the Post Office moved to Van Buren and Canal and his times working night shift ended. During the depression when many of his friends were out of work he had a secure job. He pointed this out many times to Will and I to teach us that loyalty to a job and company was important to himself and our family. He wasn't a talker, but a doer. In 1936 he was assigned to Civil Service. He proctored and gave exams for government jobs. I remember the hours he spent with my mother getting his speed in dictation up to 120 words a minute for typing and stenography tests. When he received the exalted position of Chief Examiner, he remembered several of buddies who he had "thrown" mail with and got them into the better paying jobs in Civil Service. I remember one in particular that he did this for, Chuck Derby, who never ceased thanking him for this lift. His peak pay working for Uncle Sam was $4,370/yr.

I quote excerpts from the letter that went out to his fellow workers regarding him on his retirement.

"Mr. Oscar J. Peterson is retiring from the Federal Service as of April 30, 1952. During the past 30 years he has conducted our civil service examinations and for a number of years has been the examiner in charge. He has a long record of federal service which totals more than 52 years.

I have approved a request for an office-wide collection for a gift for Mr. Peterson. It is planned to present this gift to Mr. Peterson at a Farewell Party to be held at Younkers Restaurant, at 6:30 P.M., on Friday May 2, 1952. Division Chiefs have already been advised that the expense of the dinner including tips will be $2.75 per person and that you will have a choice of either Chicken in the Rough or Baked Halibut Steak".

J.A. Connor Regional Director

Wasn't that a glorious way for them to honor 52 years of service? Sic transit Gloria!!

After being home with his gardening into the early fall he got bored and missed not going down to "The Loop" so he took a job in the mail room of the Boston Insurance Co. and worked there until he was 80!!! He loved going to downtown Chicago.

In his later years he served as a Deacon and Chief Usher at our church. He took this job very seriously and rarely missed a Sunday. He hardly ever said any thing bad about anyone. If he disagreed with some person's opinion, especially democrats, he'd say, He's n-u double t nuts. Only twice did I hear him say a curse word. As soon as he said it he asked my forgiveness and God's.

When I went to Bethel College, for the Spring Quarter of 1948, Dad went with on the new vista coached, Burlington train. To put me at ease he said that mom and he had put money away for Will and I, and they would pay my room, board, and tuition for my four years of college. He figured that would be about $4,000. I know how they did that: they scrimped and saved, denying themselves trips, new cars, etc so they could give us what they never had, a college education. In their life as one, they never took a trip out of the country. We went on the trip to Wisconsin in 1940, To N.Y. and New England in1950, and to the states of Washington and Oregon in 1955. That was it except for our cottage at Bass Lake, Ind. and a couple of trips to Florida, when they stayed with my wonderful aunt Elvira & uncle Albin. They had plans to go to Sweden in 1960, but Mom got Cancer and spent the rest of her life going in and out of hospitals.

When my mother died in October of 1964, dad died inside. You could see he'd lost the will to live. He went to live with my brother and his family in Glen Ellyn, leaving his home, garden and church. He spent a lot of afternoons watching his Cubs lose another one. I'm grateful to my brother and sister-in-law Eunice for taking on the major part of caring for him in his last years. In his middle eighties he became mentally ill with what I believe was "Lewy Bodies" disease, a branch of Parkinsonism; symptoms of which are a shuffling walk and mental delusions. When he visited us in New Jersey, he seemed to his under ten year old grandsons to be a crazy old man. This was a natural reaction for them, but it hurt me deeply. One night I sat on his bed with my arm around him as he was shaking with fear because of the man who was going through his pockets. One morning when we were having breakfast he came down and asked me to go out and pay the Halsted St. bus driver. You couldn't convince him that he wasn't in Chicago or that a bus was not out there.

In the early fall of 1971 he was taken to Dupage Hospital with heart failure. The last time I saw him he was in a deep sleep or coma, I could not waken him even though I shouted in his ear that I was Paul and I loved him. A few days later, on October 7, 1971, at age 89, this great man died. His body was buried in Oak Hill Cemetery, but his spirit went to heaven.

Alice E. Peterson

Mother's Day, May 14, 2010. I have a strong feeling of inadequacy as I tell my mother's life story. More than any other person, she had the greatest influence in molding my life.

She was born on June 19, 1898, the third child of AF and Caroline Anderson. Her older siblings were Bernard, born in 1893, and Judith, born in 1896. Two more children would be born to them, Roy in 1901 and Elvira in 1907. At the time of her birth they lived at 1216 W 59th St. in the Englewood section of Chicago. Moms' parents were founding members of the Swedish Baptist Church of Englewood located at 59th and Emerald Ave. Much of my mother's life happened in that church. The most important event she recorded in her diary: "I was converted and accepted Jesus as my own, March 8, 1908. And I was Nine years old. I have never regretted it." Her social life centered in her family and the church. She graduated from Lewis Chaplin Grammar School and Englewood High School.

From the time she was eight years old the family spent most of the summer at their cottage at Bass Lake, Indiana. Two of AF's brothers, Charles and David also owned cottages next to them so they had a lot of cousins to play with during the summer months. Bass Lake was about 80 miles from their home in Chicago. In the Forties it was a 2 hour trip by car. In 1906, when they made the first trip it took them a full day. Later trips took a half day if you were lucky. Highway 30 "The Lincoln Hwy." was a 2- lane paved road to Valparaiso, then an improved gravel road ran to Route 35, where you turned south to the lake 18 miles away. These were rutted gravel roads with several rickety bridges over streams, and at Knox, the 40- yard wide Yellow River. When the car came to these bridges the passengers got out of the car and walked across after which the driver very slowly drove across. They usually had one flat tire on the trip, sometimes two. When they finally got to the lake, the wives and kids generally stayed for the summer. The dads had to work and went back to the city on Sunday, they left one car for the wives. The dads would come back every weekend. The families would all return to the city about the first of September, as school started the day after Labor Day.

In 1917 the family moved to a luxurious home (6841 Bennett Ave) in the area of Hyde Park. In 1921 mom and her parents, with one of her grandparents made a trip back to the Sweden to visit family and friends. They also went to Denmark, Norway, Switzerland and Germany. They traveled for 79 days. I can only imagine how my grandparents must have compared their coming to America 34 years before, in steerage, and now to be traveling first class. My mother told me about this trip several times. It was to be her only trip out of America.

Mother never had a job outside the home. She spent a lot of time looking after Elvira who was nine years younger. Through out their lives they were as close as sisters could be. We shared my grandmother's cottage at Bass Lake in summers. We were together for the celebration of most birthdays, Christmas's and Thanksgivings. This beautiful relationship continued after her marriage to my Uncle, Albin Person in 1940.

When mom graduated from High School in 1916 she started a Sunday School class for teenage girls. This group formed the core for a group that grew to about 50 women that she continued to teach for the next 45 years. Only her terminal cancer stopped her teaching in 1963. She was their teacher, mentor and friend. Many served as attendants at her Wedding, on October 17, 1928.

Fourteen months and three days after the wedding my mother and I went to, The Lying in Hospital in the middle of one of Chicago's biggest blizzards, twelve inches of snow fell while my mother was in labor for twenty hours and twenty minutes. Thank the Lord she was at the "Taj Mahal" of maternity hospitals where both of us were treated royally for the next two weeks. In comparing her birthing experience with me to my brother almost three years later, she said, "I'd rather deliver 3 more Willard's than another Paul."

My memories of mother begin at 8234 Champlain Ave in 1932. There were two rooms in which she spent most of her waking hours: The kitchen where she cooked, baked and ironed; and the room off it where she prepared her Sunday school lessons, knit and crocheted. She sang her favorite hymns as she worked, with a good soprano voice. I heard her sing "Great Is Thy Faithfulness" hundreds of times. She also loved classical music. She listened to the "400 Hour" in the morning as we ate breakfast and got dressed for school. From this I got a good dose of Tchaikovsky, Rossini, Wagner and Strauss.

Several evenings a week we listened to the "Bell Telephone Hour" or the "RCA Symphony" conducted by Toscanini, and on Saturday afternoon the "Metropolitan Opera." From her I got my appreciation and love for great music. She knit sweaters, gloves and socks for us boys. Mom crocheted a couple of table cloths, one of which we have, which are made up of a couple hundred squares. She also knit dresses for herself, Aunt Elvira, and my wife, Lee, who she loved as if she were her own daughter.

Mom was a big woman, not obese, but well padded over a 5'8' frame. As a lady she never went out in public without being strung up in her corset. My dad was the bread winner, but she was the manager. She was never obvious about being head of the house, but in fact she was that. To my dad's credit he recognized her ability and let her take the lead.

The one sports event that she loved was the "Chicago Relays", the big winter track meet at Chicago Stadium. That was an atypical night for her as she cheered like a kid for the various runners. I regret that she never got to see my son Dave run, She would have been, next to me, his biggest fan.

Mom was a deaconess in the church in the 40's and 50's. Proverbs chapter 31: 10-31 describes her well. Although the Apostle Peter wrote that all believers are saints, mother was a SAINT!! The most lasting images I have of her are of she and dad kneeling at the bedside each night before they got into bed. The other is of her sitting in her favorite green chair with the sun streaming in on her auburn hair onto the Bible in her lap.

She was the best cook and baker of the relatives. On winter days I'd come into a warm kitchen with the odor of Peppakakor, chocolate chip cookies, cardamom coffee bread or Swedish "Limpa" rye bread baking in the oven. Underneath the stove lay our dog "Sharp." I'd lie down next to her and experience a sensual treat of warmth and odors. A few minutes later I'd get a taste of what was baking in the oven along with a glass of milk. It was near heaven at home. On my birthday she'd prepare my favorite meat dish, Kidney Veal Chops with a French white sauce and to top it off she'd make my favorite dessert, "Apricot Dream." She taught my wife, Lee to cook and bake many of the things I enjoyed.

Mother was quiet, had many friends and admirers but only a few close women friends who she shared with deeply. She was not the life of the party, but had a wonderful laugh. Among her closest were, Ellen Alquist, her maid of honor, Mrs Bell and Brunzell, but her closest friend was her sister Elvira. After mother died I'd call her occasionally. It was eerie, I would have sworn that my mothers voice was speaking. Carolyn pointed out recently, as I was interviewed on Shell Point TV, that I acquired the same slanted smile that my Mother had.

Mom was a very healthy person and except for her affliction with hay fever, which came on the middle of August and lasted until the first frost, she had no serious illness. Hay fever was not a minor thing for her. (This was before they gave shots to ward off allergies.) She wore filters in her nostrils treated with oil that kept some of the pollen from entering nose and sinuses. This was a miserable time of year for her that she endured. One winter she fell and broke her wrist, which bothered her some the rest of her life. She had one weakness, an addiction to coffee, which she drank all day including the evening meal. In her fifties she came down with colitis and was told by the doctor to give up coffee. She cut back some but could not give it up totally. Her severe colitis continued and in 1960 she was found to have cancer of the colon. After her first surgery and chemotherapy she began to lose weight. More radical surgery took place in 1963 which required a colostomy bag.

When I took a new job in New York City, that required our family to move to New Jersey, the hardest thing I had to do was leave her. That November she and dad flew out to visit us. It was great that my brother Will and his wife and my Uncle Albin and Aunt

Elvira could also be with us for Thanksgiving. We had a wonderful bittersweet time. One could see she was thinner and weaker and in considerable pain. (We also endured that weekend the tragedy of John Kennedy's assassination)

At Christmas time we drove back to Chicago to be with her for one more precious time. The next summer we spent two weeks at Bass Lake, and even though she was laying down most of the time, she was able to enjoy being with her grandchildren. In Chicago, with dad, we consulted with the doctor. He held out no hope for curing the cancer and said, for her sake, it would be better if it would proceed faster in order to shorten the suffering.

The last time I visited her was on the afternoon of September 12. She could barely lift the glass of water to sip from it. Among the many things she said were, "How can Jesus who I love, let me suffer like this? I want to die." I couldn't answer her. When I was about to leave to catch my flight to Newark, she asked me to pray that she would die. I did. It was the most difficult prayer I've ever prayed. I flew back and when I got home Lee met me at the door to tell me that she had died while I was flying home.